REFLECTIVE HIST

Barbara Finkelstein and William J. Reese, Series Editors

Radicalizing the Ebony Tower

BLACK COLLEGES
AND THE
BLACK FREEDOM STRUGGLE IN MISSISSIPPI

Joy Ann Williamson

Teachers College
Columbia University
New York and London

Published by Teachers College Press, 1234 Amsterdam Avenue, New York, NY 10027

Library of Congress Cataloging-in-Publication Data

Williamson, Joy Ann.
   Radicalizing the ebony tower : Black colleges and the Black freedom struggle in Mississippi / Joy Ann Williamson.
      p. cm. — (Reflective history series)
   Includes bibliographical references and index.
   ISBN 978-0-8077-4864-0 (hard cover : alk. paper) — ISBN 978-0-8077-4863-3 (pbk. : alk. paper)
   1. African American universities and colleges—Mississippi—History.   2. African Americans—Education (Higher)—Mississippi—History.   3. Racism in higher education—Mississippi—History.   4. Mississippi—Race relations—History.
I. Title.
   LC2781.W545 2008
   378.762'08996073—dc22

                                                                          2007048836

ISBN 978-0-8077-4863-3 (paper)
ISBN 978-0-8077-4864-0 (cloth)

Printed on acid-free paper
Manufactured in the United States of America

15   14   13   12   11   10   09   08   8   7   6   5   4   3   2   1

Contents

Acknowledgments

My thanks to my former colleagues at Stanford University, including Clayborne Carson, Doug McAdam, David Tyack, David Labaree, Ray McDermott, Sam Wineburg, and the history of education reading group, who read various parts of the manuscript. My intellectual colleagues at other institutions, including James Anderson, Emilye Crosby, Denoral Davis, John Dittmer, Marybeth Gasman, Philo Hutcheson, Leslie Burl McLemore, Aldon Morris, and the anonymous reviewers at Teachers College Press, contributed invaluable expertise and advice. A special thanks goes to Brian Ellerbeck for recognizing promise and nurturing it along the way. Also, Michael Dunson and Lori Rhodes, my doctoral students, culled numerous sources for pertinent information and made trips with me to Washington, D.C., and Jackson, Mississippi, in order to complete this project. I hope their involvement benefited them as much as it did me.

Many archivists and librarians went above and beyond their duties to facilitate this research and made it immeasurably easier to conduct from across the country. I owe a special debt of gratitude to the archivists at the Mississippi Department of Archives and History, especially Clarence Hunter; Alma Fisher, Minnie Watson, and Tony Bounds at Tougaloo College; Mildred Matthews at Jackson State University; and Joanna Williams at Alcorn State University. My deepest appreciation goes to my interviewees. Some of them began or ended their interviews by saying that they doubted they helped me much. I assure each and every one of them that they did. The written record on black colleges is very thin, and this research could not have been completed without their thoughts, memories, and the generous gift of their time.

I am also grateful for permission to reprint material from "'This Has Been Quite a Year for Heads Falling:' Institutional Autonomy in the Civil Rights Era," *History of Education Quarterly* 44, no. 4 (Winter 2004): 489–511; "'Quacks, Quirks, Agitators, and Communists:' Private Black Colleges and the Limits of Institutional Autonomy," *History of Higher Education Annual* 23 (2003): 49–81; and "Black Colleges and Civil Rights: Organizing and Mobilizing in Jackson, Mississippi," in *Higher Education and the*

Civil Rights Movement, edited by Peter Wallenstein (Gainesville: University Press of Florida, 2007): 230–270.

On a more personal note, my family and friends cheered me on from the sidelines. The home of my parents, Willard and Donna, sister, Julie, brother-in-law, Rich, and nephew, Silas James (a.k.a. Babycakes), provided periodic respite from the loneliness that is writing. I was glad for the distraction and reinvigorated by the downtime. And to Joe Lott Jr., my friend, partner, and colleague—this book and my life are all the better because of you.

Abbreviations

AAUP	American Association of University Professors
AMA	American Missionary Association
AMEC	African Methodist Episcopal Church
CMEC	Colored (Christian) Methodist Episcopal Church
CORE	Congress of Racial Equality
COFO	Council of Federated Organizations
HUAC	House Un-American Activities Committee
MECS	Methodist Episcopal Church, South
MFDP	Mississippi Freedom Democratic Party
NAACP	National Association for the Advancement of Colored People
RCNL	Regional Council of Negro Leadership
SACS	Southern Association of Colleges and Schools
SCEF	Southern Conference Educational Fund
SCLC	Southern Christian Leadership Conference
SISS	Senate Internal Security Subcommittee
SNCC	Student Nonviolent Coordinating Committee

Chapter One

Introduction

"The long-range effect of the rising level of education in the Negro people goes in the direction of nourishing and strengthening the Negro Protest." Gunnar Myrdal, An American Dilemma (*New York: Harper and Brothers, 1944*), 88.

This book examines black colleges against the backdrop of the black freedom struggle of the middle twentieth century, a highly contentious, and often violent, ongoing conflict between state agents and their allies determined to protect the racial hierarchy and activists equally determined to cripple white supremacy. It does so to deepen the scholarly treatment of race, power, and the pursuit of democracy. Activists demanded that colleges and their constituents play a central role in societal reformation—a distinct challenge to the notion of the ivory tower in which institutions remained aloof from direct involvement in community concerns. State agents and their allies, however, demanded that colleges distance themselves from the black freedom struggle and promised to mete out harsh penalties if they did not. By documenting how colleges resolved the tension between activism and academics and between broad constitutional rights and restrictive campus regulations, how activists transformed nonpolitical institutions into liberatory agents, how social movements emerged through the daily process of agitation and confrontation, and how campus constituents negotiated local, state, and national political pressures, the book serves as a resource for those interested in the story of campus and societal reform through the words and deeds of college activists and their enemies firsthand.

CRITIQUE OF THE LITERATURE

It might seem that there is nothing new to say about black colleges and the black freedom struggle. All of the literature on the movement mentions the pivotal role played by black college students beginning in 1960.[1] There are books on the Student Nonviolent Coordinating Committee (SNCC) written by scholars and former members.[2] Researchers have identified black colleges, along with black churches and political organizations, as movement centers:

1

organizations or institutions that enable a subjugated group to engage in sustained protest by providing communication networks, organized groups, experienced leaders, and an opportunity to pool social capital.[3] And there is a wide literature that examines black student activism in the early 1960s.[4] The problem with the existing research is that social movement studies merely mention that black colleges were movement centers and do not provide an in-depth treatment of the college campus as an organizing site, and higher educational history relegates black students and black colleges to the margins of the story of student activism and the American university.

Students as Activists, Not as Students

The existing literature provides insight and useful information about the patterns and psychology of black protest, but there are several holes in it. First, the literature extracts students from their campus reality and analyzes them as if their identity as activists preempted or was more important than their identity as students. It is a mistake to divorce students from their campus reality. These *activist* students also were *student* activists. Students did not terminate their interest in the black freedom struggle while on the college campus, nor did they terminate their student status when they participated in campaigns organized by other protest organizations. Students attended college to get a degree, to expand their intellectual repertoire, and, ultimately, to get a well-paying job, not to join the movement.

Still, black students are most often characterized as foot soldiers devoid of any meaningful institutional affiliation. For instance, Aldon Morris highlights the important role of students through what he calls the church-student network. According to Morris, the sit-ins were not a college phenomenon in the sense that students conceived them. Activists in black churches devised the tactic and relied on students to popularize it.[5] Although it is an overstatement, the point that the black church played a pivotal role in organizing students and spreading the sit-ins is a valid one. But discussions of the black college campus should not reduce the institutions to recruitment centers for off-campus activists to populate various campaigns, particularly since the sit-in movement began on campuses and was sustained by students. It is a mistake to assume that because students worked with black ministers or protest leaders, their campuses were not sites of creative organizing in themselves. The two were not mutually exclusive—students used the college campus to organize themselves into a wedge against white supremacy while at the same time they participated in campaigns initiated by other movement centers.

The same critique holds for characterizations of SNCC. The literature discusses the development of the national organization and its trajectory, mission, campaigns, and demise, but does not discuss the influence of the *student* in the *Student* Nonviolent Coordinating Committee. SNCC members are treated as if their institutional affiliation was incidental beyond the fact that their status as students protected them and allowed them to participate at a higher rate than nonstudents—an assumption that will be critiqued later. SNCC had very few full-time employees. Many were full-time students working part-time for the organization. College chapters spearheaded local campaigns, raised money for SNCC projects, and used college-owned paper and machinery to publish SNCC newspapers and flyers (though they sometimes did so without the consent of the administration). The most obvious comparison would be ministers in the Southern Christian Leadership Conference (SCLC) who used their own churches to host meetings and rallies, took up collections to provide bail for arrested activists, and employed the church infrastructure—such as phone lists, organizations, and copying machines—to advertise movement projects. This level of analysis exists for black ministers and churches, but it is missing from the literature on student activists and their colleges.[6] Students are credited with dominating the movement after 1960, but the existing literature ignores the immediate environment in which student activists functioned: the college campus.

Colleges as Monoliths

Second, the existing literature follows a structuralist argument in which black colleges are treated as a monolithic entity—i.e., the black college played an important role in the black freedom struggle. But *the* black college did not exist. Students, campus administrators, and governing boards did not share the same ideas concerning the worth of mixing academics and activism. To treat the colleges as identical incorrectly credits structures and organizations with the power to attract participants and assumes the inevitability of activism as a consequence of membership. Some of the literature on student activism provides nuance to such a structuralist argument by investigating how geographical location, level of prestige, percentage of black residents in the surrounding community, size of the student body, and relationship to the state influenced the level of campus activism.[7] This type of analysis is useful in that it offers a global framework and general patterns for student activism in a variety of campus situations. The problem with these characterizations is that they remain deterministic and static. In the case of student and college activism, the whole is more than the sum of its parts. The fact that students in urban, private, and reputable institutions were more likely to participate tells us nothing of *how* students and other activist constituents transformed indigenous resources into power resources.

To take the colleges' relationship to the state as one example, literature on the movement portrays private black colleges as shielded from overt government interference, a situation that allowed them more latitude to serve the movement. Public institutions relied on appropriations and goodwill from state legislatures determined to protect the Southern racial order, conditions that severely constrained overt participation.[8] But a college's relationship to the state did not completely dictate activism. Students at private campuses participated at a higher rate than their counterparts at public institutions, but private philanthropic support did not necessarily protect private colleges from state sanction. Also, not all private governing boards or college presidents supported the use of campus space for movement ends. Attendance at public institutions, on the other hand, did not mean that students remained removed from the movement. When college and state officials banned civil rights organizations from campus, some student activists filled the institutional void by co-opting other student groups and creating underground protest organizations. The most obvious examples of student activism at a public institution are the North Carolina A&T students who initiated the sit-ins that swept the South. Their college president refused to curtail student actions despite pressure from state officials.[9] A college's financial and political relationship to the state was important, but a structuralist argument that focuses on *the* private college and *the* public college misses the on-campus negotiation that occurred, ignores the cultural work necessary to transform colleges into movement centers, and only partially answers the question of why some campuses became movement centers while others did not.

Exaggerating the Protected Status of Students

Third, the literature overemphasizes the special status of students. Their lack of familial and occupational obligations, free time, youthful energy, idealism, or membership in an organized institution in the black community are the most common factors cited in the literature in explaining their high rate of participation when compared with nonstudents.[10] There was something unique about the college environment, generational experiences, and psychology of late adolescence that facilitated activism, but this type of discussion fails to address the intense countermovement students faced. In doing so, the literature minimizes the contentious and dangerous business of activism. While off-campus, students faced the same brutality as nonstudents. Ku Klux Klan members, white mobs, and the billy clubs carried by police did not distinguish between students and nonstudents. On some campuses, students butted heads with conservative students, faculty, and administrators who admonished them to postpone activism until after graduation. And they faced expulsion, suspension, and loss of scholarships. Also, some colleges faced reprisals, as governing boards threatened to withhold funds and fire presidents who did not punish activists, and government agencies hired informants and filed injunctions and lawsuits against institutions and individuals. To treat student participation in protest activity as a natural outgrowth of college attendance trivializes the pressure students and colleges were under *not* to participate and the consequences they faced in doing so. Participation was not an inevitable outcome of college attendance. It was an act of will.

Truncating Southern Black Student Activism

Fourth, the literature relegates Southern black student activism to the early 1960s. Whereas the sit-ins and 1964 Freedom Summer draw heavy scholarly treatment, Southern black student activism in the later 1960s and early 1970s is almost completely omitted in the literature.[11] Instead, the literature on the later 1960s focuses almost exclusively on the highly publicized activities of black and white students at white college campuses in the North. This is despite the fact that black college students of the Black Power era described their actions as part of the larger and older black freedom struggle and the fact that quantitative studies found students at Southern black colleges highly active and facing the most punitive forms of punishment when compared to any other group of students.[12]

A consequence of truncating Southern black college student participation in the black freedom struggle is that scholars credit white college students, particularly those in the 1964 Free Speech Movement at the University of California at Berkeley, for providing the catalyst for widespread student activism in the second half of the 1960s.[13] Such an analysis only holds because Southern black college students of the early part of the decade are stripped of their student identity. This misplaced credit for forcing change in higher education has resulted in a preponderance of studies regarding white student activism.[14] In 1975, Patricia Gurin and Edgar Epps lamented the absence of scholarly attention to black student activism.[15] In 1981, Charles V. Willie and Donald Cunnigen came to a similar conclusion.[16] Very little literature on black college activism has been published since.[17] White student activism certainly merits study. But the lack of attention to black colleges contributes to a pattern in higher educational research in which black colleges and their students are relegated to the margins of educational history and not seriously considered as a stimulus for any meaningful changes in American higher education.

Grafting White College Experiences onto the Black College

Fifth, and following the pattern of tangential treatment of black colleges, there is overwhelming attention to the plight of white colleges during the McCarthy era and the federal witch hunt for communists spearheaded by the House Un-American Activities Committee (HUAC). According to Ellen Schrecker, "When, by the late fifties, the hearings and dismissals tapered off, it was not because they encountered resistance but because they were no longer necessary. All was quiet on the academic front."[18] This is exactly when Southern states took the reins and sought to purge activists from black and white college campuses. Anticommunist sentiment merged with anti-integration sentiment as the black freedom struggle gained momentum, and the witch hunt continued. Legislatures and other government entities regularly violated the autonomy of public and private colleges and intimidated institutions into firing liberal faculty and curtailing activism.[19] Hostile whites cared little about the loss of accreditation and even less about the opinion of the American Association of University Professors (AAUP). The fact that many black colleges did not have tenure regulations and hired faculty on annual contracts well into the 1960s—a fact that separated them from most of their white Northern counterparts—made purging even easier. So, too, did the fact that Southern legislatures could exploit a network of terrorist organizations, police departments, banks, and other powerful groups that supported their mission. When Northern white colleges moved into a period of self-imposed quietude, black colleges faced mounting and organized pressures to curtail freedom of speech and association.

Still, some private black colleges used the latitude offered by their financial independence from the state to hire the suspected communists fired from white colleges as well as Jews fleeing Hitler's master race ideology in Europe, a fact that makes the story of academic freedom at black and white colleges all the more complicated. While Schrecker posits that white black-listed professors could only go "South, to the small, poor, denominational Negro colleges that were so desperate for qualified faculty members that they would hire anybody with a Ph.D., including teachers other educational institutions dared not touch,"[20] another interpretation would be that certain private black colleges were more radical than their white Northern counterparts in their defense of academic freedom. Yet black colleges are neither credited with attempting to protect the notion of academic freedom nor studied as a way to understand the intensity of state and financial pressure to terminate dissent. Many private black colleges refused to hire suspected communists and actively purged their campuses of activist faculty, but the liberal spirit that prompted missionary philanthropists to erect black colleges after the Civil War remained at others and influenced their choice of faculty in the middle 1960s.

This critique of the literature is not meant to demean or dismiss it. The existing scholarship is useful and has helped explain a wide variety of phenomena. The point is that the literature on social movements and the literature on higher educational history can be merged in a way to deepen our understanding of those same phenomena. This book uses the state of Mississippi to turn the familiar facts of black college involvement in the black freedom struggle into puzzles. It is a historical narrative that analyzes the unexplored territory of the college campus itself. Examining the mechanisms through which campus activists remade campuses into movement centers, the obstacles they faced in doing so, and the consequences they and the colleges faced for their actions yields different and nuanced answers to old questions.

DEEP IN THE HEART OF DIXIE: THE MISSISSIPPI CONTEXT

Any Southern state could serve as a case study, since no state was exempt from black college activism, and every state included a variety of black college configurations with different levels of activism. But the extremities of black activism and white resistance in Mississippi provide a particularly vivid picture of the battle for social, political, and economic reform. According to a survey of Southern states in the first half of the twentieth century, "Southerners, with their eye for distinction, place Mississippi in a class by itself." The state proved unique in several respects. It was the most rural of all Southern states and was the most heavily dependent on agricultural labor. It had the highest proportion of black residents of any state; as late as 1940, blacks comprised 49.2 percent of the population. The state was poorer than its neighbors on every measure. And the state demonstrated an extreme dedication to its firmly entrenched racial hierarchy. Whites in other Southern states supported segregation, subscribed to notions of black inferiority, and intimidated their black citizens into quietude, but white Mississippians, according to historian V. O. Key, "put the white-supremacy case most bitterly, most uncompromisingly, most vindictively." The state oppressed and terrorized its black residents by spending less on the education of black children than any other state, ranking first in the number of lynchings, and priding itself on having the fewest number of black registered voters. An organized and interconnected network of white Mississippi officials and their federal-level allies used legal and extralegal means to keep blacks undereducated, politically disenfranchised, and docile.[21]

Mississippi maintained its unique status during the middle twentieth century and has been described by movement contemporaries and historians as the most repressive state in the nation with regard to the black freedom struggle. Andrew Young, a member of SCLC, remembered, "We knew the depth of the depravity of southern racism. We knew better than to try to take on Mississippi." In addition to terrorist groups like the Ku Klux Klan, Americans for the Preservation of the White Race, and White Knights of

Mississippi that used violence to quell the movement, white elites formed the White Citizens' Council months after the 1954 *Brown v. Board of Education* decision. Its official literature euphemistically described its mission as "dedicated to the maintenance of peace, good order and domestic tranquility in our Community and in our State and to the preservation of our States' Rights." As Charles Payne points out, however, the organization pursued "the agenda of the Klan with the demeanor of the Rotary." The Mississippi Sovereignty Commission grew out of the same anti-desegregation spirit, and the two groups worked in tandem to defeat desegregation efforts in general and school desegregation in particular. Created by an act of the Mississippi legislature on 29 March 1956, the commission sought to "do and perform any and all acts and things deemed necessary and proper to protect the sovereignty of the state of Mississippi, and her sister states, from encroachment thereon by the Federal Government or any branch, department, or agency thereof." The commission conducted investigations, participated in the national campaign to thwart passage of the 1964 Civil Rights Act, created a Speakers Bureau to present Mississippi's case to the nation, and donated taxpayers' money to groups like the White Citizens' Council. White Mississippi law enforcement, courts, banks, proprietors, elected officials, and others joined the effort to crush the movement through intimidation, physical violence, and economic reprisal.[22]

On the other hand, black Mississippians turned the state into "a laboratory in which the civil rights movement displayed its most creative energies." Though Mississippi whites often accused outside agitators—meaning black and white race liberals from out of state—of instigating the black freedom struggle in Mississippi, local black Mississippians led, coordinated, and executed the mass movement in the state. NAACP chapters had existed in the state since 1918, but the statewide organization was energized and radicalized with the appointment of Medgar Evers as the Mississippi field secretary in 1954. Under Evers and other local NAACP leaders like Aaron Henry, the organization initiated economic boycotts, school desegregation cases, and voter registration campaigns. So, too, did the northern Mississippi-based Regional Council of Negro Leadership (RCNL) organize an offensive with economic boycotts and voter registration drives. Some black churches, local political organizations, and black colleges served the movement by hosting meetings, initiating protests, mobilizing members, and collecting money for movement projects.[23]

SNCC, an organization with chapters across the South, arrived in Mississippi in 1961. Soon thereafter, SNCC chose Mississippi as a primary target for civil rights activity because of the intensity of white resistance in the state. In 1964, the organization helped spearhead the Freedom Summer project under the auspices of the Council of Federated Organizations (COFO). The project brought hundreds of mostly white volunteers to Mississippi to register black voters and to work in Freedom Schools that educated black children about the movement as well as traditional academic subjects. By doing so, SNCC focused national attention on the horrid political, economic, educational, and social conditions in the state and catapulted the Mississippi movement into the national consciousness. Black Mississippians continued to dominate the national news when the newly created Mississippi Freedom Democratic Party (MFDP) challenged the seating of the white members of the Mississippi Democratic Party at the Democratic National Convention in August 1964. At the convention, Mrs. Fannie Lou Hamer, a staunch Mississippi activist, told the Credentials Committee about the vicious beating she received in a Winona, Mississippi, jail the previous year. With her speech broadcast to a national audience, she challenged the American citizenry, "All of this is on account of we want to register, to become first-class citizens. And if the Freedom Democratic Party is not seated now, I question America. Is this America, the land of the free and the home of the brave, where we have to sleep with our telephones off of the hooks because our lives be threatened daily, because we want to live as decent human beings, in America?"[24] Like the countermovement they inspired, black activists, political organizations, activist churches, and activist colleges were organized, connected, and vehement in their agitation.

MISSION OF THE BOOK

With the Mississippi movement as a backdrop, this book takes cues from scholars who caution against a static structural interpretation that focuses on shifting institutional rules, organizational schemes, or other factors to explain the workings of a social movement. Instead, the book investigates how activist campus constituents reconceived the meaning and purpose of black colleges and, therefore, transformed them into political entities. Because social movements necessarily arise out of contentious and ongoing negotiation between the state and a challenger, the black college and the Mississippi Sovereignty Commission, as organizations created and appropriated by activists on both sides of the movement, are major units of analysis. Yet another level of contention and negotiation existed within the black college itself as activists battled conservative campus constituents as they attempted to enlist the campus for movement purposes. To this end, diversity of opinion and the difficulty of the appropriation process are necessary to fill out a discussion of black colleges as movement centers or political opportunity structures.

This book offers several distinct additions to the analytic framework with which to understand black college involvement in the black freedom struggle.

The book takes as a premise that it is not enough simply to state that black colleges were movement centers. We must ask *how* activists appropriated and politicized the campus space for movement purposes. As Doug McAdam states regarding the role of black churches, "To turn even some black congregations into vehicles of collective protest, early movement leaders had to engage in a lot of creative cultural/organizational work, by which the aims of the church and its animating collective identity were redefined to accord with the goals of the emerging struggle."[25] The same can be said of black colleges. Scholars describe the black colleges of the 1950s as bourgeois, conservative, and authoritarian environments where campus administrators restricted freedom of speech, association, and movement.[26] That changed in the early 1960s, at least for some colleges, when constituents co-opted the campus space for movement projects. The question is *how*. In particular, the book documents how students appropriated existing organizations and created others to attack white supremacy, how activist faculty helped students organize and allowed their classrooms to be used for movement ends, and how administrators figured in the process. Activists were not always successful in enlisting the campus space as a center of political activity, but examining the (attempted) appropriation process offers an opportunity to understand how institutions are transformed into liberatory agents.

Also, the book emphasizes the variability of participation across institutions by examining the ongoing process of interaction among a range of stakeholders. It investigates the nuances of negotiation, concession, and coercion that existed within discrete campuses and the relationships—student/student, student/faculty, student/administrator, faculty/administrator, administrator/governing body, and governing body/state—that influenced a college's participation in the black freedom struggle. In some ways, the campus space resembled a miniature social movement and a unique political opportunity structure, with agitators and power brokers marshaling their forces in a fight over the role of a black college in social reform. Membership in the categories of agitators and power brokers was not fixed, and liberals and conservatives were represented in every level of the campus constituency. These differently situated constituents interacted constantly, and that interaction impacted a campus's movement center possibilities.

The colleges did not exist in a vacuum, and the intense off-campus countermovement similarly influenced variability in college participation. Hostile whites tossed bombs onto campuses, and police shot into crowds of demonstrators. The Mississippi Board of Trustees of Institutions of Higher Learning threatened to financially sanction public institutions, revoke accreditation or charters, or fire presidents. Though their private status meant that the state could not intervene directly in campus business, state pressures forced private governing boards to ask, could the college afford to be involved in the black freedom struggle? Could it financially afford to spend multiple hours and resources defending itself and its constituents? Could it politically afford to be committed to the struggle in the face of constant state pressure? An examination of the on-campus and off-campus countermovement and its impact on campus constituents complicates the picture of why some institutions participated at a higher rate than others.

The book also highlights the continuity of activism by examining the Black Power Movement in Mississippi and at black colleges. Black Mississippi activists continued to organize and agitate for political, social, and economic reform as they had in the early part of the 1960s.[27] The Black Power Movement itself was inaugurated in Greenwood, Mississippi, when police arrested several people, including SNCC member Stokely Carmichael, on a march toward Jackson in 1966. Frustrated and infuriated, Carmichael addressed a rally of six hundred people, "We been saying freedom for six years and we ain't got nothin'. What we gonna start saying now is 'Black Power!'"[28] Mississippi activists who already had been agitating for power now did so against the backdrop of a national movement that shared their agenda in an overt manner. Their actions posed enough of a threat to the state that the countermovement remained fierce in its mission to crush the movement. Activists met violent physical reprisals across the state, continued policing by the Mississippi Sovereignty Commission, economic sanction from the White Citizens' Council, and litigation prompted by newly passed Mississippi legislation meant to stem the tide of the movement.

The same holds true for Southern black college students and Black Power. The nature of their involvement shifted during the middle part of the decade, but their goals remained the same: increased power, respect, and dignity. The actions of Mississippi's black college students represent an important version of Black Power ideology. They did not receive the same amount of attention as their Northern counterparts, but their demands for representation on collegewide committees, increased academic quality of the faculty, expanded student freedoms, improved campus facilities, and courses focused on the black experience fit securely into the student movement's agenda. Rather than using their campuses as movement centers to dismantle the racial hierarchy off-campus, these students turned their attention inward and attacked the vestiges of white supremacy on an intra-institutional level. In fact, they created mini-movement centers to spar with the administration and enlisted student organizations, media, and campus space to serve the movement. Like their predecessors, they understood their activism as a part of the larger black freedom struggle and met an organized countermovement in their quest for dignity and equal opportunity.

Lastly, the book offers a reexamination of the American university during the middle twentieth century. Higher education changed in the 1960s as liberal constituents reexamined the traditionally distant relationship between institutions and American society. They heavily critiqued the concept of a college as an ivory tower and demanded that colleges use their assets to ameliorate racial, social, and economic inequality. But how did race complicate this picture? How did the historical mission of black colleges change their relationship with society, particularly during the 1960s? White and black missionary philanthropists created private black colleges as a vehicle of racial uplift, while white legislatures created public colleges to fit blacks into the existing racial hierarchy. White colleges did not share such overtly political agendas. The mission, location, and racialized nature of the black freedom struggle necessarily influenced how black colleges intersected with the movement in a way that white institutions did not experience. Therefore, an examination of black colleges during the middle twentieth century offers a different lens through which to examine how institutional autonomy was undermined or protected from state interference in times of social upheaval and how institutions resolved the tension between broad constitutional rights and restrictive campus rules and state laws.

ORGANIZATION OF THE BOOK

The chapters that follow develop these themes in greater depth. Chapter 2 provides a context for the book with a description of Mississippi's black colleges. Chapter 3 investigates students' on-campus organizing efforts and documents how activists at public and private colleges attempted and sometimes succeeded in appropriating student organizations, campus space, and media for movement ends in the early 1960s. Chapter 4 examines the experiences of faculty as campus activists and investigates how academic freedom was forfeited and protected at different types of institutions. Chapters 5 and 6 examine the experiences of private and public institutions separately, but they do not provide a blanket description of the movement possibilities at each type of campus. Rather, the chapters focus on the variability in campus involvement in the movement by documenting the different forms of negotiation, concession, coercion, and resistance that existed on individual campuses. Chapter 7 takes up the topic of Black Power at black colleges. The mission of this chapter is to examine how students continued to use campus space to organize and mobilize against white racial hegemony during the late 1960s and early 1970s. Though it is a separate chapter, it highlights the continuity with earlier student activism through a discussion of the creation of on-campus movement centers (i.e., Black Power–minded organizations); the use of tactics like demonstrations, boycotts, and other disruptive measures; the severe consequences meted against students; and the conflict between campus constituents regarding the place of a black college in a social movement. Chapter 8 returns to the themes discussed in this introductory chapter and draws larger conclusions from the battle between black colleges and the state of Mississippi.

The chapters are, in large part, thematic, and should be understood as a treatment of the diverse layers of campus activism. In fact, chapters 3 through 6 overlap in terms of the time frame examined. That students, faculty, and administrators are discussed separately does not mean that these constituents did not interact or that their interaction did not shape attitudes about and involvement in the black freedom struggle. Rather, it is a way to highlight the different status, responsibilities, and stressors faced by various campus constituents. They approached the movement in different and sometimes competing ways, and their contestation over the role of a black college in society provides a unique opportunity to examine the cultural work necessary to transform organizations into liberatory agents and the intense pressure faced in doing so.

Chapter Two

Training the Talented Tenth: A Brief History of Mississippi's Black Colleges

The end of the Civil War forced the nation to grapple with integrating freedmen and freedwomen into the social order, and reformers turned to education as the primary mechanism through which that integration would occur. The Reconstruction Era constitutions of Southern states mandated the creation of schools for all youth, and the newly created black colleges focused on teacher training to staff the black elementary and secondary schools in the different states. The colleges' duty to educate these teachers and the future leaders of the race made their curriculum and educational mission hotly contested issues. Educational reformers understood that the debate was not merely a difference in opinion on particular curricular offerings. Rather, ideas on the proper education of the black intelligentsia revealed different conceptions of black citizenship.

On one side were black and white liberals on racial issues who believed that the classical curriculum provided a discipline of the mind that would enable black leaders to guide the rest of the black community to freedom and full political and civic equality. On the other were black and white conservatives who argued that the future leaders needed to be taught practical knowledge, industrious work habits, and Christian morals through a manual training program. This type of education would socialize them to accept their disenfranchisement and make them better workers, something they could teach the rest of the black masses.[1] Colleges and boards of trustees had to choose a course of action on the end to which blacks would be educated, and their choice of curricula revealed their attitudes on the proper place blacks should occupy in the social order.

Mississippi's black colleges reflected the range of ideological positions on the question of black education and place in society. Some of the state's private institutions were very liberal on the race question, while others were entirely conservative and still others held a mix of attitudes on the issue. Tougaloo College, Rust College, and Mississippi Industrial College, the state's private four-year black colleges, and Campbell College, a private two-year black college, represented different denominational and funding patterns, which, in turn, influenced the level of liberalism or conservatism on notions of racial equality and agitation toward that end. The ideological and educational mission of Alcorn Agricultural and Mechanical College, Jackson State College, and Mississippi Vocational College, the state's public four-year colleges, was that of the white racists in the state government: education for subservience.[2] This chapter charts the history of the state's black colleges with an eye toward their racial composition, attitudes toward racial uplift, and funding sources. Their histories and genesis directly influenced their relationship to the black freedom struggle of the middle twentieth century and provide a context in which to understand why certain institutions were positioned inside or outside the movement.

BLACKS AND WHITES, LIBERALS AND CONSERVATIVES: PRIVATE BLACK COLLEGES

Against the backdrop of black disenfranchisement, poverty, massive illiteracy, and state-sanctioned white supremacy, Northern white benevolent societies and denominational bodies traveled to Mississippi at the end of the Civil War to create private black colleges. So, too, did black philanthropists build private institutions, though their colleges were less well funded than their white counterparts. The education of the future leaders of the race became the paramount concern for both groups. In the words of philanthropist Henry L. Morehouse, "In all ages the mighty impulses that have propelled a people onward in their progressive career, have proceeded from a few gifted souls."[3] Black colleges would be uniquely positioned to train these few gifted souls, who would come to be known as the Talented Tenth, to lift as they climbed.

Different denominational bodies, however, practiced varying degrees of liberalism on questions of curriculum, political agitation, and the ability of blacks to determine their own destiny. Some philanthropists, black and white, believed that blacks should be educated for political and civic equality through a liberal arts curriculum and moral training and that blacks should be trusted to run their own institutions. Other philanthropists, black and white, had faith in the intellectual and moral capacity of blacks but did not believe that blacks possessed the skills to plot a path toward liberation on their own. Still others, black and white, shied away from a discussion of political and civic equality and instead used vocational and manual training to educate blacks to find a useful place in the existing social order. Most institutions, regardless of their denominational funding, instilled racial pride and leadership skills but accepted the segregated Southern reality.

Tougaloo College: The American Missionary Association and Conservative Liberalism

The American Missionary Association (AMA) was one of the first and most important organizations that met the charge to adjust newly emancipated blacks into the social order. These missionaries brought with them a form of radical Christianity that supported the notion that all humans were created equal and that the denial of equal rights was a sin against God and man. In this spirit and in cooperation with the Freedmen's Bureau, a federal-level agency charged with supervising relief and education activities for recently emancipated African Americans, the AMA purchased a five-hundred-acre plantation on the northern outskirts of Jackson, Mississippi, to build a school for blacks in 1869. Two years later, the state of Mississippi granted Tougaloo University its charter and incorporated its board of trustees. The student body was exclusively black despite the fact that the charter did not place racial restrictions on enrollment. The board of trustees, faculty, and staff, however, were racially mixed. A combination of funds supported the new college. Tuition, AMA contributions, and individual church donations made up a small portion of its operating budget, leaving the campus perilously underfunded. For a short while Tougaloo received money from the Mississippi legislature for its teacher training program, though the state terminated its support for Tougaloo's program in 1890 when a new state law ended financial appropriations for schools that charged tuition or were controlled by private agencies. Lump-sum donations from philanthropic foundations kept the institution from bankruptcy in its early years.[4]

While AMA officials and white Tougaloo administrators were liberal in their attitudes toward the political and civic equality of blacks, they were conservative in other racial matters. The AMA refused to appoint blacks to high-level administrative offices at Tougaloo. The racially mixed faculty was also racially segregated, with black teachers in the industrial program and white teachers in the normal school. White teachers sat separately from the black students and staff in the cafeteria. And white teachers sent their children to local white schools rather than Tougaloo's own primary and secondary school, which remained exclusively black. The AMA and white Tougaloo administrators believed that blacks had the capacity to be full participants in American democracy, but the organization believed that the journey should be measured and cautious lest blacks move too quickly and repeat the "reckless rascality" and "ruin of the state" perpetuated during Reconstruction. Blacks needed proper guidance, and white Tougaloo officials sought to provide it. When students pushed too quickly and were openly critical of the racial situation in Mississippi in the late nineteenth century, the president assured angry local whites that he would counsel them to "fit themselves for intelligent citizenship, stay out of politics, and accept the Jim Crow situation as one not to be helped by 'bad spirit.'" Campus administrators counseled quiet on racial matters as a paternalistic measure to direct the path of change as well as to protect Tougaloo in an intensely hostile racial climate.[5]

Tougaloo experienced a variety of changes during the early twentieth century that forever changed the institution. In 1916, trustees renamed it Tougaloo College to reflect their more limited goals. More importantly, the spirit of the World War I era translated into an increasingly militant pursuit of equality in the black community as well as at Tougaloo. The trustees and campus administrators improved the quality of the college courses and the liberal arts track. They also hired a number of black faculty who created Tougaloo's first courses in Negro history and Negro literature. Students formed the Paul Robeson Dramatic Club, the Phillis Wheatley Writing Club, and other organizations to showcase their talents and for artistic expression. Also, an infusion of funds and a major building program boosted Tougaloo's reputation. In 1931, the college received a B rating from the Southern Association of Colleges and Schools (SACS), the accrediting agency responsible for institutions in the Southern United States. Though it did not receive an A rating, college officials considered it a victory because the B rating meant that Tougaloo secondary school students could enroll in any undergraduate college, and Tougaloo graduates could enroll in any graduate or professional school—provided those schools admitted blacks. A subsequent campaign to boost faculty salaries, the number of faculty with advanced degrees, library holdings, and endowment funds earned the institution the coveted A rating in 1948, making it Mississippi's only accredited black college, a dubious distinction it maintained until the early 1960s. It also held the honor of being the only institution with a voluntarily desegregated student body when white transfer students from Northern institutions enrolled in the early 1960s, a fact that brought Tougaloo increasing attention from segregationists.[6]

A Study in Denominational Diversity: The Methodist Episcopal Church

A different denominational body, the Methodist Episcopal Church, played the largest role in the provision of higher education for blacks in Mississippi. The church splintered at different times in its history, with each sect creating educational institutions that grew directly out of its particular stance on racial relationships. The mother church officially opposed slavery but segregated black and white congregants during its services. Many black congregants protested such treatment and formed the African Methodist Episcopal Church (AMEC) in 1816. The new church followed the same theological precepts as the mother church but adopted an aggressive stance on black equality. As the mother church moved toward integrated services, Southern white congregations revolted and split the denomination in half, with white Northerners (and some blacks who remained committed to the church) forming the Methodist Episcopal Church, North, and white Southerners forming the Methodist Episcopal Church, South (MECS) in 1844. Black congregants in the South fell under the MECS's purview and were kept in bondage and in separate church facilities. In 1870, however, black Southerners organized the Colored Methodist Episcopal Church with the consent and assistance of the MECS, which continued to support racial separation.[7] Each of these denominational splits bore fruit in higher education in Mississippi: The Methodist Episcopal Church, North, founded Rust College in 1870; the AMEC founded Campbell College in 1887; and the Colored Methodist Episcopal Church, which maintained a friendly relationship with the MECS, founded Mississippi Industrial College in 1905.

Rust College and Conservative Liberalism

The Freedmen's Aid Society of the Methodist Episcopal Church, North, joined the AMA in rushing south to adjust the freedmen and freedwomen to their new citizenship status. Like their counterparts, they held liberal notions on racial equality and created educational institutions that would train black leaders accordingly. In this spirit, two white missionaries traveled to Holly Springs, Mississippi, twenty miles from the Tennessee border and less than fifty miles from Memphis, to open a school for newly emancipated blacks in 1866. Four years later, the institution received its charter and was named Shaw University in honor of a generous philanthropist. Though it educated students toward a variety of ends, it sought to educate future teachers in particular. Financial support for the institution came from church assessments, private philanthropy, the Freedmen's Bureau, and local blacks. The institution also received support from the state legislature, which appropriated money for the school's teacher training program. When the program split from the campus to become the State Normal School in 1873, the state funneled all its appropriations to the new institution, thereby terminating its support for teacher training at Shaw University.[8]

A few local whites welcomed the school, though the majority regarded it with suspicion. Black enrollment at a school meant absence from the fields, and more importantly, the school represented a shift in the racial order. To make matters worse, the black community flocked to Shaw University. Students of all ages enrolled, though most congregated in the elementary and secondary grades with smaller numbers enrolled in the college department, normal school (which remained after the state terminated its funding), and vocational courses. The institution drew heavily from Marshall County, in which it was located, since no black public high schools existed in the county until the middle twentieth century. Its reputation drew from an even wider radius, with one student reporting a trek of over one hundred miles in the dead of winter in order to enroll. Blacks well understood the significance of the new institution. According to one observer, "when the first building . . . went up . . . a bell was installed in connection with it, and when it sounded for the first time an old colored woman shouted aloud with joy. In all her life up to that time the only bell she had heard had been the plantation bell calling the slaves to work. Now to have a real bell calling Black boys and girls to school was an experience so profound and epoch-making as to be well worth shouting about."[9] Her sentiment was made more poignant by the fact that the first campus building was erected on the site of former slave auctions.

The Freedmen's Aid Society created an institution that resembled other religiously affiliated black colleges across the South: the board of trustees included blacks and whites (though whites outnumbered blacks), a white missionary was appointed the first president, the white and Northern teaching staff outnumbered the black and Southern teaching staff, the student body remained monolithically black, and the charter opened the institution to all students regardless of religious affiliation. The institution's growth in physical plant, enrollment, college courses, and faculty during the late nineteenth century demonstrated the Freedmen's Aid Society's dedication to the education of future black leaders. Their appointment of a majority white trustee board, administrators, and teaching staff revealed their paternalistic attitudes toward that end. The school, renamed Rust University in honor of Richland S. Rust in 1890, was considered a flagship institution. The Freedmen's Aid Society regarded Rust as "one of our best schools, with a splendid grade of students . . . the influence of the school has been very great in furnishing leadership to the colored people of the South . . . the proportion of advanced students here is very large, and this foundation will grow to be a permanently great school."[10]

The institution was transformed in the first half of the twentieth century, including another name change to Rust College in 1914, and was influenced by the more aggressive New Negro spirit in the wake of World War I. Demands for more black control translated into a shift in the racial composition of the campus. By the 1923–24 academic year, twenty-one of twenty-five faculty were black. The board of trustees, still an interracial group, appointed Rust College's first black president in 1920. By the 1940s, there were no whites on campus in any capacity. The college also began to focus more on higher education and worked toward accreditation with SACS, a move that necessitated an increased endowment, a larger number of holdings in the library, a higher percentage of faculty with advanced degrees, and higher faculty salaries. The sudden increase in student attendance with black

World War II veterans enrolling with the aid of the GI Bill, higher faculty wages, and a flood and subsequent fire rocked the campus and complicated efforts to upgrade the institution. The lack of funding was acute. Church subsidies grew from $6,736 in 1897 to only $7,222 in 1942, an increase of less than $500 over the course of forty-five years. Other financial sources did not match the cost of inflation, and the institution grew poor. The elimination of the elementary and secondary departments provided a temporary financial boost, and the college celebrated receiving an A rating from the accrediting agency in 1949, only to struggle to maintain it and then lose it in 1957. Rust finally regained accredited status in 1962.[11]

Campbell College and the Race Rebels

The AMEC, the members of which split with the Methodist Episcopal Church over the issues of segregation and racial discrimination, also sought to educate blacks. The denomination traveled south via free blacks before the end of the Civil War. The number of AMEC churches remained small in the South and not all of its members were militant and outspoken about their attitudes toward the evils of slavery, but the common worship between free blacks and some enslaved blacks certainly informed an antislavery spirit. The end of the Civil War meant the AMEC could become more aggressive in attracting black Methodists and converting others outside the denomination. They were in large part successful and set up conferences under which to organize the new Southern congregants. The church gained a foothold in Mississippi in the 1870s and formed two conferences in the state: the North Mississippi Conference and the Mississippi Conference.[12]

In 1890, the Mississippi Conferences "decided that it was of the utmost importance that there should be established by them a college for all, regardless of creed or denomination, who would like to avail themselves of the opportunity to secure an education. To this end, committees from both conferences were appointed to select trustees and determine upon a suitable site. In honor of one of our esteemed and venerable bishops, J. P. Campbell, the college was named." Originally located on two different sites in Vicksburg and Friars Point, the campuses combined and moved to Jackson in 1898. The entire Campbell College constituency, from its trustees, faculty, administrators, staff, and students, was black. The twenty-five elected trustees selected twelve prominent white Mississippians sympathetic to their educational mission as honorary trustees, though blacks controlled the board.[13] Racial separation was not an anomaly in Mississippi, but black control of a higher educational institution was.

Most students were AMEC members from Mississippi, with a smaller number from other denominations and from surrounding states. The institution was largely a primary and secondary school when it began, though a sizable number of pupils enrolled in the teacher training course. The curriculum focused on liberal arts, with the upper grades enrolled in classes like Latin, English, mathematics, science, history, logic, psychology, and ethics. In 1922, an AMEC member described the college's growing focus on higher education: "Campbell College plans to meet the educational needs of the Negro youth of the twentieth century by offering them the advantages of a Christian education through its Normal, Industrial, Scientific, Collegiate, Missionary, and Theological Departments. Training in these, coupled with practical work in the domestic economy, will enable them to lead productive lives." By the 1930s, Campbell College granted bachelor's degrees to those who completed the collegiate and scientific courses and diplomas to those who completed the normal school. However, the institution never morphed into a full-fledged four-year institution. It focused instead on secondary education and junior college–level work, particularly teaching training. High school students boarded at the institution while junior college students commuted.[14]

The new institution began and remained in poverty. Various reports described the immediacy of the situation with buildings in need of repair, a fire that destroyed campus buildings, money owed to teachers, and a mortgage debt. The AMEC National Board of Education raised the money for general appropriations from an 8 percent tithe on conference fundraising events, maturing life insurance and endowment policies, special church collections, and private donations. But each conference bore the brunt of financing its local institutions. For some more wealthy conferences in the North and Midwest, this funding structure was not a problem. The poorer Mississippi conferences struggled to support Campbell College, particularly since the college received half the amount the Board of Education appropriated to the AMEC's four-year institutions. The college owned land in Bolivar and Coahoma Counties in northwest Mississippi, but could not capitalize on its use since it was over 150 miles from the Jackson campus. Trustees considered relocating to that area in order to take advantage of cultivating the rich Delta land and its location in the Mississippi black belt. But the campus never relocated or capitalized on the use of its acreage. Instead, it continued to struggle in Jackson.[15]

Mississippi Industrial College and the Racial Conservatives

The third Methodist denomination, the Colored Methodist Episcopal Church (CMEC), also gained a foothold in the South. And, like its counterparts, it created institutions that mirrored its theological and political principles. The CMEC split with the Southern branch of the church in 1870. Unlike the contentious rift in the Northern church, the division between the Southern branches was amicable. Both groups considered it a victory. The division allowed Southern black church officials the power to ordain their own bishops and ministers, while Southern whites won institutionalized segregation and maintained a large degree of control over the CMEC. In particular, white church officials strongly influenced the black denomination's attitude toward racial equality and social activism toward that end. The relationship between the denominations and their attitudes toward racial agitation were revealed in the founding charter of the CMEC: "We shall for ever hold in grateful remembrance what the Methodist Episcopal Church, South, has done for us; we shall forever cherish the kindliest feeling toward the bishops and General Conference for giving to us all that they enjoy of religious privileges. . . . Let our churches be plain and decent, and with free seats, as far as practical; they shall in no wise [sic] be used for political purposes." This position on political neutrality and racial accommodation placed the church in stark contrast to the attitudes of the Northern church and the AMEC, which blasted the CMEC as "a fit place for nobody but such as prefer to be in slavery and ignorance rather than free and educated."[16] Regardless of the criticism, the CMEC proliferated in Southern states with the aid of the MECS, and for the most part remained quiet on matters of race and admonished members to focus on evangelization rather than politics.

The CMEC conferences of the state of Mississippi organized the Mississippi Theological and Industrial College, later Mississippi Industrial College, in Holly Springs in 1905. The founders were far from activist, but they were interested in racial uplift. Bishop Cottrell, the first chairman of the board of trustees, conceived of the school after Governor James K. Vardaman vetoed legislative appropriations for and effectively closed the State Normal School, the same school in Holly Springs that split from Rust College. With church donations and black community support, the institution was built on 110 acres near the campus of Rust College and finally opened in 1906 with 200 students in attendance. The new college focused on teacher training through heavy doses of Christian ideals and vocational and technical work. Its mission and curriculum mirrored that of Booker T. Washington's Tuskegee Institute, which encouraged the creation of a productive black labor force in lieu of political and social equality. The school remained underfunded, as Mississippi Industrial received only a small share of the communal CMEC funds and the Mississippi conferences struggled to support the college.[17]

The constituency at Mississippi Industrial mirrored that at Campbell College, with an entirely black board of trustees, faculty, and student body. And its charter looked similar to that of its neighbor, Rust College, in that both institutions sought to educate future leaders, and future teachers in particular, toward racial advancement. Mississippi Industrial, however, understood racial advancement as bounded by the segregated Southern reality, while Campbell and Rust educated students for full political and civic equality. Also, its counterparts trained future teachers through the classical liberal arts curriculum, while Mississippi Industrial trained those same future leaders through an industrial course. In short, Mississippi Industrial, like its founding denomination, took a conservative stance on the adjustment of blacks to the racial hierarchy, a fact that revealed the heavy influence of the MECS and Southern white attitudes toward the proper form of education for black leaders. To some, the brand of education at Mississippi Industrial seemed the extension of the "plantation mission ideology of paternalism with its mutual obligations and reciprocal duties that reinforced black subservience." Others considered it "a practical model for racial comity and cooperation with southern whites for the mutual benefit of both races."[18]

The CMEC grew more liberal in its attitudes toward advocating racial equality toward the middle of the twentieth century. The term "Colored" in the name of the denomination became a source of concern. Many members wanted to replace it with a more inclusive label and objected to its use as an antiquated and offensive term that reminded them of the signs that hung over restrooms, waiting rooms, and other facilities that segregated the races in the South. The time was right, these members contended, to see a name "that would remove some of the stigma that adheres to the political subordination, economic depression, social ostracism, and personal disfavor" of blacks. At the annual conference in May 1954, the Colored Methodist Episcopal Church became the Christian Methodist Episcopal Church. The body did not adopt radical rhetoric or positions on racial equality and activism, but the name change signified a willingness to engage with political concerns.[19] This sentiment affected the CMEC colleges. By the early 1960s, Mississippi Industrial was still conservative when juxtaposed against schools like Tougaloo, Rust, and Campbell. The continued relationship between the CMEC and Southern whites and CMEC history curtailed any major shift in ideals and practice, and campus administrators refused to allow students to use the campus for movement ends.

BLACK CONSTITUENTS, WHITE CONTROL: PUBLIC BLACK COLLEGES

The Mississippi legislature created public black colleges toward a completely conservative mission. On the heels of the Civil War and black emancipation, the 1890 federal Morrill Act provided each state with funds to sustain one of its public universities. Southern states, including Mississippi, anticipated the 1896 *Plessy v. Furguson* decision and used the land-grant funds to set up a dual system of college education to preserve racial segregation as state laws

and customs demanded. While black Republican legislators of the Reconstruction era were in office, these colleges received their share of the federal
funding, followed the classical curriculum, and advocated an education that
provided black students with the skills to dismantle the racial hierarchy. When
the white Democrats rose to power, however, these schools were all but dis-
mantled. Newly elected white officials gutted the financial coffers of the black
colleges, altered the curriculum away from intellectual to manual training,
and reoriented the colleges to discourage any activities that disrupted white
supremacy. States set up additional publicly supported colleges as blacks
demanded access to higher education and the need for black elementary and
secondary school teachers continued to rise, but these institutions, like their
land-grant counterparts, remained pitifully funded and substandard.[20]

Alcorn A&M College: The Black College and White Politics

Mississippi legislators established Alcorn University, the first black land-grant
institution in the nation, in 1871, in a remote location eighty miles southwest of the capital of Jackson near the Louisiana border. Governor James L.
Alcorn, a Republican for whom the institution was named, and other whites
in the government recognized the need to support the education of newly
emancipated blacks. Their motives, however, were not purely altruistic since
they also wanted to stall the growing movement to integrate the University
of Mississippi. Black legislators worried that the creation of a black college
would provide "a precedent which we were working hard to break down—
that of separate institutions for the races," but they relented when the legislature appointed an all-black board of trustees and named Hiram R. Revels,
the first African American to serve in the United States Senate, as Alcorn's
first president. With the support of friendly black and white Republicans,
the new institution received three-fifths of the federal land-grant funds and
generous support from the state legislature. All students received an education that mirrored the normal school programs at private religiously affiliated colleges, with an emphasis on classical subjects and a small amount of
industrial training.[21]

Three years later, the young institution was plunged into chaos. President Revels, who began his career as a conservative Republican, switched
his alliance to the Democratic Party. His politics and practiced deference to
whites angered the students and faculty at Alcorn, who boycotted classes and
registered complaints with various officials. At the same time, Revels found
himself the victim of the political whims of newly elected Governor Adelbert
Ames, who resented Revels's support of Governor Alcorn. With campus
unrest and as retribution for Revels's allegiance to the former governor,
Governor Ames fired him along with the entire board of trustees and fac-

ulty. The school struggled for two years with temporary leadership and a massive student exodus until the white Democrats, who had recently risen to power in the legislature, reinstated Revels in 1876. The faculty and students remained monolithically black, but the board of trustees now included white and black members, revealing the changing tide in black control of the institution.[22]

In 1878, the newly elected Democrats in the state legislature gutted the institution by reducing annual appropriations, abolishing state-funded scholarships, downgrading the curriculum, and renaming the institution Alcorn Agricultural and Mechanical College. College-level work was almost wholly dropped from the institution's mission, as the legislature mandated a curriculum that provided "scientific and practical knowledge of agriculture, horticulture, and the mechanical arts, also in the proper growth and care of stock, without, however, excluding scientific and classic studies, including military tactics." In the early twentieth century, Governor James K. Vardaman used his position to discourage black aspirations at any opportunity and further weakened the institution by reducing the salaries of Alcorn's academic faculty and raising the salaries of its vocational faculty. According to Vardaman, "There is no need multiplying words about it, the negro will not be permitted to rise above the station which he now fills," since education only "renders him unfit for the work which the white man prescribed." Alcorn had been reduced from a bachelor's degree–granting university to an agricultural science and industrial arts college to an institution that trained students for menial labor under the guise of teacher education. The curriculum, along with Alcorn's isolated geographical location and reputation as a local rather than statewide institution, made it unattractive for college-age black Mississippians, and enrollment remained low.[23]

The legislature consolidated Alcorn and Mississippi's public white institutions under a single Board of Trustees of Institutions of Higher Learning in 1910, an act that terminated black trusteeships at Alcorn. The legislature initially barred elected officials from serving on the board to prevent abuses of power and the politicization of higher education in the state, but it repealed the regulation two years later, fearing that complete autonomy would exempt the institutions from the popular will of taxpaying citizens. The board became a tool for each subsequent sitting governor, who appointed trustees and became an *ex officio* member of the board himself. In 1930, Governor Theodore Bilbo rid the white state colleges of his political enemies and appointed his own board of trustees, which fired 179 faculty, including a college president, and jeopardized the positions of 233 others. According to an article in the *New Republic*, Alcorn, the only public black college in the state, was safe from Bilbo's wrath only because "there are no Negro voters in Mississippi to be punished or rewarded." Bilbo's actions angered the national press, infuriated the faculty and administrators at Mississippi's white colleges, and plunged Mississippi higher education into chaos. The SACS, AAUP, Association of American Law Schools, and American Association of Medical Schools suspended each of Mississippi's white public institutions. Alcorn escaped the sanctions because it was not accredited by any agency and was not considered a true college.[24]

To make matters worse, the board of trustees, legislators, and governor regularly meddled in Alcorn's affairs. Since the institution's founding, white officials had either fired or intimidated into resignation each of the college's presidents, a fact that increased the instability of the institution. By the 1940s, some considered Alcorn beyond repair, and an official in the state department of education recommended it be closed. It remained open less because whites considered blacks educable and more because the 1890 Morrill Act required Southern states to maintain black colleges along with white colleges or be forced to desegregate higher educational institutions. The curriculum remained driven by industrial pursuits. When a president "leaned altogether toward arts and sciences" at the expense of vocational training, he joined the ranks of fired Alcorn presidents.[25] The legislature paid little attention to upgrading the college, which focused on teacher training, mechanical arts, and agriculture into the 1950s. Small enrollment continued to plague the institution because of its geographical isolation, and it remained unaccredited until 1962.

Jackson State College: From Liberal Roots to a Conservative Reality

Jackson State College, the state's second public black institution, began with radical roots. A group of black Baptist ministers in Mississippi organized the Baptist Missionary Convention in 1869, and discussed the formation of a theological school. At their second convention, the organization's president stated,

> I now come to the subject of education, and what I believe to be the destination of the colored race. To elevate that race, and to save it from idolatry and corruption, we must educate. Corruption follows hand in hand in the path of ignorance, and to prove this, had the Southern people been educated up to that high and moral standard that should characterize the civilized world, all this war and devastation, and carnage, would not have happened in our midst. But instead of that, they were educated to believe that they were the peculiar and favored work of God's hand, and that the poor African race was born to be their slaves. That made them believe that a Negro had no rights that a white man was bound to respect. But we praise God from whom all blessings flow, we find in the face of all that heathenish teaching, that slavery is dead; and as such we all ought to be engaged in building up the old waste places.[26]

The new seminary would train ministers to correct the twisted Christianity propagated by whites that encouraged blacks to be subservient and docile. In 1877, Northern white Baptists, through the American Baptist Home Missionary Society, joined with black Mississippi Baptists in their cause, and together they erected Natchez Seminary in Natchez, Mississippi.

The new institution included a normal school, a theological department, and a preparatory department for those youngsters who might aspire to the higher departments. Much like other private religiously affiliated colleges, students enrolled in English, Greek, Latin, history, theology, moral law, public speaking, rhetoric, and science. The racial composition of the institution also mirrored that of some of its counterparts: the entire student body, which included males and females, was black, and the board of trustees, faculty, and president were white. The institution got its first black faculty member in 1882, a biracial board of trustees in 1899 (along with a name change to Jackson College), and its first black president in 1911. Sixty pupils enrolled in the first year of operation, though numbers soon swelled to the point at which trustees moved the institution to a larger site in a more central location on the outskirts of Jackson. Animosity toward the institution grew in the white Jackson community almost immediately and was exacerbated by the exponential growth of the capital city; the expansion of the city limits, which placed the college near the center of town; and the fact that the area in which the institution was located had been transformed into an elite white neighborhood. In 1890, Millsaps College, a private white institution, opened near the new campus and white students resented the presence of blacks, especially those receiving an education, in such close proximity. Hostility toward the college rose to such a level that Jackson College's president received threats on his life.[27] Despite black protests against the move, the campus relocated to the western part of the city directly across the street from AMEC-supported Campbell College in 1902.

The year Jackson College got its first black president, 1911, the institution also transitioned to an entirely black faculty. The outgoing white president and the board of trustees elected to move toward racial homogeneity—at least on campus, since the board of trustees remained mixed—because black student resentment against white paternalistic attitudes had grown to a point at which the board did not feel that whites could govern the institution. Enrollment increased dramatically after the change of leadership, and the new black staff worked to upgrade and expand the curriculum to a point at which, in 1927, the institution became capable of conferring bachelor's degrees. The tide changed, however, when Baptists decided to terminate appropriations for the institution in the face of financial woes. After convincing the state legislature that Mississippi needed another black teacher training school, the Baptists eventually transferred control to the state of Mississippi and the all-white Board of Trustees of Institutions of Higher Learning.[28]

In 1940, the Mississippi legislature adopted responsibility for the institution but demoted it to junior college status and changed its name. As one state representative put it: "What a 'Nigra' needed to learn was how to work—how to run a middle buster. I am against calling this school a college; I move that we name this institution the Mississippi Negro Training School." The motion passed. By 1944, however, the legislature supported a measure to reinstate the institution's four-year program and changed the name to Jackson College for Negro Teachers. The all-white board of trustees selected black administrators and faculty who would not encourage agitation against the racial hierarchy. Legislators only minimally supported the newest black public college in the state, and for the first two years under state control the institution received more money from private sources like the Julius Rosenwald Fund and the General Education Board than from the state itself.[29]

In 1956, the again-renamed Jackson State College expanded its curriculum to include general liberal arts. The expansion of Jackson State was not a mark of legislative support for black higher education. Rather, the United States Supreme Court's rulings in *Gaines v. Canada* (1938), *Sipuel v. Board of Regents* (1948), *McLaurin v. Oklahoma State Regents* (1950), and *Sweatt v. Painter* (1950) threatened the legality of racially segregated public colleges. As the number of rulings mounted, the Mississippi legislature buttressed public black colleges to forestall desegregation. As a preemptive measure, the board of trustees took steps toward the accreditation of public black colleges by reconstituting them in 1951. Alcorn continued to integrate teacher training with vocational training, while Jackson State became a liberal arts college. Jackson State's new status meant more financial support and legislative commitment to bolstering the faculty, facilities, and curriculum. By the 1960–61 academic year, Jackson State enrolled 1,301 full-time undergraduate students, making it the largest student body at a black college in the state. The changes made Jackson State the most prestigious public black college in Mississippi, though it remained unaccredited until 1962.[30]

Mississippi Vocational College: The Black College as an Afterthought

In the same spirit of delaying desegregation, the legislature chartered Mississippi's third public black college, Mississippi Vocational College, in 1946, and finally opened it in 1950. The legislature chose an abandoned cotton plantation in Itta Bena, the heart of the Delta, as the location of the new institution. In 1945, the Delta housed almost half of the state's black population but had few black primary and secondary schools and even fewer qualified black teachers. The legislature originally contemplated relocating Alcorn, but the desperate need for black teachers and the legislature's desire to stall desegregation at the primary and secondary level led to the creation of a new institution for black teacher training. Rather than being a liberal arts college, Mississippi Vocational College's mission was to educate black students "in all branches of study which pertain to industrial training, health and rural and elementary education." The curriculum would fit black students into their appropriate place in the Southern social order and "be correlated with the plantation system of farming." According to the college catalogue, "basic in the philosophy of the college is the objective of attaining economic and social adjustment through vocational competence." When the board of trustees reconstituted the state's public black colleges in 1951, the mission of Mississippi Vocational remained true to its name.[31]

The campus began in pitiful conditions. Its first classes met on the grounds of the Negro High School in the summer of 1950 because no classroom buildings existed on the college site. The campus also suffered from a lack of proper drainage, roads, electricity, faculty housing, student housing, and adequate toilet facilities. It more closely resembled a swamp than a college in the early years. Despite its location in the heart of Mississippi's black population, the number of full-time students remained low. Only twelve students graduated in the first class of 1953. Most students were part-time and were practicing teachers who attended the college's summer program or night school. A large number of students enrolled in vocational classes and other coursework that did not lead to a bachelor's degree. Its pattern of enrollment and low status, even when compared to the state's other public colleges, left the institution in dire straits. President James H. White attempted to persuade the board of trustees to invest additional funds in the college, but he was forced to court private sources to offset the cost of "building the college from the ground up."[32] His efforts yielded enough funds to construct several classroom buildings and student dormitories, and by 1954 the institution could call itself a functioning college, though it remained unaccredited by SACS until 1968.

SIMILARITIES AND DIFFERENCES BETWEEN THE COLLEGES

Such was the condition of Mississippi's black colleges by the middle twentieth century. All the institutions had monolithically black student bodies either because whites refused to patronize black private institutions or because whites were explicitly barred from attending black public institutions. All colleges, both private and public, suffered from a lack of funding that left them in a vulnerable state when the black freedom struggle gained momentum and black students sought to enlist their campuses for the cause. White Mississippians had come to accept the higher education of blacks as inevitable but worried about the end to which blacks were educated, and powerful whites sought to monitor and direct the nature of that education away from racial agitation and toward a respect for the racial order. The nature of financial support meant that racists in the Mississippi legislature and on the board of trustees easily controlled the public institutions. Private institutions received no state funding and elected their own boards of trustees without state interference, but they still had to eke out an existence within the confines of Mississippi's white supremacist system.

There also were important differences between institutions. The public institutions shared widely different status. Alcorn A&M College was the oldest public black college in the state, but the board of trustees focused its attention on upgrading Jackson State College in the middle twentieth century. Jackson State became a liberal arts institution with better facilities, an enlarged library, and a more highly trained faculty. Its improved status attracted some of the brightest students from across the state who wanted to pursue a bachelor's degree in a rigorous academic environment. Alcorn, because of the board's actions, could not compete with the academic programs offered at Jackson State. It therefore continued to serve the local black college-going community and remained less selective in its student body. Alcorn received accreditation from SACS during the same year as Jackson State, 1962, but the board continued to focus most of its attention on bolstering Jackson State as a tactic to assuage the black community's call for equal educational opportunity. Mississippi Vocational received even less of the board's support than Alcorn. For the first several years Mississippi Vocational more closely resembled a community college in that it admitted every student who applied, offered several nondegree courses, had many commuter students, and drew students almost exclusively from the local area. The board of trustees authorized the college to grant bachelor of science degrees to those full-time students enrolled in a four-year course in vocational and technical training, but did not build the liberal arts curriculum or authorize bachelor of arts degrees until the early 1960s. The board renamed the institution Mississippi Valley State College in 1964 to reflect the newly broadened focus, but even with the increased support the institution was not accredited by SACS until 1968 because of its poor facilities, pitiful library, paucity of funding, and largely untrained faculty.

The location of the public colleges also marked them as different. Alcorn and Mississippi Vocational were in rural parts of the state. Alcorn was located in Claiborne County, in the southwest part of the state near the Louisiana border, where, according to the 1960 census, black residents outnumbered whites by a ratio of over three to one, were overwhelmingly concentrated in the agricultural sector, and had an average of only 6.6 years of schooling. Mississippi Vocational was located in Leflore County, in the north-central part of the state. As in Claiborne County, Leflore's black residents outnumbered whites, were agricultural laborers, and had a paucity of schooling, with an average of 5.1 years. Conversely, Jackson State was located in the most heavily populated county, Hinds County, and in the state's largest city, Jackson. Blacks in this area fared better than their rural counterparts in terms of occupational diversity, home and business ownership, and educational levels. For instance, blacks in Hinds County attended school for an average of 7.6 years, a fraction of the time of blacks in Northern states but still the highest average black educational level of any county in Mississippi. Also, the number of whites and blacks in Hinds County and Jackson was more balanced, with whites slightly outnumbering blacks, a fact that political scientists believe contributed to more muted (though still pronounced) white antipathy toward black advancement when compared to those counties in which blacks far outnumbered whites.[33] Jackson State's proximity to the state capitol, legislature, board of trustees, and other black colleges (Campbell was directly across the street, and Tougaloo was a mere nine miles away) also meant that the institution was differently positioned than Alcorn and Mississippi Vocational when activists in the black freedom struggle began to form a network of movement centers.

The state's private institutions demonstrated even more variance. Two colleges, Rust and Mississippi Industrial, were located in Holly Springs in Marshall County, a rural county in northern Mississippi where the status of blacks matched that in Claiborne and Leflore counties. The context in which Tougaloo, located in Madison County, found itself closely matched that at Campbell and Jackson State, which were located in neighboring Hinds County.[34] More importantly, each of the four colleges was created by a different group of religious philanthropists who translated their particular religious and political beliefs into an educational program, which, in turn, meant that some institutions were more liberal on the notion of agitation against the racial hierarchy than others. Tougaloo College was the least tied to a particular denomination, since the AMA was a nonsectarian organization that maintained a Christian mission but did not tie funding to particular church doctrine. Rust College, Campbell College, and Mississippi Industrial College were more closely affiliated with denominational funding. The Freedmen's Aid Society of the Methodist Episcopal Church, North, much like the AMA at Tougaloo, was an interracial group that was less denominational than nonsectarian, however, which meant that it was more loosely tied to denominational control than Campbell or Mississippi Industrial. Also as at Tougaloo, Rust's white philanthropists advocated racial equality, though they often did so in a patronizing manner. Campbell and Mississippi Industrial, on the other hand, were intimately tied to denominational funding that resulted in distinctly different positions on racial amelioration. The AMEC's radical interpretation and use of Christian doctrine toward liberatory ends directly influenced the nature of education and activism at Campbell, while the CMEC's conservative theology and stance on agitation translated into minimal involvement with the movement at Mississippi Industrial.

The racial composition of the leadership at private colleges also varied. Blacks controlled the board of trustees at Campbell and Mississippi Industrial, while whites outnumbered blacks on the Tougaloo and Rust boards. And only Tougaloo had a white president or employed any white faculty members by the early 1960s. To some observers this marked Tougaloo as radical: to have black and white people living and working together as colleagues was anathema to state laws and social mores. To others, Tougaloo's practice of hiring white faculty and presidents smacked of white paternalism, though this sentiment became more prominent in the late 1960s rather than the early part of the decade. The exclusively black campus leadership at Rust, Campbell, and Mississippi Industrial did not necessarily represent a radical position on political, social, or racial issues. Campbell, because of its particular denominational history, was the most militant in terms of its choice to maintain an all-black faculty and leadership. Rust's interracial board of trustees did not intentionally exclude whites from campus and hired white faculty members in the middle to late 1960s, but it did make a conscious choice to appoint black presidents. Mississippi Industrial, the most theologically conservative of the colleges, hired black faculty and black presidents less as a political gesture and more because of the fact that the CMEC was an entirely black denomination.

The private colleges also differed in their level of status. Tougaloo, the most prestigious private or public institution in Mississippi, attracted students from across the state and other states. Its location on the outskirts of the capital city of Jackson increased its visibility and further augmented its prominence. Rust College, the next most prestigious private college, received enough funding to compete with Tougaloo, but its location in rural northern Mississippi negatively impacted its ability to attract faculty and students from a broad constituency. Though Mississippi Industrial was located across the highway from Rust in Holly Springs, it could not compete with its neighbor in terms of funding and facilities. Its choice to remain oriented toward vocational and teacher training also negatively influenced its status. Campbell College, a junior college, did not compete with the four-year institutions for students and could not compete with them in terms of curricular offerings, but its location in the city of Jackson (not to mention its proximity to Jackson State and Tougaloo) helped increase its status when compared to other black community colleges in Mississippi.

CONCLUSION

There are generalities that can be drawn about black colleges as a whole on the eve of the black freedom struggle. And there are appropriate generalizations about private institutions and public institutions. But focusing too closely on the broad classifications of the colleges obscures important distinctions between them. The differences in structural characteristics outlined in this chapter offer a springboard with which to understand the diversity of college involvement in the movement. At the same time, it is important to remember that simple categories labeled "kinds of institutions that participated in the movement" and "kinds of institutions that did not participate in the movement" do not exist. Funding patterns, racial composition, location, theological identification, level of prestige, and attitude toward racial agitation differently influenced the colleges. The particular combination of these factors could facilitate or hinder campus participation in the black freedom struggle. However, it is necessary to look beyond structural factors and examine the particularities of each campus's constituents, their attempts to transform their campuses into movement centers, and the countermovement they faced in order to understand why some institutions were integral to the movement and others remained outside it.

Chapter Three

From Bourgeois to Activist: Students and the Radicalization of the College Campus

Movement centers, including black churches, political organizations, and colleges, maintained vital resources for sustaining the black freedom struggle. Logistically, they were institutions with a pre-organized group of constituents, established leaders, media outlets, networks, and meeting spaces. Emotionally and ideologically, they bolstered collective enthusiasm, built on a common mission, and served as an outlet for discussion and social expression.[1] The fact that many enjoyed financial independence from hostile whites made them particularly important. Still, the transformation of these institutions into liberatory agents was not inevitable. The political organizations already advocated societal reform, while black churches and black colleges did not. Churches and colleges served the black community and many advocated racial equality, but they often did so within the confines of the Southern racial hierarchy. Their conversion into movement centers actively plotting against white supremacy was made possible by constituents determined to use any and all means for their cause.

This chapter examines how activist students co-opted and politicized the campus space and resources, with a particular focus on student organizations. It does not detail participation in off-campus campaigns organized by civil rights groups, since other scholars chronicle the activities of these groups and student participation in them.[2] Nor does it examine all instances of student activism. And it does not discuss the entirety of the countermovement colleges faced, which is a topic that reappears in later chapters. Instead, the focus is on student organizations enlisted for movement ends. The student organizations often had overlapping membership and worked in concert on different campaigns with off-campus groups. For instance, Leslie Burl McLemore, a student at Rust College, was the president of the Student Government Association, the president of the campus chapter of the NAACP, a member of SNCC, and a delegate in the MFDP. Still, it is in campus-based organizations that students most easily blended their identities as students *and* as activists. And it is through these organizations that the full weight of student participation in the movement is understood.

34

THE MISSISSIPPI MOVEMENT

Before launching into a discussion of campus-based activism, it is important to illustrate conditions in Mississippi and the genesis of the black freedom struggle in general. Blacks began to organize against white supremacy in the post–World War II period as veterans returned home and reaped none of the benefits for which they fought abroad, namely freedom and democracy. They and other blacks joined groups including the NAACP and the newly formed RCNL and Progressive Voters League to agitate for first-class citizenship rights. The 1954 *Brown* decision emboldened them, and agitation became more aggressive. The most striking events occurred outside the state of Mississippi as the 1955 Montgomery Bus Boycott and the 1957 desegregation of Little Rock's Central High School made national headlines and presaged the forcefulness with which blacks would advance their demands. In Mississippi, Medgar Evers's appointment as Mississippi field secretary for the NAACP—which followed his failed attempt to enroll at the University of Mississippi School of Law the day after the Supreme Court decided *Brown*—further radicalized local black movement centers. Desegregation of public facilities, including schools, became a major campaign. No state spent less on the education of its black residents than Mississippi, which spent $122.93 per white child and $32.55 per black child in 1950, a ratio of almost four to one.[3]

Racist whites also organized. To them, the defense of white supremacy was not only a biblical and social mandate that protected the sanctity of the master race, it was uniquely patriotic since it represented a stand against communism and the Soviets, with whom the United States had been battling in a Cold War since the 1940s. Convinced that the concept of desegregation was a part of a communist plot to destroy America from the inside out (an unfounded and egregious claim), racists attacked it at every turn. In the words of a Mississippi white college president, "Communism, as you well know, is based upon Karl Marx's doctrine of internationalism and the classless society and the obliteration of all national and racial distinctions and the final amalgamation of all races."[4] Whereas anticommunist witch hunts focused on Hollywood, labor unions, and white universities in the 1940s, white Southerners enlisted them against the black freedom struggle in the 1950s, 1960s, and into the 1970s.

Such sentiment, in addition to a well-organized countermovement against the black freedom struggle, existed in other Southern states, but Mississippi earned the reputation of being the belly of the beast. Public officials used their preexisting interconnected networks at the local, state, and national level to plot against activists and organizations and created the Mississippi Sovereignty Commission to employ covert mechanisms to destroy them. The White Citizens' Council organized its first chapter in the heart of the Mississippi Delta and soon spread throughout the state and the South. And the Ku Klux Klan, Americans for the Preservation of the White Race, White Knights of Mississippi, and other private citizens' groups joined the battle and terrorized activists, or any black person who had the audacity to step out of line, for that matter. The most brutal incident in the immediate post-*Brown* era was the 1955 murder of Emmett Till, a fourteen-year-old boy who was beaten, shot, and thrown into a river with a seventy-five-pound cotton gin tied around his neck with barbed wire after he whistled at a white woman. An all-white jury acquitted his murderers.

In the early 1960s, the black freedom struggle escalated across the South. In 1960, black college students formed SNCC and used the organization to spearhead desegregation and voter registration campaigns. In 1961, Freedom Riders, an interracial group, traveled across the South to test a Supreme Court decision and the Interstate Commerce Act, which forbade discrimination in interstate transportation. The same year, the University of Georgia, located in one of the last states to hold out, admitted its first black student. Two years later, federal marshals forced Alabama's governor, George Wallace, to move from the schoolhouse door as they escorted the University of Alabama's first black students onto campus (this left Mississippi as the only state yet to desegregate its public higher educational institutions). National organizations such as CORE, SCLC, NAACP, and SNCC, local organizations like the Montgomery (Alabama) Improvement Association, the Albany (Georgia) Movement, and Mississippi's RCNL, activist churches, and activist colleges worked together and employed both civil disobedience and legal maneuvers to undermine white supremacy. Their efforts also made national news and garnered sympathy for the movement as many Americans watched, horrified, at the brutal and sometimes deadly force with which racists defended the racial hierarchy.

As the black freedom struggle progressed, Mississippi remained most committed to protecting white supremacy. It was known as a dangerous state in which whites defended the racial hierarchy with fanatical zeal. As the president of the Jackson White Citizens' Council stated at a rally held on the anniversary of what racists called Black Monday, the day *Brown* was decided, "The Negro agitators, left-wing pressure groups and other advocates of racial violence and lawlessness have met a solid wall of resistance in Mississippi, and every move to force racial integration has only served to strengthen the determination of our people that there shall be no integration forced upon us." Conservative black leaders counseled activists to be patient in such a hostile atmosphere. Percy Greene, the editor of Jackson's conservative black newspaper, the *Jackson Advocate,* warned that civil disobedience created "a deepening of the animosities towards the Negro and a widening of the gulf between responsible Negroes and Whites."[5]

Militant activists ignored the advice. Medgar Evers organized an Easter boycott of downtown Jackson stores to protest poor treatment and discrimination in 1960. Local college and high school students canvassed door-to-door to solicit support, but only for a short while and with limited success. The same April, NAACP members on the Gulf Coast organized a wade-in in Biloxi to protest regulations that prevented blacks from patronizing beaches along the Gulf of Mexico. A white mob chased and assaulted the swimmers as police watched. In 1961, Jackson became the center of increasing civil rights activity after nine Tougaloo College students staged a sit-in at the whites-only public library in March (the details of which will be discussed later). The sit-in inaugurated a period of sustained and massive civil disobedience across the state and in Jackson in particular. Between 1961 and 1964, activists in Jackson launched another longer-lasting and more effective boycott of white stores; conducted sit-ins, pickets, mass marches, and letter-writing campaigns; and initiated a school desegregation lawsuit. Local NAACP branches, the RCNL, and other interested individuals and groups organized and executed a variety of attacks on segregation and discrimination in the rest of the state over the next few years. The movements in McComb, in southwest Mississippi, and in the Delta, the heart of the black Mississippi community, were especially bloody.[6]

The escalating black activism infuriated whites, who vowed that the compromises made in other states would never be made in Mississippi. Jackson's mayor even announced that he was "fully confident massive demonstrations similar to those touched off in Alabama will be avoided"—a statement he was forced to recant a short time later. Local papers sounded the alarm by warning readers that, as one article title put it, "STATE CALLED NO. 1 TARGET OF CIVIL RIGHTS GROUPS." Medgar Evers's promise that "the pace of the past seven years was altogether too slow. This year [1962] there will be stepped-up civil rights activity in Mississippi," added fuel to the fire. Racists savagely beat or killed activists (including George Lee and Gus Courts in 1955; Herbert Lee in 1961; Jimmy Travis in 1962; Medgar Evers, Fannie Lou Hamer, Annell Ponder, Euvester Simpson, and Lawrence Guyot in 1963; and Louis Allen in 1964) to stem the tide of protest. They also bankrupted, evicted, intimidated, and harassed organizations and individuals through state apparatus or with state sanction. "The communistic aim is race and religious genocide for Anglo-Saxon Christians," one white citizen warned. "God have mercy on the apathetic, gutless souls of stupid Americans."[7]

Mississippi's dismal record on civil rights brought increasing media attention in 1963 and 1964. Freedom struggle luminaries like Dr. Martin Luther

King Jr., Dick Gregory, James Baldwin, and members of the NAACP Legal Defense Fund repeatedly traveled to the state with reporters in tow. In 1963, local SNCC and CORE activists executed Freedom Vote, a hugely successful mock election for governor that demonstrated to Southern and Northern whites that blacks were, indeed, interested in participatory democracy. During the summer of 1964, SNCC and COFO spearheaded the Mississippi Summer Project, which caused a media frenzy. Organizers hoped to force the state to change its racist policies or coerce federal intervention, highlight the rabid resistance to racial equality, and develop local leadership to sustain the movement. The project brought hundreds of mostly white volunteers to Mississippi to teach in Freedom Schools and to work in voter registration alongside local activists. The brutal murder of James Cheney, Andrew Goodman, and Michael Schwerner, three civil rights organizers working with the project, increased the intensity of press coverage, particularly since two were white. The same summer the MFDP, the political party formed during the 1963 mock election, lobbied unsuccessfully to unseat the Mississippi Democrats at the Democratic National Convention in August. Their appearance at the convention, however, drew a national television audience and increased pressure on Mississippi to change its racist ways.[8] The passage of the 1964 Civil Rights Act, which barred segregation in public facilities, and the 1965 Voting Rights Act, which extended voting privileges by prohibiting racially motivated barriers to the franchise, further emboldened Mississippi activists, who continued to push forward.

This truncated account of the early years of the black freedom struggle in Mississippi is meant as a backdrop against which to position campus activism. It is the first layer upon which subsequent chapters build. The next four chapters examine different groups of campus constituents and overlap with the chronology offered here. Though the book does not focus on the cross-fertilization between college constituents and other movement centers, it will highlight certain moments of intersection to remind the reader that the off-campus movement and campus-based activism occurred simultaneously and deeply influenced one another.

DEMOCRACY BY EXAMPLE:
STUDENT GOVERNMENT ASSOCIATIONS

Thomas Jefferson, one of the first proponents of student self-government, believed that giving students real power to create rules and mete out disciplinary action would encourage conscientious democratic leadership. At the founding of the University of Virginia, Jefferson asked the Board of Visitors "to devise and perfect a proper system of government, which, if it be founded in reason and comity, will be more likely to nourish in the minds of our youth the combined spirit of order and self-respect, so congenial with our political institutions, and so important to be woven into the American character." According to Jefferson, to invest students with a measure of responsibility encouraged a healthy respect for law and order through benign rather than punitive methods. Such proposals democratized the traditionally hierarchical structure of the university. Student governments spread from Virginia to other white campuses throughout the nation and acted as a bridge between the student body and administrators. Though black colleges lagged behind white colleges in the creation of Student Government Associations, by the 1930s, most black colleges allowed students to form such organizations.[9]

At black colleges, students found themselves in the paradoxical situation in which they could run for office and vote in campus elections but not local, state, or national ones. The incongruity of encouraging political participation on campus but not in American society was not lost on black students. Nor was the fact that black colleges practiced a paternalistic control over their students, including their dress, personal conduct, co-educational activities, and ability to leave the campus, that was unmatched at most secular white institutions. Student Government Associations attracted these politically minded students who sought power as well as changes to the campus regulations and climate. Though student governments most often focused on grievances against the dress code, strict supervision of male–female contact, and lack of student representation on campus committees rather than black enfranchisement, their arguments mirrored the burgeoning black freedom struggle's demands for participatory democracy. Black public colleges and Mississippi Industrial prohibited the formation of rights-oriented groups, particularly in the late 1950s and early 1960s as the black freedom struggle gained momentum, but administrators could not curtail political interests.

The Basic Right to Organize

Students at Mississippi Vocational College initiated a boycott to demand the right to create a Student Government Association in February 1957, marking the first large-scale disruptive event initiated at a black college in Mississippi during the middle twentieth century. Their actions did not directly attack white supremacy, but they were influenced by the increasingly aggressive nature with which blacks advanced their grievances in the immediate post-*Brown* era and the boycott tactics popularized in the Montgomery Bus Boycott, resolved only two months earlier. Forty percent of the Mississippi Vocational student body staged a thirty-six-hour walkout to demand their own student government to act as a liaison with the campus administration. A joint faculty–student committee existed, but students wanted more autonomy. Adding insult to injury, all of Mississippi's other black colleges had student-run organizations. President James H. White and the board of trustees promised to discuss the issue with students, and the walkout ended peacefully. However, President White stalled action on the issue for four years. Not until the 1961–62 academic year were students allowed to create such an organization, and even then it was heavily censored.[10] Mississippi Vocational students never stated an intention to use the group for off-campus political aims. The movement had yet to gain a foothold in Mississippi at the time of the boycott, and students were more interested in campus advocacy issues. But their demand for a democratic voice on campus rattled the trustees and campus administrators and demonstrated that students would take drastic steps to achieve their ends. If students were willing to stage a boycott over a student government, the trustees worried, perhaps they would do the same for civil rights issues.

On Strike, Burn It Down!

Events at Alcorn substantiated the trustees' fears about student co-optation of registered student organizations for political aims and their willingness to enlist civil disobedience. One month after the boycott at Mississippi Vocational, members of the Alcorn Student Government Association spearheaded the second large-scale disruptive action at a black college in Mississippi. In early March 1957, Clennon King, a minister and instructor of history, angered the Alcorn student community with a series of articles commissioned by the *State Times*, a white Mississippi newspaper known for its racism. In his articles, King associated the NAACP with communism, called Adam Clayton Powell a "dupe to Northern race trickery," provided a thoroughly cleansed interpretation of American slavery, and expressed his admiration for the character of Uncle Tom in *Uncle Tom's Cabin*. The fact that pictures of Alcorn students appeared with King's articles did not help his cause, nor did his derogatory attitudes toward women in his classroom. The same day as the third installment of King's series, 6 March, students boycotted King's classes and demanded his resignation or his firing. The boycott spread to other classes on campus the following day, and President Jesse R. Otis recommended King's dismissal to the board of trustees. President Otis, according to rumors printed in the *State Times*, supported the students' critique of King and took action against King for drawing Alcorn into controversial issues.[11] The final decision on King, however, was left to the all-white board of trustees.

Members of the board traveled to Alcorn to assess the situation on 7 March. They met with students and then issued an ultimatum: If students did not return to classes, the board would expel all the protesters and close the campus. The offending students could not use dining rooms and dormitories—a major blow because of Alcorn's isolated location—and would receive a pro rata refund for tuition and housing expenses for the month of March. Students were furious, and one trustee recalled an angry student yelling, "I don't give a damn if you burn [Alcorn] down!"[12] At the end of the day, the situation remained deadlocked. Students refused to return to class until the board fired King. The board refused to negotiate until students returned to class. Emotions continued to run high the following day when students held a rally at the chapel, at which King spoke. King begged students to return to class and attempted to explain his statements in the *State Times*. Students were not swayed and minutes later filed out of the chapel. On the steps, Ernest McEwan, the student body president, read a statement endorsed by 489 of the 571 Alcorn students:

> We the student body of Alcorn A&M College of sound mind feel certain that Mr. Clennon King has inflicted a great injustice upon us by using our students' pictures in support of his series of articles. We feel that every man is entitled to express his opinion. Every person has freedom of speech, the press. But we believe that it is unprofessional and unethical for any person to prescribe or use another's name, picture, institution in support of his convictions. The student body was not informed of this submission of the articles to the *State Times*. Therefore we were denied our freedom of speech. There is an apology owed to us by Mr. King. The only circumstance under which we will accept his apology is by the offer of his resignation. The damage that has been done to us by Mr. King cannot be repaired without a blemish. We do not wish under any circumstance to have Mr. King remain on our campus. This should give you a brief summary of the event that occurred today. At 11:55 am the oldest land-grant college in America for Negroes, which was founded in 1871, died.[13]

The board followed through on its threat to close the campus, fired the president because trustees believed students had "taken over, by and with the acquiescence, if not the consent and approval of the President," and asserted its ultimate authority by renewing King's contract. Those students who wanted to reenroll were forced to meet with the new president, John D. Boyd, and sign a statement vowing never to participate in activism again. Governor James Coleman promised he would open the school with an entirely new student body if they did not comply. Most students signed the statement and reenrolled, but many were furious with Boyd and dubbed him a "white man's tool." Those who did not sign the statement or were identified as leaders in the walkout, including Ernest McEwan, were refused readmission. The entire affair drew national attention, as some ousted students traveled on a speaking tour across the country. Black newspapers, students at other black colleges, and activists applauded the students for their bravery. Their comments mirrored those of Medgar Evers, an Alcorn alum, who recalled, "[Their actions] shocked the very foundation that the white supremacists thought they had reinforced so very substantially. (Imagine Negro students defying an ultimatum issued by a Board of Trustees in the State of Mississippi who happened to be white!)" The national office of the NAACP, the RCNL, and the Elks Club offered financial assistance for the students to attend other universities outside Mississippi.[14]

The forced truce between the administration and the students did not last long. Every year for the next several years, Alcorn students registered their discontent with Boyd's iron-fisted control of campus life. In 1958, Boyd suspended several women after a minor scuffle and expelled the president of the dorm for calling a meeting for residents to discuss the issue. He also expelled several women who attended a public dance, although the dance took place during the semester break and each had parental permission to do so. In 1959, Boyd expelled another woman and a male student for riding in the same car together from the local bus station to the campus (college regulations prohibited female students from riding in cars with males without permission). The last straw was his interference with the election of Miss Alcorn and the student council. Boyd appointed a committee to oversee the elections and warned them, "You should be satisfied, as a committee, that such persons, as are nominated for positions, possess the right attitude toward law and order on the campus, as well as proper attitude toward responsibility of the administration in dealing with campus problems."[15] The black freedom struggle was yet to be in full swing in the state, but President Boyd and the trustees vowed to keep students under control and uninvolved in political and social issues.

President Boyd's actions prompted a second student boycott in October 1959. Students submitted a list of grievances to the administration and demanded the right to establish an autonomous student government, student representation on the Discipline Committee, expanded social privileges, and improved cafeteria and dormitory conditions. True to form, Boyd responded by closing the campus, expelling the student leaders, and calling the state police to escort students to buses waiting to transport them off-campus. When the campus reopened three days later, Boyd required seventy-three students to turn their identification cards over to the Highway Patrol so that they could be monitored. According to a black newspaper and student materials, he also asked that the offending students be denied financial aid—including federally funded National Defense Student Loans—and be fired from their campus employment. Boyd granted the students a hearing for their grievances under the guise of due process, and a committee granted several of their requests. Still, Boyd maintained autocratic rule over the campus, and very little changed.[16]

Alcorn students characterized the president's actions as overly punitive. They complained about the ineffectiveness of the student government and the administrative attitude toward students, which was apparent in that "the majority of the students based their justification for demonstrating upon their notion that there existed no machinery whereby a representation would have been recognized and, hence, effective." A joint faculty-administrative committee, on the other hand, argued that proper channels existed and warned, "The committee wishes it to be made crystal clear to the students that leniency will not be shown, as has been done in this instance, to any future demonstration since it has been brought to everyone's awareness that there are appropriate channels for airing grievances. It cannot but be strongly emphasized that mass demonstration can never be condoned as a becoming pattern of behavior in any college society."[17] Demonstrations may not have been flattering behavior, but Alcorn students enlisted the tactic several more times in the coming years.

In March 1960, the same month as the attempted wade-in in Biloxi and a month after the first student sit-ins in Greensboro, North Carolina, Alcorn students again boycotted classes and issued a list of grievances that closely mirrored the 1959 list. Smaller demonstrations occurred over the years until a two-week boycott rocked the campus in 1964. By this time, the movement in Mississippi was full-blown, with demonstrations, boycotts, sit-ins, and litigation, and SNCC and COFO were planning to bring additional federal attention to the state through the upcoming Freedom Summer campaign. Bolstered by the escalating black freedom struggle's demands for participatory democracy off-campus, hundreds of Alcorn students gathered on the football field and demanded to see the president. Their list of demands included old requests, like "a student government free of administrative domination," and new ones like a relaxed dress code, more competent instructors, and expanded library hours. (The press, however, deliberately misrepresented and trivialized the demonstration by stating it "came as a result of expulsion of students accused of theft from the college bookstore.") Boyd repeated his past behavior and had all students rounded up and escorted off-campus by Highway Patrol. This time, perhaps made more wary of student unrest with intensifying civil disobedience off campus, Boyd required that parents attend a meeting with their child in order to reenroll—quite a request, since some students' parents lived as far away as Chicago and Detroit.[18] The tactic was a way to ensure that students would submit to administrative discipline, since many parents were horrified that their child, often a first-generation college student, participated in a demonstration that put his or her academic career in jeopardy. It is not clear that the student government played a role in organizing the demonstrations after the 1957 crisis, particularly since the administration had a stranglehold on the organization and students indicted it in their lists of grievances. But politically minded students did play a role. Boyd could not kill their aspirations to participate in a democratic environment, despite his best efforts.

The Dissolution of Democracy

To the horror of the Jackson State administration and the board of trustees, Jackson State students appropriated the Student Government Association for civil rights activities in a way that neither Mississippi Vocational students nor Alcorn students had. Their first organized act of defiance occurred when Jackson State students mobilized in support of the Tougaloo College students arrested at the library sit-in in March 1961, discussed in depth later. Seven to eight hundred black youth, including some not affiliated with Jackson State, congregated on-campus near the Jackson State library the evening of the Tougaloo library sit-in. According to James Meredith, a Jackson State student at the time, President Jacob L. Reddix attempted and failed to disperse the crowd. Reddix became so frustrated he began "snatching students at random and shoving them toward a [campus] policeman or dean with orders to expel them." To make matters worse, rumors spread that Reddix slapped a female student. Meredith remembered, "This incident introduced another factor into the demonstration, because it reminded the students of their many long-standing grievances against the administration."[19] The demonstrators finally dispersed with word that city police were on the way, but protests continued the following day with a twofold focus: support for the Tougaloo students and grievances against the administration.

Governor Ross Barnett threatened to close the campus, and President Reddix threatened expulsion if students persisted. Students disregarded the threats, boycotted classes, and planned a march to the city jail. The Student Government Association spearheaded the carefully orchestrated demonstration in which fifty students volunteered to march. According to Walter Williams, president of the Jackson State student body and member of the intercollegiate chapter of the NAACP, "This was SGA sponsored. Medgar [Evers] knew we were going to do it. We had passing NAACP support, but it was a student thing." Organizers asked all other students to attend a rally on-campus to draw attention away from the marchers. While students at the rally sang songs and prayed, the marchers moved in a single-file line on each side of the street to avoid arrest for blocking traffic. Police swiftly and violently reacted to the demonstration with blockades, tear gas, billy clubs, and— for the first time in Mississippi civil rights history—attack dogs. Dorie Ladner, a Jackson State student and participant in the march, remembered, "The police were running all around the alleys and around the houses with these dogs and looking for people. It reminded me of what I had read about slavery, a runaway, you know . . . with them pursuing you." Henry Johnson, another student, agreed: "We were stopped by the police, and a very fierce chase with nightsticks [ensued]. . . . We ran to try and protect ourselves. . . . we feared that the danger might lead to the severest harm to many of the demonstrators." Reddix and the board of trustees clamped down on students, enforced stiff rules and penalties regarding student conduct, and dissolved the Student Government Association after accusing it of "embarrassing" the school. Reddix also expelled Walter Williams and created a dummy government in the student government's stead.[20]

It was fitting that students at Mississippi Vocational, Alcorn, and Jackson State would demand a student government and enlist it as a change agent and that their efforts would be thwarted. A student government, some black college officials and many whites worried, would do just what Thomas Jefferson had hoped: represent a shift in the hierarchical structure of the university and give students a measure of authority and input. It was not that Mississippi's white officials and public black college administrators believed that citizenship training was irrelevant. In fact, Mississippi Vocational, Alcorn, and Jackson State included the notion of education for proper citizenship in their mission statements. Such learning, however, was supposed to be confined to discussions in the history, government, or economics classroom. Students challenged this assumption when they deigned to translate republican theory into practice by demanding the right to form an advocacy organization and using it to challenge the administration and white supremacy. The boycotts at Mississippi Vocational and Alcorn took place before the black freedom struggle gained a foothold in the state, but the all-white Board of Trustees of Institutions of Higher Learning was not so naïve as to believe that black students were uninterested in organizing for social and institutional change.

The Promise and Peril of Student Governments at Private Institutions

Mississippi Industrial College students did not co-opt the Student Government Association for movement ends, since the attitude of the administration at Mississippi Industrial more closely mirrored that at the state's public colleges rather than its private-college counterparts. Students did, however, enlist it for specific projects. In 1961, Clark White, president of the student body, approached Leon Roundtree, a white theater owner, about segregation polices that forced black patrons to sit in the balcony. Roundtree responded to the request by saying, according to White, that "we could sit either downstairs or upstairs but that there would not be any whites attending" on the theater's Negro days. Though the resolution was not what the students wanted, their request was a radical move, since the city of Holly Springs practiced a firm commitment to segregation and many local blacks counseled them against it. In White's words, "The response of the president, as well as our parents and community people—black community people—was that they thought it was most unusual in that we were stepping into an area that had caused people to be killed!" The reason President Edgar E. Rankin did not block their efforts was because Rust College students, not Mississippi Industrial students, took the lead after Roundtree derailed the initial demands.

Another Mississippi Industrial student government–sponsored initiative was a march to hear Dr. Aaron Henry, state president of the NAACP, give a talk at Rust College. Emma Louise Anderson (now Anderson Crouther), a student at the time, remembered, "We organized, and the student council plotted to go. It was going to happen on a Sunday afternoon, so the plan was to get lunch on Sunday and leave the cafeteria and march straight over to Rust, which many of the students did. Of course, the student council was in trouble for having plotted it." President Rankin did not dissolve the organization, though he warned students against future actions. Anderson kept her academic scholarship but was forced to move off-campus during her senior year because of her attendance at the talk. Mississippi Industrial students joined in local activism, but neither the Student Government Association nor any other campus group could organize a sustained campaign against the racial hierarchy.

The Rust College Student Government Association, many members of which also were members of the NAACP and SNCC, organized a more aggressive attack on white supremacy in Holly Springs. Shortly after Mississippi Industrial students approached Leon Roundtree, the white theater owner, the Rust student body sent him a letter declaring their intent to boycott if he did not desegregate in good faith and permit blacks and whites to attend movies concurrently. Worried about the loss of revenue and the possibility that the boycott would spread to students at Mississippi Industrial—which it did—Roundtree arranged a meeting with the Rust Student Government Association. He offered to build a colored theater of equal quality, but students rejected this compromise as well. They demanded, "Permit us to sit where we please, by whom we please, and use the same facilities that everyone else uses." Roundtree refused, and Rust students inaugurated the boycott.[21]

In December 1962, Rust students and SNCC and NAACP members expanded the boycott to include local drugstores. Rather than encouraging patrons to avoid the stores, the boycott called for sit-ins. Activists visited each drugstore and made polite inquiries asking the druggists "to permit the Rust College students to be served at the fountain and to sit at the tables the same as white people." None of the druggists agreed to desegregate, and one threatened to "remove his tables and chairs from the drug store, as he did not care to be the center of a controversy which could cause serious trouble and further that Holly Springs was not ready for such a venture." The students held meetings on Rust's campus to discuss the issue and invited each druggist to attend. None accepted the invitation, and the boycott continued.[22]

Local blacks, including Mississippi Industrial students, joined the initiative, further crippling white businesses in Holly Springs.

The Student Government Association at Tougaloo did not play a role in organizing for the off-campus movement. Instead, the government focused on particular campus issues and employed the organization in a manner consistent with Thomas Jefferson's conception of it: to advocate for more decision-making power and a flattening of the campus hierarchy. Two disruptive clashes initiated by the government occurred against the backdrop of massive civil disobedience in Jackson, the state of Mississippi, and across the South. The first was a proposed student strike to increase the minimum wage paid to student workers in March 1964, the second a sit-in at the college library to protest its early closure so that nonstudent library staff could attend cultural events on campus in April 1964. Students invoked the notion of participatory democracy consistent with the voter registration efforts occurring off-campus in both instances by complaining that "the students have 'their place' and that decisions are something that students have no right getting involved in," and emphasizing "the importance of Tougaloo students having the right to make a choice." They also drew a firm link between on-campus rights and off-campus democracy. As Gershon Konditi, the 1963–64 student body president, wrote the college president, "I think our school is well known and has been highly commended for its just and reasonable attempt to make people of this state understand the principles of American democracy and to demonstrate to them how to respect human dignity. It is quite absurd to learn that this is almost a mere preaching of words we do not really subscribe to."[23]

Freedom of the Student Press

Administrative control over student organizations similarly impacted student publications. At public campuses, student newspapers could not advertise upcoming demonstrations or boycotts and rarely mentioned student involvement in the movement. The tear-gassing, beating, chase, and arrest of Jackson State students during their march to the city jail in March 1961 received fifteen lines of coverage in the college's *Blue and White Flash* that euphemistically described what happened and ended with the thoroughly cleansed, "They were intercepted and dispersed by City police."[24] The yearbook ignored the demonstrations and the dissolution of the Student Government Association altogether. Neither did the newspapers nor yearbooks at Mississippi Vocational or Alcorn mention the boycotts that shook those campuses. On the other hand, Tougaloo, the most active of the campuses, published two papers, *The Voice of the Movement* and *The Student Voice*, and a college yearbook, *The Eaglet*, that discussed and celebrated the movement. And the 1961–62

Eaglet printed a several-page spread on the students arrested at the white library. Rust's *Bearcat* similarly advertised Rust's involvement, while the yearbook included pictures of NAACP officers and Aaron Henry's campus visit. The newspapers and yearbooks from Campbell College and Mississippi Industrial have been lost, but there is little doubt that the amount of coverage mirrored administrative attitudes toward the movement. Restrictions on the student press did not, by themselves, preclude activism, particularly since students were well informed about movement projects through other means. But they revealed the iron grip that some administrations had on students, and curtailed the campus's movement center possibilities.

APPROPRIATING OFF-CAMPUS ORGANIZATIONS FOR THE CAMPUS-BASED MOVEMENT: THE NAACP

In the first half of the twentieth century, the NAACP was the most important rights organization in Mississippi. The national office followed a legalistic strategy that fought white supremacy in the courts, but local chapter leaders like Medgar Evers often employed direct-action tactics, including sit-ins, boycotts, and demonstrations. College students sometimes created campus-based chapters, while others joined citywide youth chapters and still others joined both organizations, since membership in the different NAACP chapters was fluid. The organization was barred from Mississippi's public colleges as well as Mississippi Industrial, but Tougaloo, Rust, and Campbell developed strong and very active campus chapters. Still, membership in the NAACP was dangerous business. Anne Moody, a Tougaloo student, reflected on the perils of being attached to the organization in her autobiography:

> I thought about Samuel O'Quinn. I thought of how he had been shot in the back with a shotgun because they suspected him of being a member. I thought of Reverend Dupree and his family who had been run out of Woodville when I was a senior in high school, and all he had done was to get up and mention NAACP in a sermon. The more I remembered the killings, beatings, and intimidation, the more I worried what might possibly happen to me or my family if I joined the NAACP. But I knew I was going to join, anyway, I had wanted to for a long time.[25]

A handful of Tougaloo students organized a campus branch of the NAACP parallel to the Jackson NAACP Youth Councils in 1960. The groups functioned with the support of Medgar Evers, worked together on different projects, and shared membership. Participation in both chapters remained small in the beginning but grew along with the black freedom struggle in Jackson. Colia Liddell, a Tougaloo student and president of the North Jackson NAACP Youth Council, approached new white Tougaloo political science professor John Salter Jr. about becoming involved in 1961. She considered the campus chapter too small and ineffective. According to Salter, "It wasn't doing much, and some of the Tougaloo students were actually more closely identified with Colia's group." Salter wholeheartedly accepted her invitation and became chapter advisor. Within a year, the organization claimed roughly five hundred members, including students from Tougaloo, Campbell, Jackson State, and black high schools. Tougaloo students also rejuvenated the campus chapter. The various youth branches helped publicize the 1960 Easter boycott organized by Medgar Evers and Charles Jones, the dean of religion at Campbell College. The boycott failed to produce any changes in white business practices in Jackson, but student participation in it became on-the-job training for activists interested in plotting a coordinated attack on the racial hierarchy.[26]

Nine Tougaloo NAACP members staged a sit-in at the whites-only Jackson Municipal Library on 27 March 1961—the same incident that sparked the demonstrations at Jackson State and precipitated the dissolution of its student government. According to Sam Bradford, a Tougaloo student and participant, the sit-in "was by no means something that was hazardly blown together. As a matter of fact, we planned it. It emanated from the youth chapter of the NAACP." Medgar Evers was fully involved in the planning, as was John Mangram, Tougaloo chaplain and NAACP chapter advisor, who helped students select a site and trained them in proper tactics and behavior. Students visited the black George Washington Carver Library and requested books they knew it did not carry, alerted national media outlets in the hope that the attention would dissuade Jackson police from physically attacking them, and arranged for bail. Only then did they travel to the white library, where police arrived soon after the sit-in began. Per their training, the students remained peaceful and refused to leave the library until police arrested them. The Tougaloo Nine, as they were called, spent the night in jail and were released after being charged with intent to provoke a breach of the peace. The sentences carried a possible fine up to $500 and six months in jail.[27] Their actions inaugurated massive and sustained civil disobedience in the state of Mississippi (the last state to experience it) and earned them the enmity of racist whites.

Another major blow struck by Tougaloo NAACP members was the sit-in at the whites-only Woolworth's lunch counter on 28 May 1963. Tougaloo students Anne Moody, Memphis Norman, and Pearlena Lewis denied organizational affiliation, but the entire affair occurred with the assistance and careful planning of the NAACP Youth Councils. The sit-in turned violent when white youths attacked Norman and beat him unconscious. Moody remembered, "A man rushed forward, threw Memphis from his seat, and slapped my face. Then another man who worked in the store threw me against an adjoining counter. Down on my knees on the floor, I saw Memphis lying near the lunch counter with blood running out of the corner of his mouth. As he tried to protect his face, the man who'd thrown him down kept kicking him in the head. If he had worn hard-soled shoes instead of sneakers, the first kick probably would have killed Memphis." Moody struggled back to her stool and was joined by Joan Trumpauer, a white SNCC member and transfer student to Tougaloo; Lois Chaffee, a white Tougaloo faculty member; a high school student; and a CORE worker. The mob pelted them with catsup, mustard, salt, pepper, and sugar.[28]

Word of the chaos reached John Salter and Medgar Evers at the NAACP office. Both men originally stayed behind, since their presence linked the sit-in with the NAACP. Evers remained in the office for strategic purposes, but Salter rushed to the scene where, in Moody's words, "the moment he sat down he was hit on the jaw with what appeared to be brass knuckles. Blood gushed from his face and someone threw salt into the open wound." Salter remained at the counter and tried to make small talk with his fellow demonstrators while being called a "nigger-lover," "communist," and "red." A short while later, Tougaloo's president, Adam D. Beittel, arrived. According to Salter, "A huge white man came up to the Tougaloo president and asked him who he was. Dr. Beittel looked at him, hard into the eyes, and the white man backed away. A. D. Beittel then sat down at the lunch counter." Beittel also demanded police protection for the entire group. After three hours of physical brutality and verbal abuse the sit-in participants finally filed out of the store, where Tougaloo's new chaplain, Ed King Jr., and President Beittel drove them to safety. News outlets broadcast the episode across the nation, and photos of the incident remain iconic of the bravery on the part of black freedom struggle activists in contemporary times. In 1963, however, the Woolworth's sit-in put Tougaloo at the center of another firestorm and inspired rabid racists to devise ways to undermine the institution.[29]

At Campbell College, students were energized by the growing activism in the city of Jackson and across the South. Alfred Cook, president of the student body, had worked closely with Medgar Evers and Charles Jones to publicize and organize the 1960 Easter boycott. Also, Campbell students formed a college chapter of the NAACP, though they maintained close contact with Evers and had overlapping membership with citywide Youth Councils. Johnny Barbour Jr., president of the Campbell NAACP chapter, joined three students from Jackson State who were members of the intercollegiate NAACP chapter in a bus sit-in on 19 April 1961. According to Barbour, "I can remember that day . . . when we got on that bus and got on those front seats. And they asked us to get up and we wouldn't get up. The bus driver begged us to get up and we wouldn't get up. And then he went and called the police and they put us in that jail downtown." The students were charged with breach of the peace and faced sentences identical to those of the Tougaloo Nine. Shortly thereafter, other NAACP members from Campbell and citywide NAACP youth chapters initiated a sit-in at the Jackson Zoo, where local laws prohibited blacks from sitting on benches or drinking from water fountains. Like their predecessors, police arrested the demonstrators and charged them with breach of the peace.[30]

At a rally shortly after the Tougaloo library sit-in and subsequent Jackson State and Campbell College student activism, Medgar Evers stated that student actions marked "the beginning of the fight to make us first-class citizens in Mississippi. In the past few days there has been history made in Jackson and Mississippi and we will move ahead from this point on." He was right. Activism in Jackson steadily escalated. Police arrested more than six hundred people in 1961 and 1962 alone.[31]

The year 1963 was a particularly active time in the struggle, with the Freedom Vote campaign in Mississippi, the desegregation of the University of Alabama, President Kennedy's submission to Congress of what would become the 1964 Civil Rights Act, SCLC's Birmingham campaign to desegregate local stores, the March on Washington, massive civil disobedience in Cambridge, Maryland, and other disruptive campaigns that reached across the entire South. It was also a particularly bloody time. Police attacked children with fire hoses and police dogs in Birmingham and severely beat Fannie Lou Hamer, Annell Ponder, Euvester Simpson, and Laurence Guyot in Winona, Mississippi, on their way home from a voter registration training workshop. The Klan killed William Moore, a CORE worker, while on a one-man march to deliver a letter to Mississippi's Governor Ross Barnett denouncing segregation. The Klan also dynamited a church in Birmingham, destroying it and killing four little girls attending Sunday school. Two white youths shot another black youngster on their way home from a white supremacist rally after the church bombing. At the federal level, J. Edgar Hoover approved a counterintelligence program to investigate and discredit Martin Luther King Jr., and an assassin's bullet killed President Kennedy.[32]

Medgar Evers's assassination on 12 June 1963 added a particularly horrific punctuation to the violence. For Mississippi activists, racists had gunned down the most prominent freedom fighter in the state, a well-known and beloved man revered for his bravery. The press, on the other hand, implicated activists for his assassination: "The professional agitators of the NAACP, CORE and the SCLC must share some of the guilt."[33] Students across the state were as furious as other activists. Those at Campbell and Tougaloo had frequent contact with Evers because of the proximity of his office to their campuses, and Evers also visited Rust. Even students at Jackson State, who were warned to stay out of the movement, slipped off-campus to visit him regularly. Some had known him since their high school days. Anne Moody's recollection highlights the desperation felt by all of them:

> Dorie Ladner, a SNCC worker [and fellow Tougaloo student], and I decided to run up to Jackson State College and get some of the students there to participate in the march. I was sure we could convince some of them to protest Medgar's death. . . . We begged students to participate. They didn't respond in any way. . . . "Every Negro in Jackson should be in the streets raising hell and protesting his death," I said in one class. . . . As we were leaving the building, we began soliciting aloud in the hall. We walked right past the president's office, shouting even louder. President Reddix came rushing out. "You girls leave this campus immediately," he said. "You can't come on this campus and announce anything without my consent." . . . I didn't say anything to him. If I had I would have been calling him every kind of fucking Tom I could think of.[34]

The demonstration did occur, though. Adding insult to injury, police armed with nightsticks, fire hoses, and dogs stood ready to attack the marchers at any provocation.

Highlighting the fact that student NAACP members and campus chapters played an important role in the movement is not meant to diminish the role of adult NAACP members or off-campus Youth Councils in the freedom struggle. A large degree of cross-fertilization existed between off-campus movement centers and student-initiated projects. For instance, Medgar Evers's presence and influence were pivotal. His office in the Masonic Temple was blocks from Campbell and Jackson State (as was the COFO office), and he was fully aware of sit-in and demonstration plans prior to their occurrence and facilitated in organizing several of them. At the same time, Evers's office was not the only physical space enlisted for NAACP projects. Students simply could have joined citywide chapters, but many decided to create campus-based chapters as well. They used the campus space to hold NAACP meetings, where they organized and recruited their fellow students for future NAACP campaigns. Evers's presence was key, but students were not his mere foot soldiers.

THE CREATION OF RADICAL
CAMPUS-BASED ORGANIZATIONS

Black college students also created their own particular rights organizations on their campuses. At places like Tougaloo, Rust, and Campbell, students did so openly, and their student presses proudly broadcast student involvement in activism. The same was not the case at the other colleges, where activist students were forced to create underground organizations, and discussions of student activism—or the movement in general—were almost wholly nonexistent in student newspapers. School papers and aboveground organizations were not the only mechanisms through which students learned of previous and upcoming demonstrations, however. The black colleges were small and self-contained, which forced students into close proximity. Students lived in the same dorms, ate in the same cafeteria, and attended the same classes. Even when they left the campus they visited black homes or black establishments where talk of activism was unfettered. Private conversations were not enough to transform black colleges into movement centers, but they could serve the movement.

A Clandestine Attack

James Meredith, who spent a year at Jackson State before applying to the University of Mississippi, described how informal friendship groups sustained his interest in activism. Meredith found like-minded students he called the In Group on the campus. These students worked together without official university status to plan activities, discuss issues, and for mutual support. According to Meredith, "There is little reason for me to doubt that this group kept me thinking of definite action. I imagine that at some time in the month preceding the decision to apply every possible course of action had been explored by the group." One hundred twenty-eight Jackson State students signed a letter of support for his application to Ole Miss after it became public. Self-identification was risky, and their signatures demonstrated their dedication to the cause.[35] Links to off-campus activists and organizations like Evers and the NAACP cemented Meredith's dedication to complete the application process.

Similarly, the dissolution of the Student Government Association at Jackson State did not terminate student interest in political issues. Students had created the Mississippi Improvement Association of Students (MIAS), a clandestine organization, in January 1961, two months before the Tougaloo Nine library sit-in but after the formation of the Tougaloo NAACP chapter. The MIAS platform mirrored that of other organizations: "to unify ourselves against powerful opposition here in Mississippi. Which display it presents by biased attitudes, unequal job opportunities, unequal public facilities, disrespect to Negro ladies, unequal educational opportunities, and financial aid to organizations which stimulate such acts." Jackson State students dominated its membership, which was in large part why the members remained anonymous. According to James Meredith, who was a member, "loyalty was irrevocable. It was literally impossible for an oath member to betray the organization or any of its members. Only security such as this would encourage a Negro in Mississippi to venture into the forbidden realm of 'White

Supremacy.'" Tougaloo students supported MIAS by printing its literature on Tougaloo's campus—an impossibility at Jackson State. The organization was short-lived, but it created enough consternation in its short existence to garner attention from the Mississippi Sovereignty Commission, which collected its literature and monitored the organization.[36]

Though MIAS literature often focused on off-campus issues, the organization turned its attention to on-campus concerns when President Reddix dissolved the Jackson State student government and ordered it reconstituted in October 1961. His refusal to hear student grievances and his threat that they either abide by the rules or leave Jackson State infuriated students. They lamented, "Where can a Mississippi Negro go if he can't go to a Negro school? MIAS feels that if the student is not satisfied, he has the right to let his dissatisfaction be known, and without expecting harsh, unfair treatment, such as losing his job or scholarship." Reddix's creation of a temporary student–faculty committee to devise a new constitution and initiate new elections made matters worse. MIAS literature admonished students to boycott the election: "We, as students at JSC, are facing one of our most critical moments. What we do now will affect our lives for years to come. Because of this MIAS feels that the student body of Jackson State College should not participate in the scheduled election for a new Student Government Association. Our pride and our future rest on this decision."[37]

Jackson State students, like their counterparts at Mississippi Vocational College and Alcorn, recognized the importance of a student advocacy organization invested with autonomy and power. They could not fathom how an institution that did not trust its students or allow them the opportunity to develop leadership skills and democratic attitudes could be a true college. MIAS asked, "Are [administrators] too steeped in their own insecure and misguided endeavors to realize that the student body is the school and that all good schools have a good thinking student body? We feel that a browbeaten student body can never be a good student body."[38] The problem, of course, was that activists used the student government to plan civil disobedience thereby fulfilling the fears of the board of trustees.

A Full Frontal Assault

Tougaloo College students created the most aggressive campus-based organization to attack racial domination, the Tougaloo Movement. The organization maintained a close affiliation with SNCC, which arrived in Mississippi in 1961, and was led by two SNCC veterans, Joyce Ladner, a black student who had transferred from Jackson State, and Joan Trumpauer, the white transfer student attacked at Woolworth's in March 1963. Tougaloo students staffed and ran the organization, which waged three major campaigns. The first was an attack on segregated entertainment at Millsaps College, the same private white college that displaced Jackson State College in the late nineteenth century. Tougaloo and Millsaps developed a cordial relationship beginning in the 1920s. Millsaps allowed white Tougaloo professors to teach at Millsaps (though they could not bring their black students with them because of the institution's position on racial segregation), students from both institutions participated in the Intercollegiate Fellowship of the Young Men's Christian Association, and a few Millsaps professors and students attended events at Tougaloo. The relationship felt hollow to Tougaloo students barred from attending public events at Millsaps reserved for white patrons only.

The Tougaloo Movement organized interracial groups of Tougaloo constituents to visit Millsaps and test the institution's segregation policy in early 1963. Protesters politely refused to leave the events, forcing embarrassed Millsaps administrators into calling the police to arrest professors and students from a neighboring institution. To make matters worse, Tougaloo Chaplain Ed King, a Millsaps alum, often participated in the demonstrations. Millsaps trustees responded to cries from concerned constituents and the white public by promising that "segregation always has been, and is now the policy of Millsaps College. There is no thought, purpose, or intention on the part of those in charge of its affairs to change this policy." For certain members of the student body, however, trustees' assurances were not enough. In the *Rebel Underground*, the racist publication subsidized by the White Citizens' Council, students blasted the trustees: "Last month William Hutchison, 'white' professor of speech at Tougaloo, brought three niggers to the Christian Center. We ask the gentlemen of the Board of Trustees if this is not integration? What is the meaning of the phrase 'segregation always has been and is now the policy of Millsaps' when niggers and their white cohorts come and go with impunity to our white college?" The moderate attitudes of key Millsaps administrators and faculty and the constant harassment by Tougaloo constituents precipitated a voluntary departure from racial protocol in the fall of 1963. Black patrons could attend public events at Millsaps, though the institution retained its policies on an all-white student body until the 1965–66 academic year.[39]

On the heels of their success at Millsaps, the Tougaloo Movement launched a second offensive against segregation at public facilities in downtown Jackson. The Cultural and Artistic Agitation Committee of the Tougaloo Movement, headed by Austin Moore, initiated a massive letter-writing campaign to dissuade entertainers from performing in front of segregated audiences in the city auditorium. The committee contacted artists, agents, and management to support their cause: "The issue is no longer one of merely appearing before a segregated audience. To appear is to endorse and condone segregation *in toto*." One of the biggest blows came when the Original Hootenanny

U.S.A., a traveling folk company, cancelled its appearance. Tougaloo students Austin Moore and Stephen Rutledge, a white transfer student who was the president of the Tougaloo student body, met the artists at the Jackson airport and convinced them not to play in the segregated city auditorium. Instead, Tougaloo's chapel hosted a free and integrated concert while original ticket holders stood in line for refunds. In early 1964, the stars of the popular television show *Bonanza* cancelled their appearance. A formal statement read, "We have been advised that the state coliseum . . . will be in fact segregated. Unless you can demonstrate to us without equivocation that our information is incorrect, this will constitute our notice of withdrawal." The white Jackson community, including the mayor, vowed never to watch *Bonanza* again. One angry citizen wrote the local paper, "Who gives a tinker's dam about Hollywood stars. . . . If the actors from Hollywood do not want to come to our wonderful state, I say good riddance." The Cultural and Artistic Agitation Committee scored other successes with cancellations by Al Hirt, a jazz trumpeter, Stan Musial, former baseball star and director of the President's Committee on Physical Fitness, and Gary Graffman, a pianist.[40] The passage of the Civil Rights Act in the summer of 1964 gave legislative and legal weight to their demands.

The Cultural and Artistic Agitation Committee became so successful that off-campus organizations attempted to co-opt it. After Medgar Evers's assassination in 1963, his brother, Charles, became the Mississippi field secretary of the NAACP. When the campaign against segregated entertainment gained momentum and national publicity, Charles Evers attempted to position himself and the NAACP as the point of contact for artists entertaining visits to Jackson. When Evers negotiated with Birgit Nilsson, a Swedish operatic star, that she would perform in front of a segregated audience but donate her fee to an integrated institution for children (none of which existed in Mississippi), Tougaloo activists were furious. Austin Moore told the *New York Times* that he could "not understand the reasoning that led the NAACP to accept the compromise suggested by [Nilsson]. At a time when the civil rights issue is so titanic, Miss Nilsson's appearance would have been interpreted by the people of Jackson as an endorsement of their racial practices." The Cultural and Artistic Agitation Committee demanded that the concert be cancelled and confronted Evers, who changed his mind and endorsed cancellation. Evers's actions alienated members of the Tougaloo NAACP chapter who had continued to work with him after his brother's death. According to Ed King, the Tougaloo chapter "had become so discouraged and disgusted with the NAACP [after the incident] that they broke their affiliation and became a SNCC chapter." The new group merged with other campus organizations, continued to serve the black freedom struggle, and used the Tougaloo campus space and resources to do so.[41]

The third and least successful Tougaloo Movement campaign was the desegregation of white churches, some of which Tougaloo professors attended. Together, white Tougaloo professors, black and white students, sympathetic white ministers from Northern states, and other activists carefully planned visits to prominent Jackson churches in the summer of 1963. Catholic and Episcopal churches admitted them, while Lutheran churches were erratic in their policies and other Protestant churches refused to bow. Student efforts intensified when the entire student body returned for the fall semester. Each Sunday, interracial groups of Tougaloo constituents and their allies targeted a white church, where they confronted church ushers who barred their entrance. They would then question the ushers about the incompatibility of racial discrimination and Christian values and open their Bibles to read silently until police arrived and arrested them.[42] The 1964 Civil Rights Act, which prohibited segregation in public facilities, did not impact churches, which were a private entity. Despite student efforts, Sunday mornings remained the most segregated day and time in Mississippi.

Battering the Status Quo

Rust College students also created campus-based organizations. Students, with the help of SNCC workers, created a Speaker's Bureau that dispatched its members to local black churches to discuss voting rights issues. The idea for it grew directly out of their success in the 1961 and 1962 boycotts of local establishments and their interest in branching out to other forms of agitation. Leslie Burl McLemore, a Rust activist, remembered, "We would dress up in our nice clothes and target different churches in the surrounding areas. . . . We were setting up these voter registration and education classes in churches and on the campus at Rust. . . . We would bring literacy forms with us. . . . Then we would ask who would be interested in coming back the following week to go through a voter registration class. Or, if people were already conversant with the form, we'd ask who would need a ride to the courthouse." The local sheriff came to know McLemore, as did the Sovereignty Commission, as a particularly active student. When questioned on the steps of the courthouse on one occasion, McLemore informed the sheriff of his intention to become a lawyer. The sheriff threatened him, "Let me tell you this. If you don't stop bringing these people down here [to register] I don't think you'll ever be able to go to law school." Frank Smith, an SNCC organizer sent to Holly Springs to help with voter registration, was impressed by what students like McLemore accomplished. According to Smith, "The image of students knocking on doors, the fact of their speaking at churches on Sundays, and the threat of demonstration have served to build respect for them and has challenged the local ministers to no end. They see this and are beginning to work to try to build their images and redeem themselves."[43]

In early 1964, Rust's SNCC activists plotted a trip to the University of Mississippi, only a short distance from Holly Springs. Their efforts paralleled those of Tougaloo's Cultural and Artistic Agitation Committee and occurred against the backdrop of intense movement work in northern Mississippi. Ole Miss had been resegregated after James Meredith graduated and the only other black student on campus, Cleve McDowell, had been expelled for carrying a weapon for self-defense. Rust students, in collusion with sympathetic Ole Miss students, tested Ole Miss policies on desegregation by attending a public lecture. In Ed King's words,

> Several Ole Miss students secretly went up to Holly Springs to talk to Movement students at the black school there, Rust College. The Black and white students worked out a plan to send Negro students to a "public" lecture at Ole Miss. Word leaked of the plan and the university officials were alerted— which was probably good since campus police acted properly and helped break up a mob of white students which started attacking the Negro students when they attempted to walk in the campus auditorium. The four Negro students were allowed to enter and joined 200 whites to hear a talk by TV commentator, Howard K. Smith. The University officials did not want to publicly turn Negroes from a neighboring college away from public lectures. But they did not want to upset the Mississippi state legislature or their more rabid students either. So the Chancellor issued an order that all future "public" events on the campus would be limited to faculty, staff, students, and their personal guests. This naturally meant that all whites and no Blacks could attend since for any liberal white faculty or students to publicly claim a Negro as his personal guest meant ostracism and trouble for the teacher, violence and possible death for the students.[44]

In fact, the white student most involved in bringing the Rust activists to campus did face severe penalty. Once identified as the ringleader, his fellow classmates engaged in constant harassment. According to a report, the student returned to his room one night and "found sheets and bedding which had been defecated on and his typewriter which had had water and mouth wash poured into it," endured forty-five minutes of Coke bottles and toilet tissue being lobbed at him, and was beaten and pushed down the stairs when he tried to escape. In the following days his fellow classmates warned him, "There is no dormitory on campus in which you can live. . . . We don't like niggers in [this dorm]. Move now. Avoid suffering later." He finally moved off-campus for his own safety. The racist campus newspaper, the *Rebel Underground*, supported the actions against the student and vowed to protect white supremacy on campus by proclaiming, "We will, as always, hold to our theme the words of Thomas Jefferson, that *resistance to tyranny is obedience to God*"[45] (emphasis in original).

Back at Rust, students displayed increasingly aggressive actions in their own classrooms. Clarice Campbell, a white faculty member hired in 1960, invited a liberal-minded professor from the University of Mississippi and five of his curious students to visit her class at Rust. The session soon became heated. According to Campbell,

> Our students seemed to just let all their damned up grievances tumble out. It occurred to me that we were doing all the talking, so I leaned forward and whispered to the student seated in front of me, "direct a question to one of the visitors because we're monopolizing the discussion." This student, himself most guilty of monopoly, proceeded to tell a story of some officers who were traveling with handcuffed prisoners on the bus. When the passengers stopped for lunch, the prisoners went in the front door and the colored passengers on the bus went in the back door. Then, obedient to my suggestion, he asked, "how do you feel about that, Mr. Washburn?" You never saw such a red face as poor Mr. Washburn's, and I concluded students might do better without my help.[46]

The aggressive nature of the exchange reflected the tenor of the black freedom struggle outside the campus. These Rust students, emboldened by the uncompromising challenge to white supremacy, acted it out on an intrainstitutional level.

CONCLUSION

Not all black students participated in the movement or the organizations on campus. In fact, student activists remembered that only small numbers of students actually participated in civil disobedience. They remained outside the freedom struggle for several reasons, not the least of which was the violent white countermovement. Police regularly arrested, intimidated, and abused student activists. The Mississippi Sovereignty Commission kept files on Rust's Leslie Burl McLemore, Campbell's Alfred Cook, Tougaloo's entire Cultural and Artistic Agitation Committee, Jackson State's MIAS, and activists from other colleges. The state filed litigation and injunctions against individual students requiring them to halt their activities or face imprisonment.[47] A loose network of other groups like the Ku Klux Klan and the White Citizens' Council policed college campuses and reported suspicious behavior to white authorities. And the white press worked to cement hostile attitudes toward the movement. White college students entered the fray with the *Rebel Underground* and the Association of Tenth Amendment Conservatives, a campus-based organization that vowed to meet the Northern white volunteers arriving for the 1964 Freedom Summer in order to disabuse them of their race-liberal notions: "We will prepare to personally show these students just exactly why segregation is the time-honored and history-proven custom which allows the two races to live in peace and tranquility where a large Negro population is present."[48]

Black student activists also faced opposition on campus. Balancing activism and academics was no easy feat. Participation in demonstrations meant absence from class, which could incur harsh penalties because of the strict demerit system at many of the colleges and the attitudes of conservative administrators, faculty, and trustees who frowned on student involvement. After the repeated expulsions of Alcorn students and the dissolution of the student government at Jackson State, students at public institutions were fully aware that the board of trustees and college presidents would take drastic action. As Jimmy Franklin, a Jackson State student, recalled, "Even the most innocent act, I mean walking across the street to Campbell to a rally, could have been an egregious act against the racist system." Neither were activists at private colleges immune. Some students who relied on scholarships and other financial aid felt compelled to curtail their activities or be forced to leave school. Others had unsympathetic parents who could not comprehend how they would involve themselves in the dangerous business of activism. Anne Moody remembered her mother's response when Anne told her she planned to attend an NAACP convention: "She said if I didn't stop that shit she would come to Tougaloo and kill me herself. She told me about the time I last visited her, on Thanksgiving, and she had picked me up at the bus station. She said she picked me up because she was scared some white in my hometown would try to do something to me. She said the sheriff had been by, telling her I was messing around with that NAACP group. She said he told her if I didn't stop it, I could not come back there any more."[49] Activism was a choice, and those students who made that choice used campus-based organizations, media, and resources toward political ends.

Examining such organizing efforts provides a fuller picture of student and black college participation in the movement. Scholars of the black freedom struggle point to the fact that it had two phases. In the organizing phase, activists created long-term strategies to sustain the movement. During the mobilizing phase, activists initiated large-scale, short-term, disruptive, and public events to bring daily life to a halt and draw attention to their grievances.[50] Students, commonly relegated to the mobilizing phase in the literature, also exploited campus space, media, and formal and informal networks to strategize and plot against white supremacy. In doing so, they helped transform an institution not meant for political purposes into an aggressive agent of liberation. Some campus-based organizations were short-lived and did not have much impact, while others successfully destabilized the racial hierarchy and attracted national media attention. Regardless, the cumulative effect of their coordinated attack made black college campuses primary targets in white Mississippi's bid to defeat the movement.

Also, an examination of campus-based organizing forces a reevaluation of student activism writ large. When black college students are examined as activists *and* students, their efforts to change their campuses become important in the history of student activism. Black college students themselves understood their campus demands as closely related to the larger black freedom struggle's mission to transform democratic rhetoric into reality. And their campus-based activism was just as dramatic as that of white students in the Free Speech Movement at the University of California, Berkeley, in 1964. They did not garner the national media attention heaped on Berkeley students, but black students were trailblazers in the perilous job of on-campus advocacy. The student boycotts at Mississippi Vocational and Alcorn were extremely radical, particularly since they attended institutions under the thumb of racist white legislators and trustees, and sanctions, expulsions, and death threats occurred regularly. Black students were not as successful as Berkeley students since, in part, the Berkeley faculty vocally and politically supported student activists while the faculty at some black colleges was forced into silence (a topic discussed in the next chapter). Still, black students were able to mobilize hundreds of people, attract media attention, and bring their colleges to a grinding halt. The fact that they did so under such oppressive conditions adds a new dimension to the nature of student activism, institutional reform, the black freedom struggle, and the racial transcendence of the entire country.

Chapter Four

Testing the Boundaries of Acceptable Dissent: Faculty Activism and Academic Freedom

Students played the largest role in transforming college campuses into movement centers, but they were not the only activist campus constituents. A handful of faculty also participated in the black freedom struggle and used the campus space to organize and mobilize. And, like their student counterparts, some faced opposition to their involvement while others enjoyed the freedom to participate at will. The AAUP's 1940 "Statement of Principles on Academic Freedom and Tenure" provided guidelines that freed the professoriate from institutional censorship and guaranteed the right to free speech, but the role of black colleges in the black freedom struggle made the guidelines null and void on many of those campuses. Black and white faculty often faced severe repercussions for airing opinions counter to those of the white Mississippi establishment.[1]

The literature on the loss and maintenance of faculty rights draws heavily on the experiences of Northern white colleges, but Southern institutions faced a different set of stressors than their counterparts damaged by the federal-level anticommunist witch hunts of HUAC and SISS during the McCarthy era. Unlike Northern institutions, where loyalty oaths and Fifth Amendment rights dominated the debate in the 1940s, Southern colleges faced a different issue, namely the battle for First and Fourteenth Amendment rights as the black freedom struggle escalated in the late 1950s and early 1960s. White Southerners, in the wake of the *Brown* decision and in reaction to increasing black demands to participate in the political process, used the banner of democracy to advocate for states' rights and white control of political institutions. The Southern platform blended anticommunism and anti-integration and found a national audience with the likes of Mississippi senator James Eastland, SISS chairman, friend of Joseph McCarthy, and rabid racist. But it was on the state level that the battle became most contentious. According to Jeff Woods, state-based efforts, "far more than their federal counterparts, were dedicated to massive resistance through the exposure of Communists in the civil rights movement." All organizations and institutions that supported the black freedom struggle were suspect, including black colleges and their faculties.[2]

The mission of this chapter is to explore the variability of faculty participation in the movement and to analyze how race and region influenced the boundaries of political dissent on the part of faculty. The first part of the chapter inserts faculty into the discussion of activist campus constituents, since they are often ignored in treatments of the college campus as a movement center. It also provides an analysis of how the faculty at Tougaloo College politicized the campus space and a discussion of why certain faculty participated while others did not. The second section documents how the SACS, AAUP, Board of Trustees of Institutions of Higher Learning, White Citizens' Council, liberal-minded faculty and administrators, and others collided in a test of wills and left faculty caught in the middle. Examining how academic freedom was negotiated, how it was lost, and how it was preserved at private and public institutions offers a different lens through which to understand patriotism, nationalism, and constitutional protections during a time of massive social and political upheaval.

UNDERSTANDING FACULTY ACTIVISM

Faculty represented a range of opinion on activism and in their participation in the black freedom struggle. Some were highly involved. Reverend Charles Jones, the chaplain and dean of students at Campbell College, fueled his activism with the radical theology of the AMEC, used the campus space to organize, and participated heavily in Jackson campaigns until the college closed in 1964. Mrs. Naomi Nero, a professor at Rust, earned the label "well-known agitator" from the Sovereignty Commission by voicing her liberal attitudes and support of the movement. The faculty at public black colleges were necessarily muted in their support. James Meredith remembered being encouraged, though quietly, by the faculty during his transfer from Jackson State to the University of Mississippi, and Jimmy Franklin, another Jackson State student, remembered that his basketball coach "never tried to arm-twist me, but he cautioned me." And at Alcorn, trustees reported getting "no support" from the faculty when students pitted themselves against the board during the battle over Clennon King's inflammatory remarks in the *State Times*.[3] At repressive Mississippi Industrial, Emma Louise Anderson recalled that "there were faculty members who pushed us to be involved, to do what we could do and still not get kicked out of school. There were faculty members who had to do what they could do and not lose their jobs." Quiet support was not enough to transform a college campus into a movement center, but it could feed and sustain student activism.

Other faculty actively worked against the movement. José Cid, a Cuban refugee teaching chemistry at Tougaloo, fed the Sovereignty Commission's fears of communist infiltration of the black freedom struggle by accusing particular professors of communist sympathies. John Held, a white professor of religion and philosophy at Tougaloo, bristled at the mixture of academics and activism and supplied the Sovereignty Commission with information that contributed to a charter controversy and the firing of the president in 1964 (the details of which will be discussed in the next chapter). According to Held, "I am in favor of the Negro having every right that he can obtain—but I do not believe it to be the purpose of Tougaloo College to sponsor agitation." The same year, at least three Rust faculty became informants for the Sovereignty Commission and played a role in the commission's quest to crush the movement and curtail the activities of black college students. One faculty member was particularly inflamed by the fact that President Earnest Smith's support of the movement seemed to drive a "wedge between the college and the white community in Holly Springs." And Clennon King, the faculty member who precipitated the 1957 boycott at Alcorn, became a hero in the white community.[4]

Personal proclivities alone did not dictate faculty involvement in or absence from movement projects. Like students, faculty found themselves constrained by the autocratic rule of the president and a lack of due process or grievance procedures. Like off-campus activists, faculty faced sanctions by the white power structure in the form of police, banks, merchants, and others that could negatively influence anyone who dared challenge the racial order. The overwhelming possibility of punishment made structural protections pivotal. Financial and political autonomy from the state was important in this regard, but it was not enough. Presidential support and liberal theological/denominational roots were a more likely marker, since Tougaloo, Rust, and Campbell faculty participated in movement projects while the president of Mississippi Industrial dissuaded faculty from participating in civil disobedience. Tougaloo offered several other safeguards for activist faculty, and liberal-minded professors took full advantage of them. Tougaloo provides a useful case study of how and why faculty could help transform a campus into a movement center.

TOUGALOO COLLEGE AS AN OASIS OF FREEDOM

Tougaloo had, by far, the most politically involved faculty of any college in Mississippi, and it is no coincidence that its structural characteristics set the college apart from its black college counterparts.[5] Not only was it independent of state funding, it was the most prestigious black college in the state, the only accredited black college in Mississippi until 1962, and had the highest percentage of faculty with doctoral degrees. Other factors marked Tougaloo as more progressive than many white colleges with regard to faculty protections in that its trustees adopted a tenure policy that resembled AAUP prescriptions as early as 1954, trustees adopted a resolution regarding academic freedom lifted directly from the AAUP's 1940 "Statement of Principles on Academic Freedom and Tenure" in 1959, and faculty organized a campus chapter of the AAUP in 1963. Research on 1960s student activism found that high-status institutions had higher rates of student participation in the movement. Apparently, the same could be said of faculty.[6]

Activism Through Off-Campus Direct Action

Tougaloo also employed a particular type of faculty and staff who translated the structural protections of the college into a shield for activism. The chaplains, much like the activist ministers in SCLC, used their faith to bolster and propel their involvement in the movement. Reverend William Albert Bender, a Tougaloo graduate and chaplain in the 1940s and early 1950s, served as president of the state NAACP. While serving in both capacities, he and two Tougaloo students traveled to the Madison County courthouse in an attempt to vote in the Democratic primary but were told "niggers haven't any business voting." When guards threatened to shoot him, Bender relented, though he later filed a complaint with the state attorney general and provided federal testimony against the seating of Senator Theodore Bilbo, the winner of the election. Hostile whites burned a cross on the Tougaloo campus in retaliation. His successor, Reverend John Mangram, who also served as an assistant professor of philosophy and religion, participated heavily in the NAACP and helped organize the campus chapter in 1960. Reverend Ed King, Tougaloo's first white chaplain, who served from 1961 to 1967, participated in countless sit-ins, boycotts, and demonstrations and used the campus space to help students and others organize different campaigns. Informed by Bender that "this is what the Chaplain is supposed to be doing," he became the most visible white activist in the state when he accepted the lieutenant governor nomination in the 1963 Freedom Vote mock election organized by SNCC and COFO. His activism infuriated racist Mississippians, who accused him of being doubly a traitor: he was white, and he was from Vicksburg, Mississippi. For his efforts, King was arrested and beaten by police, slandered in the press, stalked and harassed by the White Citizens' Council, monitored by the Sovereignty Commission, which tried to get him fired, litigated against by the state of Mississippi, and excommunicated from the white Conference of the Methodist Church.[7]

Other faculty also took advantage of Tougaloo's liberal ethos and institutional protections. Mississippi's second most visible white activist, John Salter Jr., taught in the Political Science Department from 1961 to 1963. He and his wife, Eldri, came to Mississippi after watching the arrest of the

Freedom Riders and the Tougaloo Nine on television, seeking a way to get involved in the movement. During his short time at Tougaloo, Salter worked closely with Medgar Evers and the NAACP, SNCC, and CORE; was a primary organizer of the boycotts that crippled white businesses in Jackson in 1962 and 1963; and offered students the use of his home, affectionately dubbed Salter's Coffee House, as a meeting space. When confronted by faculty doubtful that students could balance academics and activism, Salter argued that "those students who became involved in civil rights activities soon found themselves 'sparked' . . . and motivation for learning was being tremendously increased." He came to national prominence when he was pictured with students at the Woolworth's sit-in in 1963, bloody and covered in catsup and mustard. Like Ed King, who was a good friend, Salter was beaten, arrested, harassed, stalked, and litigated against. The fact that he had ties to the Southern Conference Educational Fund (SCEF), considered a communist front by the Sovereignty Commission, HUAC, and SISS (an unsubstantiated claim SCEF officials vehemently denied), infuriated white Mississippians who believed that the black freedom struggle was infiltrated and led by communists seeking the destruction of America. The Sovereignty Commission and the white press publicized Salter's relationship with SCEF members as a way to intimidate Tougaloo into taking action against him. President Adam D. Beittel refused to fire Salter—Salter left of his own volition to work full-time with SCEF in 1963—but Salter's relationship with the organization marked Tougaloo as a primary target for racist whites.[8]

Activism Through On-Campus Structures

No other faculty, black or white, at any other college, private or public, matched the overt participation by King and Salter. Other faculty chose less public ways to support the movement. One of the most important at Tougaloo was Ernst Borinski, a Jew who fled Nazi Germany in the late 1930s. He arrived at Tougaloo in 1947 and became head of the Social Sciences Division. He used his training as a sociologist and legal scholar to inform his work, and his personal history as an expatriate Jew influenced his interpretation of the Southern racial reality. Borinski was no raging radical and never participated in any demonstrations. Instead, he believed that blacks should exploit their status as citizens to enact a legalistic strategy to dismantle white supremacy. His presence and support of the movement, however, were vital. According to Salter, Borinski "always played a very significant role in getting people together, and sewing [sic] the deeds of discontent, in his very kindly and professional way." Students remembered his influence similarly and recounted how Borinski created "an atmosphere in which white moderates and blacks might debate the issues of segregation integration, inequality, the movement, world affairs, what have you. He maximized his outsideness as a Jew in Mississippi among blacks without ever overtly appealing, as he might have, to some special notion of kinship."[9]

Borinski also created institutional mechanisms that politicized Tougaloo. A year after his arrival, Borinski created the Social Science Laboratory, in which students connected their classroom learning to current social conditions. By doing so, he helped make the walls around the ebony tower more porous. Borinski remembered, "We noticed that in our courses in sociology the students became very eager to apply their learning and experiences to acute social problems of their daily life. The Southern Negro student is an alert and sensitive observer of social situations. . . . The students that enter our sociology classes expect to be guided toward the best possible solutions of their problems." While developing academic skills, students put their learning to use by writing to the United Nations about the Marshall Plan, to the Supreme Court about restrictive covenants, and to local newspapers about domestic issues. It was Borinski's Social Science Forum, however, that made the biggest impact and helped transform the campus into a full-blown movement center. Organized in 1956 with support from the Field Foundation, Borinski created a speaker series that brought Ralph Bunche (a black activist, scholar, and Nobel Peace Prize winner), Eudora Welty (a celebrated white Mississippi author and Pulitzer Prize winner), James Baldwin (a black activist and author), and other renowned speakers to campus to speak about race, society, and democracy. At Borinski's invitation, a handful of faculty and students from Millsaps College participated in the Forum, as did black and white students from other colleges in the state. Both the liberal content and the integrated nature of the audience marked it as radical.[10]

Faculty Activism in Black and White

What emerges in the public record of faculty involvement at Tougaloo is a generalized picture of activist whites and absent blacks, particularly in the 1960s. Where were the black faculty?[11] It is important to remember that black professors at Campbell and Rust (not to mention black colleges in other states) were publicly involved in the movement, so black faculty were not dormant. At Tougaloo, however, black faculty were overshadowed by the activities of certain white faculty. Black professors may have opted out of civil disobedience because they were members of what E. Franklin Frazier described as the black bourgeoisie, an apathetic black middle class more interested in emulating whites than altering the conditions of the black community.[12] But dismissing them in this way trivializes the immediate and virulent dangers of the white countermovement and the probable difficulty of securing future employment in the event they were fired. After all, police incarcerated and physically brutalized activists on a regular basis, and black professors were constrained in their job opportunities because Northern and Southern white institutions refused to hire them.

Also, such a narrow interpretation does not allow for a broad definition of activism. Many black faculty did not participate in demonstrations or sit-ins but supported the movement by donating money to political organizations, allowing students to use the classroom to discuss movement issues, and refusing to punish students for their involvement.[13] Others believed their role in the movement was to keep the college open. In the words of Ed King, "The people who were hostile had good reasons. Tougaloo was there to lead our students North. The second level was to get some of the students to come back as an occasional doctor or lawyer. The third was to train people to work in the public schools. Education was the only way up and out. For people to risk that going to jail and to jeopardize the college itself, that was very heavy." Educating students in a rigorous academic environment that enabled them to lift the black community as they climbed, many black (and white) faculty believed, was itself a form of activism. Their lack of involvement could say less about their personal attitudes and more about the fact that they did not believe the structural protections offered by Tougaloo provided enough shelter for them to participate in the movement without retribution.

Neither did all of Tougaloo's white faculty participate in the movement. Tougaloo hired Salter and King, but it also employed Held. Salter and King were outliers for all faculty, black or white, with regard to their activism. Each pursued employment at Tougaloo because of its role in the movement and the high level of student activism. Borinski did not set his sights on altering the racial reality of Mississippi, but he understood the role he could play at a black college. As he told an AMA hiring committee, "I cannot say that I want to go into black education, but I want to go into education where I can use my talents [including] a wide range of personal and social experiences, a wide range of experiences with people, experience of persecution, experience of army, experience of success and failure." These and a few other white faculty came to Tougaloo with a social mission facilitated by Tougaloo's structural protections. It is plausible that black faculty may not have shared such a mission and were attracted to Tougaloo because employment at a black college was their only option and Tougaloo was the most prestigious institution in the state.[14]

By these measures, the activist faculty experience at Tougaloo mirrored the generalizations drawn by scholars of the era. A study of faculty political attitudes on black and white campuses conducted in the middle 1950s—before the black freedom struggle escalated but during the McCarthy era—found that colleges of higher quality maintained resources and working conditions attractive to distinguished faculty members who often held permissive notions that lent themselves to activism and to an openness with regard to how society should function.[15] Tougaloo's endowment, library holdings, and facilities could not match those of many of its white counterparts, but the college outranked the other black colleges in the state on those same measures and offered a liberal-minded constituency the structural protections necessary to act on their convictions.

BATTLING REDS AND BLACKS: ACADEMIC FREEDOM IN A SOUTHERN CONTEXT

Faculty and student activism took place against the backdrop of an escalating black freedom struggle and the concomitant rise of the Southern brand of anticommunism. Feeding off the frenzy of federal-level investigations and alarmist propaganda regarding Russia's attempt to destroy America by fostering social and economic crises, the white South married the anticommunist fight with the anti-desegregation battle. Southern legislators and committees, facilitated by HUAC and SISS lists that identified countless civil rights organizations as communist fronts or dangers to the state, considered theirs a moral and constitutional duty to defend the southern way of life.[16]

In large measure, the federal-level witch hunts disregarded black colleges. HUAC and SISS focused most of their attention on Northern white institutions in hearings on communist infiltration in higher education, and they interrogated black rights and labor organizations when attempting to root out communism in the black community. Still, black colleges did not completely escape their attention. HUAC called Charles S. Johnson, president of Fisk University, a private AMA institution, to testify regarding communist attempts to recruit black college students in 1949. However, it was at the state level that black colleges—and Southern white colleges—found themselves under siege. Freedom of speech and association undermined the racial hierarchy as far as Southern legislatures were concerned and, like their federal-level counterparts, Southern whites attacked colleges as progenitors of liberalism and sought to curtail campus and faculty dissent in the name of national security. In the words of South Carolina governor George Bell Timmerman, "When academic freedom supersedes loyalty to one's country, loyalty to one's state, and to our trust in God, it becomes an instrumentality of treason that profanes the faith of our nation."[17]

The AAUP became the primary organization through which faculty sought to ensure their First, Fifth, and Fourteenth Amendment rights. The organization adopted the German notion of *Lehrfreiheit*, the guaranteed right of free speech, research, and publication for faculty, as it refined a definition and defense of academic freedom. At first, the AAUP focused more on creating professional standards than parsing out acceptable limits on the breadth of political dissent, but the Cold War forced the organization to turn its attention to academic freedom issues soon thereafter. Its 1940 "Statement of Principles on Academic Freedom and Tenure" made more explicit the organization's support for freedom of speech (a First Amendment issue), due process (a Fourteenth Amendment issue), and tenure (an employment issue). AAUP guidelines did not, however, protect members of the Communist Party, since it was considered a danger to the American state, and many college presidents and trustees succumbed to external pressure or voluntarily sanctioned dissidents in the name of national security.[18]

Another limitation of the AAUP protections emerged in Southern higher education in the 1950s and 1960s. As historian Walter Metzger says about the AAUP's 1915 "Declaration of Principles,"

> by defining a violation of academic freedom as something that happens *in* a university, rather than as something that happens *to* a university . . . nothing was said in this document about the relations of the academy to state authority . . . nothing was said about the external enemies of the university, though history made available such impressive candidates. . . . Nothing was said about the threats to the autonomy of the university that were not, at one and the same time, threats to the livelihood of its members; indeed, it was not even clearly acknowledged that a corporate academic interest, as distinct from an individual academic's interest, existed and had also to be preserved.

The same could be said of the AAUP's 1940 "Statement of Principles on Academic Freedom and Tenure." Even a 1957 resolution that recognized the potential destruction of academic freedom in the racialized wake of the *Brown* decision focused on individual rather than corporate rights.[19] The AAUP's limited authority to force institutional compliance further muted its effect. That the organization relied on the power of persuasion through censure and public condemnation in the *AAUP Bulletin* was laughable to Southern states willing to endure public humiliation to maintain the racial hierarchy.

AAUP prescriptions gained some weight from Supreme Court decisions that took cues from the organization's definition of and support for academic freedom. In the 1950s, the Court issued decisions highlighting the particular importance of teachers in a democracy. In 1952 in *Wieman v. Updegraff*, the court found that "the nature of the teacher's relation to the effective exercise of the rights which are safeguarded by the Bill of Rights and by the Fourteenth Amendment, inhibition of freedom of thought, and of action upon thought, in the case of teachers brings the safeguards of those amendments vividly into operation." Five years later in *Sweezy v. New Hampshire*, the Court reversed a contempt conviction against a professor who refused to answer questions regarding his involvement in a leftist organization and about the content of one of his lectures. Issuing a strong statement regarding the worth of unfettered inquiry, the Court argued that "no one should underestimate the vital role in a democracy that is played by those who guide and train our youth. To impose any strait jacket upon the intellectual leaders in our colleges and universities would imperil the future of our Nation."[20]

Still, the definition of and provisions for academic freedom remained in flux. A 1961 survey of the legal status of academic freedom found a discussion and defense of it almost wholly absent in the appellate courts and only recently included in *Words and Phrases*, a word usage guide for the legal profession. Also, the breadth of a faculty member's right to political dissent was not limitless. Legal decisions circumscribed an institution's ability to fire or punish faculty but allowed public institutions to prescribe acceptable limits on public utterances and political affiliations. By doing so, the courts drew a distinction between freedom of speech and academic freedom. Academic freedom was just that, a *freedom*, not a *right*, in that it provided protection against institutional sanction but did not command institutional subsidy for a faculty member's individual interests or opinions. Nor were the courts completely friendly to faculty or other campus constituents advancing academic freedom claims. Judicial reluctance to intervene in institutional business and overrule administrative authority translated into an array of campus policies that varied from institution to institution.[21]

Academic freedom at private colleges was another matter. The faculty at private institutions enjoyed only the freedoms provided by their employment contracts, since the constitutional protections and safeguards offered by *Wieman v. Updegraff* and *Sweezy v. New Hampshire* only extended to institutions under the control of the government. The AAUP pressed private institutions to adopt AAUP prescriptions, but nineteenth- and early-twentieth-century judicial decisions that solidified private institutional autonomy from government interference also meant that private college administrators retained the authority to limit academic freedom in the 1960s.[22]

Appeals to lofty constitutional ideals or notions of academic freedom fell on deaf ears in Mississippi as the black freedom struggle accelerated and whites adopted a siege mentality. Since *Brown*, the state had faced litigation to desegregate its primary and secondary schools, increasingly aggressive civil disobedience, the arrival of the Freedom Riders, James Meredith's enrollment at Ole Miss, Freedom Summer, and implementation of the 1964 Civil Rights Act and 1965 Voting Rights Act. The fact that many whites believed each of these was part of a communist plot to precipitate America's ruin though a race war heightened anxieties. Those in power, including the governor, legislature, Sovereignty Commission, board of trustees, other government officials, and their allies, worked diligently to maintain the racial hierarchy, legal and AAUP protections be damned. As the AAUP noted, "In this atmosphere

of intensely conflicting feelings, arising out of the encounter between a rap-
idly changing social situation and an almost pathological xenophobia concerning ideas which are believed to be subversive of the traditional way of
life, conditions of academic freedom are precarious."[23] Public institutions
and private institutions experienced the external pressures differently, but
both faced the state of Mississippi's frontal assault on academic freedom.

INSTITUTIONAL AUTONOMY VERSUS STATE SECURITY: ACADEMIC FREEDOM AT BLACK AND WHITE PRIVATE INSTITUTIONS

The potent mix of the black freedom struggle and the fear of communism
touched both black and white institutions. In Mississippi, the first major threat
to academic freedom occurred at Millsaps, the private white college in Jackson
from which students and faculty traveled to Tougaloo to attend Ernst Borinski's
Social Science Forum. In March 1958, several years prior to Tougaloo's assault
on segregated entertainment at the institution, the Millsaps Christian Council
sponsored a series of debates, one of which was entitled "Christianity and Race
Relations." The Council invited Borinski, since Millsaps barred blacks from
campus at the time, and he was "the closest to black they could get." In his
address, Borinski called segregation un-Christian and infuriated segregationists. Two days later, local papers reported Borinski's comments and announced that a "second integrationist," Glenn Smiley, field secretary of the
Fellowship of Reconciliation, was coming to Millsaps. Adding insult to injury,
the papers reported that a Millsaps professor addressed Borinski's integrated
Social Science Forum the same day.[24]

President H. E. Finger cancelled Smiley's visit, but his action was not
enough to quell the concerns of the Mississippi legislature, which initiated
an investigation of Borinski and his links to the NAACP. The White Citizens' Council considered the invitations representative of a larger issue and
blasted Millsaps in the local press. Ellis Wright, president of the Jackson
chapter, wrote in a letter to the editor of the *Jackson Daily News,* "The public,
contributors to the college, its friends, students and parents of students want
to know, and we want to know the answer to the one simple question. Where
does the administration stand on segregation?" The issue, of course, was not
simply Millsaps's stand on desegregation or segregation. "The closed society," as Mississippi historian James Silver named it, linked freedom of speech
to an assault on white supremacy. Could administrators curtail student rights
to hear different opinions on controversial topics, concerned Mississippians
asked? And should outside parties like the White Citizens' Council and the

legislature have the power to curtail a (private) college's right to maintain its own affairs for the sake of national and state security?[25]

The debate over these issues became high drama, and the public registered its opinions with scathing editorials in the local press. Some pitted freedom of speech against national and state security in the spirit of the HUAC and SISS hearings of the McCarthy Era: "The Citizens' Councils and other patriotic public officials are engaged in a life and death struggle for our very existence against an enemy with whom there is no compromise. It is intolerable for Millsaps College, right here in the heart of Mississippi, to be in the apparent position of undermining everything we are fighting for. I tell you frankly and without rancor that the time has come for a showdown." Another angry citizen wrote, "The institution's faculty should screen the topics which are to be discussed. Some people will cry that this will stifle freedom of speech. There is a time and place for all things. A college campus in America is not the place to extol the virtues of Communism. We are engaged in a 'cold war' of survival with the Soviet Union. No red-blooded American needs to hear both sides in order to make up his mind."[26]

Other citizens appealed to constitutional freedoms and defended students' First Amendment rights. "Russia is not the only place dominated by Dictatorship. Mississippi is caught in the tentacles of a mighty octopus, better known as the Citizens' Councils. Free speech is not allowed here. Democracy is out, it's dead, the Citizens' Councils censor who can speak, who to Preach and who to teach. They control the Politicians and the elections, just as the Communists do where they are in control." Hodding Carter, Pulitzer Prize–winning author and editor of the *Delta Democrat-Times* in Greenville, entered the fray by appealing to Jeffersonian ideals, accusing the Citizens' Council of "Nazi-like conformity of thought," and calling Ellis Wright "pathetic." Even Millsaps constituents stepped up to defend the institution, though at least one student did so anonymously for fear of retribution.[27]

President Finger walked a fine line. He promised that Millsaps would remain segregated until the board of trustees decided otherwise and assured a nervous white public that the "College Administration will urge all committees inviting guest speakers to exercise care and caution in the selection of appropriate personnel." But he argued that students had the right to hear different points of view. In a letter sent to the local newspapers and to Millsaps alumni, Finger elaborated, "In an age when we are alarmed at the increasing controls of government, we should be strengthening those institutions which support and preserve freedom of speech. It is better to have freedom of speech abused now and then than not to have it at all."[28]

In 1962, four years after the Millsaps debacle, Tougaloo found itself in a similar situation. Otto Nathan, a lifelong pacifist and socialist who escaped

Nazi Germany, spoke to Ernst Borinski's Social Science Forum. He heavily criticized HUAC in his address and argued at other events during his week on campus that freedom fighters should persist in their efforts "until we have real integration and a complete end of racial discrimination." The white press was furious and harangued Nathan. "Is this the same Dr. Otto Nathan," the *Jackson Daily News* asked, who was "known to have associated with communists and officials from Iron Curtain countries; and as having refused to answer questions with reference to conversations with representatives of Communist nations?" President Beittel not only verified that it was the same Otto Nathan but refused to apologize for Nathan's comments or review Borinski's invitations to controversial speakers in the future. Adding a final insult, Beittel stated that he would not hesitate to invite Nathan to Tougaloo for future events. According to Beittel, "Education depends on contrary points of view. When you censor a speaker because he disagrees with you, you get only propaganda. I'm afraid that too much of that is happening in this area."[29] Nathan's talk did not garner as much public attention as Borinski's speech at Millsaps, possibly since the segregation issue added fuel to the Millsaps fire, but his presence and Beittel's refusal to take action rankled white racists who considered the episode proof that Tougaloo was a danger to the state.

A parallel between the events at Millsaps and Tougaloo is instructive in a discussion of academic freedom, particularly at private colleges. Both colleges were religiously affiliated and considered liberal when juxtaposed against their respective white and black counterparts. Administrators could curtail academic freedom without violating constitutional protections. Both speeches took place at a time of heightened apprehension: Borinski's speech at Millsaps occurred in the immediate post-*Brown*/Little Rock era amid fears of a communist conspiracy to force integration on whites, and Nathan's talk at Tougaloo occurred when Tougaloo students were heavily involved in the Jackson Freedom Movement. Cold War rhetoric flourished in both cases. And local whites couched their argument for limits on freedom of speech in the paternalistic language of protection for impressionable students.

Still, the situations played out very differently. Though Tougaloo was the weaker of the two institutions in terms of status, endowment, income, and national reputation, Millsaps voluntarily (though reluctantly) forfeited a measure of institutional autonomy, while Tougaloo aggressively asserted its own. With these examples, only Millsaps fits into the story that historians tell about liberal academics faltering when given an opportunity to transform faith in academic freedom into an institutional reality. According to an AAUP report, Tougaloo had "*no* problem at all" with regard to restrictions on classroom teaching, public utterances by faculty, or invitations to outside speakers (emphasis in original). Instead, the report found the major issues to be the state's continued attempts to interfere in college affairs and the fact that recruitment efforts were hindered by the hostile racial situation and poor public schools for faculty with children.[30] The story of this small black college in Jackson, Mississippi, therefore, complicates the traditional story of institutional capitulation to political pressure.

The Tougaloo example challenges other generalizations in the literature as well. For instance, of black colleges during the McCarthy era, Ellen Schrecker states, "These schools, though so far outside—and below—the mainstream of American higher education that they could hire politically undesirable professors, did not completely eschew the blacklist." Schrecker is correct: many black colleges were wary of hiring faculty called to testify before HUAC or SISS during the 1940s and early 1950s. However, black colleges did not have the latitude in hiring that she assumes. Tougaloo was outside the mainstream with regard to federal pressures and scrutiny, but it was central in white Mississippi's mission to crush "agitation and militant and belligerent activities . . . against the peace and harmony of the State of Mississippi." Mississippi officials kept close watch as concerns about the black freedom struggle and communism merged in the late 1950s and 1960s. By then, HUAC's mission to root out communists had been translated into a state-level agenda, and black colleges like Tougaloo faced mounting pressure to purge their faculties of politically undesirable professors. Tougaloo's refusal to fire Salter, King, Borinski, and other faculty despite the fact that the Sovereignty Commission was "thoroughly convinced that communist front individuals had infiltrated into the activities at Tougaloo" was not the act of a desperate institution but a mark of bravery and a defense of academic freedom.[31]

Events at Millsaps and Tougaloo also force a broadened definition of the phrase "the state" in treatments of academic freedom during this era. First, the phrase is often used to imply federal meddling, with a focus on HUAC or SISS hearings as intimidation. But the harassment of Southern institutions in the post-McCarthy era also came from Southern state governments. In Mississippi, hearings did not exist, and dissidents were not allowed the opportunity to address their accusers—if, in fact, they even realized they were being accused in the first place. Second, "the state," in the Southern context, should be extended to include terrorist groups like the White Citizens' Council. Though a private citizens' organization, it received funding from the Sovereignty Commission, and members were represented in every level of government.[32] The fact that Council members held leadership positions in the community as bankers, lawyers, and business owners extended "the state's" reach. In short, "the state" was not simply elected officials and government agencies. In the South, the state's tentacles enabled a coordinated attack on the black freedom struggle in both the public *and* private sectors.

WHITE SUPREMACY AS STATE POLICY: THE PARTICULAR VULNERABILITIES OF PUBLIC INSTITUTIONS

The all-white Board of Trustees of Institutions of Higher Learning worked in collusion with government officials willing to sacrifice academic freedom for white supremacy and regularly meddled in institutional business. The board did, at least, pay lip service to the provision of academic freedom. In August 1959, it issued a statement that "there should prevail at our universities and colleges an atmosphere of freedom in their research, teaching programs, and services and that there should be no political or subversive propagandizing in the academic programs. It is proclaimed with equal fervor that academic freedom does not mean academic license. With freedom there must be responsibility for statements, speeches, and actions."[33] The statement resembled the AAUP's 1940 "Statement of Principles on Academic Freedom and Tenure" in that it referenced acceptable limits on dissent. The AAUP and the board, however, diverged on what type of speech and association should be protected and found themselves adversaries as they battled over academic freedom at several of the state's public institutions.

Firing Faculty with Impunity

The lukewarm protection offered by the board was tested less than a year after the adoption of the 1959 policy. In 1960, Alcorn's president, John D. Boyd, fired Corrine Craddock Carpenter, an assistant professor, and eleven other faculty and staff, including her husband. Professor Carpenter served Alcorn for nineteen years, several of them as a full-time professor, but was dismissed late in the 1959–60 academic year without notice. The entire affair occurred against the backdrop of the SNCC-sponsored sit-ins spreading across the South, nascent civil disobedience in Mississippi, and the 1959 and 1960 demonstrations at Alcorn. Boyd, determined to keep the Alcorn campus out of the fray, warned the faculty that "any demonstrations at that time might be misjudged as attempts at sympathy (or worse) with the 'sit-in' demonstrations." In building his case against Carpenter, Boyd offered no evidence of poor work performance but harangued Carpenter for undermining his authority and encouraging student unrest. Boyd began his assault on Carpenter by arguing that the 1959 faculty committee's recommendation of clemency for students protesting conditions on campus was an affront to his authority and told Carpenter, who was a member of the committee, that she "should and could have influenced the committee to act differently." The temerity with which the committee would suggest leniency demonstrated that they "did not have any sense." He also blamed her for a student boycott of his inauguration, a charge she vehemently denied. Boyd was particularly inflamed by student actions at a concert at which Carpenter presided. According to Carpenter, "I asked that we give a 'big hand' to the President and his First Lady. They stood, and in the background a few students 'booed.'" Boyd considered the fact that she did not eject the students and close the affair (which had just begun) evidence that she sanctioned his public humiliation. Carpenter bristled at Boyd's accusations and complained to the board of trustees that "my work was above reproach—he just felt I wasn't with him."[34]

The AAUP launched a full-scale investigation. A member of the team arrived in Mississippi the same day as the Freedom Riders, a fact that was not lost on him. In conference with the president, Boyd offered conflicting statements. One, he refuted Carpenter's accusations and argued that her views on student protest were not an issue. But he explained that he could not offer advance notice regarding her firing because it would have divided the institution, already rocked by student unrest, and that the quiet of the 1960–61 year was proof that his plan worked. Two, according to the AAUP official, "He stated in one breath it was ignorance not defiance of the 1940 statement, but in another breath stated he would handle future cases like Mrs. Carpenter's in precisely the same fashion, guided strictly by what he thought would be best for the institution."[35] The board of trustees had hired him to quell dissent, and Boyd took his job seriously despite the damage to academic freedom or constitutional protections.

The final AAUP report was a scathing indictment. Of Boyd, an AAUP official observed, "his system of arbitrary dismissals has generated in the faculty deep insecurity and a strong reluctance to express opinions openly. Faculty participation in government, consequently, is at an absolute minimum. Many department heads do not even have a voice in such a fundamental issue as the hiring of new men in the department, or in determining departmental salary increases and promotions." The AAUP also took aim at the board of trustees, which refused to be swayed and never rehired Carpenter or the other faculty and staff dismissed without due process. In fact, the investigating committee found "no evidence that the Mississippi Board of Trustees was concerned with academic due process." Trustees cared little about external pressures, especially from those insensitive to the racial climate in Mississippi, and Alcorn remained on the AAUP censure list until 1973.[36]

Accreditation, Race, and Academic Freedom at a White Institution

On the other hand, trustees did worry about the status of Mississippi's white colleges and its flagship, the University of Mississippi, in particular. While the AAUP investigated events at Alcorn, James Meredith submitted his application to transfer from Jackson State to Ole Miss. The fallout put the state's support of white supremacy in stark relief. White racists rallied behind the board of trustees, which refused to enroll Meredith. A Jackson news outlet declared, "Their decision is one of not just preventing a negro from entering the University. It will be one to set the precedent that Mississippi is a State of integrity." It also assured the board that "never have men in the history of Mississippi had such unity behind them." Similarly, Governor Ross Barnett addressed the citizens of Mississippi: "We must either submit to the unlawful dictates of the federal government, or stand like men and tell them NEVER!" The White Citizens' Council added, "We hereby serve notice on the racial perverts and ruthless politicians who would destroy the South: 'We have only begun to fight.'"[37]

Meredith's application, by putting Mississippi higher education in a national spotlight, also pitted white racists against SACS and the AAUP. SACS put *all* of Mississippi's black and white public institutions on probation after Governor Ross Barnett interfered with the board of trustees (which struck a deal with the governor so they would not be indicted themselves) and the University of Mississippi regarding Meredith's enrollment. The AAUP acted similarly when several faculty resigned in protest of the university's handling of the Meredith crisis and others expressed concern about retaliation for liberal views. The faculty feared reprisal from both the board of trustees—which could fire them—as well as more immediate persecution by the White Citizens' Council, which inundated liberal and moderate faculty with "honorary nigger" postcards, engaged in a "long siege of harassing telephone calls to faculty at inconvenient hours," and dismissed AAUP concerns by declaring, "This is no question of 'academic freedom.' It is rather, a simple matter of morality." Despite the AAUP's active involvement in the case, SACS sanctions carried the most weight, since the loss of accreditation meant that diplomas were useless for those students pursuing further education, while AAUP censure was simply a public shaming as far as trustees were concerned.[38]

The board scrambled to rectify the situation and wrote to SACS officials promising "in the strongest possible terms that it will observe the constitution and standards of the Southern Association of Colleges and Schools and will continue to be assiduous in its efforts to secure the integrity of the institutions under its control, to safeguard their ability to achieve their purposes without political interference, and to preserve and advance their standing in the educational world." The board also concocted a policy meant to soothe SACS and AAUP concerns about the lack of institutional autonomy in 1962. The new policy included a probationary period of at least three years for faculty, something unheard of at black public colleges, where faculty, staff, and administrators worked on annual contracts. The policy also included tenure regulations in which a continuing appointment would be in effect at the end of the probationary period and with a letter from the president. And any fired professor was guaranteed at least one semester's notice before final termination. The board's policy, however, was disingenuous. When put to the test, and despite the fear of SACS penalties, the state of Mississippi cared more about maintaining a racial hierarchy than the status of its higher educational institutions.[39]

The board's dedication to its 1962 policy was put on trial the following year with the case of James Silver, a tenured full professor of history at Ole Miss since 1936. With the black freedom struggle in full swing and on the heels of James Meredith's enrollment, Silver delivered the Southern Historical Association's presidential address, "Mississippi: The Closed Society," in November 1963, and published it in book form the following year. In the book Silver wrote,

> Mississippi has erected a totalitarian society which to the present moment has eliminated the ordinary processes by which change may be channeled. Through its police power, coercion and force prevail instead of accommodation, and the result is social paralysis. Thus, the Mississippian who prides himself on his individuality in reality lives in a climate where non-conformity is forbidden, where the white man is not free, where he does not dare to express a deviating opinion without looking over his shoulder. Not only is the black man not allowed to forget that he is a "nigger," but the white moderate must distinctly understand that he is a "nigger-lover."[40]

The tenor of the book, and the fact that he blamed whites for the riot at Ole Miss when James Meredith enrolled, was an act of treason as far as the governor, legislature, Mississippi Sovereignty Commission, and board of trustees were concerned.

In retaliation, legislators introduced resolutions demanding Silver's firing and prohibiting him from speaking on racially charged topics. According to John Bell Williams, state representative and future governor, "Accreditation or no accreditation the time has come to fumigate some of our college staffs and get those who will teach Americanism and not foreign ideologies." The director of the Sovereignty Commission wrote the board of trustees asking them to fire Silver despite the repercussions. Even Ole Miss students recommended that the university withdraw from SACS: "The best way to deal with a BLACKMAILER is to Refuse to do business with him and DEFY him to do his worst." Despite certain sanction, the board of trustees prepared to fire Silver for making inflammatory statements they believed were calculated to increase racial tension. In doing so, trustees directly violated the constitution of SACS, the 1940 AAUP "Statement of Principles on Academic Freedom and Tenure," Supreme Court rulings, and their own 1962 policy, which provided that a tenured faculty member could only be fired on the recommendation of a tenure committee. Silver actively pursued the case with the

AAUP, but the complaint was closed in 1965 because he left for a faculty position at Notre Dame.[41]

Firing Faculty with Impunity Revisited

The second major test of the 1962 policy came at a familiar location: Alcorn. As with Corrine Carpenter—as well as James Silver—any support for the black freedom struggle was considered grounds for dismissal. In 1964, President Boyd fired Frank Purnell, a physical education instructor and head football coach, after five years of service. The president claimed that the football team's poor performance precipitated Purnell's firing. Purnell and others suspected it had more to do with the 1964 student boycott that rocked the campus, and he contacted the AAUP for assistance. Purnell told the AAUP that he received a letter of reappointment in March 1964, weeks before the boycott. However, Boyd called a meeting of all the department heads, administrators, and coaches after the boycott and "coerced them to sign a statement asserting their complicity with him in the action taken against the students on April 21, 22." Though the faculty were not consulted before Boyd called the Highway Patrol, they signed the statement after an administrative officer threatened to fire them if they refused to comply. When Boyd demanded they sign a second statement to the same effect, Purnell refused. In Purnell's own words, "I could not in a clear conscience sign a statement which in fact was untrue, that is, sign another such statement." Boyd fired him two days later.[42]

The AAUP saw Purnell's case intertwined with Carpenter's, particularly since trustees dismissed AAUP concerns by arguing that they did not "feel that any constructive results could be obtained by reopening the case of Corrine Craddock Carpenter" and instead hoped "that as time passes the procedures at Alcorn A & M College will prove satisfactory in this respect." When an AAUP investigator contacted Boyd directly, Boyd responded by stating that everything that could have been done for Carpenter had been done (which was nothing) and that Purnell's department head recommended he be fired—a switch from the first rationale, that the football team's losing record precipitated Purnell's firing. The AAUP reminded Boyd that Purnell "does not seem to have even received the notice to which he was entitled under institutional regulations. To state that you, as President of the College, were simply following the recommendations of a department head in this instance does not excuse what appears to be a total disregard of standards acceptable to the world of higher education." The AAUP also contacted the board of trustees about the continued abuses at Alcorn. Boyd and the board refused to take any action. A full year later, the AAUP reported back to Purnell and lamented, "There is little to be gained by conducting a full-scale investigation of conditions of academic freedom and tenure at an institution already censured for failing to abide by proper standards. On the other hand, the apparent new violation does underscore the conditions which led to the original censure action."[43]

The AAUP as a Liability

The AAUP's ineffectiveness and the board's disregard for academic freedom also came to a head at Mississippi Valley State College, formerly Mississippi Vocational College. In 1964, President James H. White fired several faculty members in direct violation of the 1962 board of trustees policy that guaranteed an employee three months' notice of termination. Paul Taylor, one of the fired faculty, and his wife were members of the AAUP. Though President White listed "contumacious conduct" as the reason he fired Taylor, Taylor and others believed that their AAUP membership was the actual root of the problem. By this time, the board of trustees had been battling the AAUP for years, and the chairman of the board admitted as much in a conversation with Taylor, stating, "your trouble is the AAUP," railing against the organization, and warning Taylor "not to pursue" the complaint. In response, the AAUP warned the board that their and President White's actions put the institution in jeopardy: "If the administrators are permitted to flout the regulations which affect themselves, is not the reaction among faculty members and students likely to be one of cynical disregard, if not contempt, for an authority which expects more of them than it does of themselves?"[44]

E. R. Jobe, the executive secretary of the board of trustees, responding to AAUP accusations arising from both Alcorn and Mississippi Valley, replied, "The Board of Trustees has not authorized these violations, but has come to the conclusion that the welfare of these institutions and the students involved require that the actions of the Presidents should be sustained in these several instances." He further explained to the AAUP investigator "that the situation at the Negro colleges in Mississippi was very different from the situation in the white colleges. . . . He said that if early notice was given, the new militant spirit among the Negroes would be likely to arouse the students to rebellion, and late notice was therefore a safeguard against such student action." Instead, the board declared that it anticipated no further violations. The AAUP was left toothless. Investigators promised to publicize the infraction but informed the Taylors that there was little the association could do, since "the President of the school remained insensitive to such action and was supported by his Board."[45]

The Battle at the State Level: Mississippi Trustees versus the AAUP

Firing faculty, curtailing free speech, and lack of due process were standard fare at black colleges in other states. Administrators at Fisk University (1955), Allen University (1958), Benedict College (1958), and Alabama State College

(1960) had been intimidated into action by trustees and racist public officials who feared that "the Communist menace is a very real menace, and most of all to education." But Mississippi's aggressive disregard for institutional autonomy shocked the national academic community. Not since Mississippi governor Theodore Bilbo's purge of higher educational institutions in 1932 had a state so sweepingly undermined the concept of institutional autonomy. The AAUP, which made little headway on an institutional level, enacted a broader strategy. In 1964, the organization sued the state of Mississippi over the fact that the board of trustees required faculty at public institutions to list the organizations of which they were members and to which they contributed funds. The policy flew in the face of Supreme Court rulings that established such requirements as unconstitutional. The AAUP found no evidence that the information had been used against faculty members but considered the files "a powder keg in the midst of a crowd of people some of whom have been known to toss matches." The state attorney general and trustees fought the issue in court, but a judge found in favor of the AAUP in 1966.[46]

The AAUP also initiated a statewide investigation, the first conducted by the organization, in 1963, and published its report in 1965. AAUP officials were shocked at the academic and professional conditions across the state. They found that none of Mississippi's public colleges, black or white, except the University of Mississippi, had maintained tenure regulations until the board issued its 1962 policy. Even then, individual campus administrations interpreted and implemented them differently, as evidenced by events at Alcorn and Mississippi Valley. To complicate matters, tenure was not official simply because a faculty member had served a term of years, as would have been the case under AAUP regulations. Instead, receipt of a letter from the president bestowed tenure, and black college presidents often withheld letters as retribution or to encourage faculty members to comply with presidential demands. At Jackson State, faculty reported that they were not clear on who had tenure or even how to receive it. Nor did all the campuses, private or public, black or white, have AAUP chapters to act as a watchdog and advocacy group for such protections. Of the black colleges in the state, only Tougaloo and Jackson State had campus chapters, though the other institutions had individual members. Not surprisingly, the organization considered the absence of AAUP chapters evidence of hostility toward the rights of faculty.[47]

When interviewed by AAUP officials, E. R. Jobe again defended the board. He offered as evidence the fact that trustees did not interfere in the faculty's choice of materials, though the White Citizens' Council and the Daughters of the American Revolution pressured them to do so. The faculty at some of Mississippi's public institutions concurred with Jobe's assessment when interviewed by the AAUP committee, but those interviewed at Jackson State pointed to subtle intimidation by stating that "there is a set of explicit and subtle directives beyond which [we] are not supposed to go." Public utterances were even more contentious and were highly restricted, a fact that did not bother trustees. As a member of the AAUP committee remembered of her conversation with Jobe, "They do not want 'reformers' on their faculties who try to change Mississippi ways. They do not mind different ideas being presented as a part of subject matter and on a factual basis, but not to use educational process to 'reform.' He believes education is to inform and *not reform*" (emphasis in original). Faculty understood the consequences of their actions. One, they could be fired. And, two, in the words of the report, "not many faculty members want to risk having happen to them what happened to Medgar Evers."[48]

To make matters worse, the board of trustees passed a speaker ban in August 1964, in the wake of the Freedom Summer Project that brought hundreds of volunteers to the state to work in voter registration and Freedom Schools. All Mississippi public colleges were affected. The speaker ban blended the themes of anti-integration, states' rights, and the threat of communism. It specifically referenced an "invasion" of Mississippi by hostile "outside agitators" for the purpose of overthrowing local government and race rioting. The resolution vowed to "protect student life from undue pressure by those engaged in activities contrary to the laws of the State of Mississippi and to the image of the citizenship of the state; and that all things be had and done which may be considered proper to eliminate development of socialistic and communistic trends among the college or university youth." It also required college presidents to investigate and approve campus speakers and forward their recommendations to the board of trustees for review.[49] By taking the power out of the hands of students, faculty speaker's committees, and even college presidents, the board of trustees demonstrated the lengths to which it would go to maintain white supremacy and quash dissent.

The AAUP also responded to the rise in *student* activism. While the organization focused most heavily on *Lehrfreiheit* and the rights of faculty, the administrative backlash against students prompted the organization to issue a statement in support of *Lernfreiheit*, the student's right to learn and study in an open environment without sanction. The AAUP's "Statement on Faculty Responsibility for the Academic Freedom of Students" positioned faculty as the purveyors of First Amendment freedoms on campus. With regard to freedom of speech the AAUP explained, "Faculty responsibility for the academic freedom of students stems from the recognition that freedom of inquiry and expression are essential attributes of a community of scholars." With regard to freedom of assembly, the AAUP admonished faculty to support student participation in the student government as "a valuable means

for the exercise of the rights and obligations of students as campus citizens."
It also asked that faculty support students who joined or created other political, educational, and cultural organizations, a declaration that, presum-
ably, spoke to the fact that NAACP and SNCC chapters were barred at all
public institutions.[50]

Following AAUP prescriptions was no easy feat for the faculty at black
colleges in Mississippi. The lack of tenure regulations, hostility, and willingness to violate policies on the part of the board of trustees, the collusion of
college presidents, and the ineffectiveness of the AAUP meant that all campus constituents who dared confront the racial hierarchy faced severe penalties. The AAUP may have been correct to assert that "the faculty has an
obligation to insure that institutional authority and disciplinary powers are
not employed to circumvent or limit the rights of students as members of the
larger community."[51] But in an environment where faculty were relatively
powerless to protect even themselves from the rabid and violent malfeasance
that ran amok in Mississippi, it is hard to imagine that they could have been
effective at protecting the rights of students.

CONCLUSION

Between 1957 and 1965, the AAUP censured fifteen Southern institutions,
eight of them for firing faculty who espoused liberal attitudes on race. The
institutions sometimes worked to resolve AAUP grievances, but legislators
and government officials dragged their feet and were motivated more by
growing national pressures and SACS sanctions than AAUP demands. Academics and the AAUP recognized the association's limitations. First, its statement on the breadth of protected dissent was vague in that it both supported
the faculty's right to speak freely regarding their specializations and warned
faculty of making "hasty or unverified or exaggerated statements, and to
refrain from intemperate or sensational modes of expression." Second, as
historian C. Vann Woodward, who conducted a survey of academic freedom and Southern institutions, stated, "The AAUP cannot take the initiative against politicians and pressure groups who are causing the trouble. An
aroused public opinion informed by exposure of outrages and abuses should
count in the long run."[52] In the long run, public humiliation did count. But
the Southern purges left academic victims across the South in the meanwhile.

Black colleges were particularly prone to external pressures because of
student and faculty participation in the movement. In many cases in which
public college faculty found themselves fired, they merely expressed sympathy with the movement and did not participate in any civil disobedience.
Faculty were caught between the status of American citizens protected by

the United States Constitution and state employees bound by state laws and social codes; Mississippi's long history of asserting states' rights over federal protections and defense of white supremacy bled into limits on academic freedom. Private campuses, on the other hand, often accepted the faculty's right to free speech but debated if the institution could afford to allow faculty (much less students) to participate in the movement if that participation brought state harassment and scrutiny. Some private colleges sacrificed institutional autonomy and academic freedom to avoid constant state harassment, while others, like Tougaloo, refused to capitulate. The combination of anticommunism and white supremacy proved a powerful mix. Enemies of the movement understood that academic freedom and campus activism went hand in hand, and the closed society demanded total compliance in its battle against the black and red scares.

Chapter Five

"Cancer Colleges":
The Battle on Private College Campuses

As institutions outside the direct purview of the state legislature, some private colleges became havens for freedom struggle activities. The structural protections of financial and political independence from the state, however, did not necessarily transform a campus into a movement center. Presidents and boards of trustees heavily influenced the ability of activist campus constituents to recruit, organize, and mobilize. At some private institutions, administrators punished students who participated in movement projects, kept a tight rein on faculty, and refused to allow activists the use of campus facilities. Even the most liberal campuses had to deal with conservative students, faculty, and administrators who did not believe that academics and activism could mix. Presidents and trustees found themselves in a bind as they worried about the academic integrity of the colleges as activism escalated. They reminded activists that campuses could not perform the same role as other movement centers like the NAACP, SNCC, or certain black churches. The colleges had an educational mission, not a political one. The point at which presidents and trustees believed that line was crossed varied at different institutions.

The situation was all the more perilous because the private colleges were not completely immune from external influences. The public role of the private colleges made them enemies of the state. The local press went so far as to describe them as "cancers" that needed to be destroyed or contained in order to save Mississippi from ruin.[1] Mississippi's agency of choice, the Mississippi Sovereignty Commission, vowed to preserve and defend white supremacy at any cost. The commission never succeeded in destabilizing any of the colleges by itself, but it created conditions under which private black colleges weighed the benefits and costs of remaining involved in the black freedom struggle. Its success hinged on its ability to act as a parasite that capitalized on institutional vulnerabilities. The weakest institutions suffered dire consequences, and none of the colleges was immune to the commission's agenda. The colleges fought back, and in some ways were successful, but the tug-of-war for ultimate control of campus affairs exacted a stiff toll.

SIMILARITIES AND DIFFERENCES BETWEEN THE COLLEGES

In 1960, Campbell College, Tougaloo College, Rust College, and Mississippi Industrial College educated approximately 1,500 students total. An even smaller number participated in active protest. Their enrollment numbers meant less than the fact that their private status preempted direct state intervention, a source of consternation for enemies of the movement. Segregationists and their allies railed against what Lieutenant Governor Carroll Gartin called havens for "quacks, quirks, political agitators and possibly some communists."[2] The Sovereignty Commission enlisted the assistance of campus informants and sponsored court injunctions to prevent campus constituents from participating in direct action. The White Citizens' Council initiated its own investigations and accused various campus officials of conspiring with communists to overthrow the United States government. Local police regularly visited the campuses and recorded license plate numbers in an effort to gather information and to harass campus constituents and off-campus activists. In extreme cases the legislature itself entertained creative sanctions against the colleges. The state's organized and interconnected network marshaled its forces to intimidate the colleges into compliance with state laws and social codes.

Though private status buffered the colleges from these external attacks, institutional vulnerabilities provided the entrée through which the state and its allies forced the private colleges to reevaluate their role in the black freedom struggle. Campbell, Tougaloo, Rust, and Mississippi Industrial were not wealthy institutions. Defending the campuses and their constituents from constant state harassment diverted funds away from college development projects. Also, the state exploited dissension on campuses. Individual campus constituents maintained different ideas on the path and pace of social reform. Conservatives accused activists of hijacking education for civil rights aims and transforming the colleges into centers for political activity. The colleges differed in their ability to withstand the internal and external pressures threatening to undermine them.

Campbell College and Mississippi Industrial College were the most vulnerable. A variety of factors set them apart from Tougaloo and Rust. First, they were supported by and affiliated with black religious philanthropy. Their entire constituencies, trustees, faculty, administrators, staff, and students, were black. More importantly, the particular nature of funding made them vulnerable to Sovereignty Commission aims and external pressures. The colleges were uniquely quite poor. The Eighth Episcopal District of the AMEC, consisting of Louisiana and Mississippi, supported Campbell. The AMEC had a nationwide network, but different districts took on the financial responsibilities of particular schools. Campbell, a combined high school and junior college, received little national AMEC attention, as the denomination concentrated its funds and energies on its four-year institutions. Mississippi Industrial suffered a similar financial fate. The CMEC's flagship institutions received the bulk of the collective denominational support, and Mississippi Industrial had to rely on state and locally based aid to subsidize the institution. Because both schools maintained small student bodies and received few funds through tuition and fees, Campbell and Mississippi Industrial had only a small pool of money on which to rely for support. The limited funding networks and the ease with which government agents sanctioned black residents of Mississippi and other Southern states created siege situations that negatively influenced the colleges' ability to withstand state pressure.

Second, all four colleges were religiously affiliated, but Campbell and Mississippi Industrial were more closely aligned with a particular denomination's ideological principles. AMEC doctrine supported full racial equality and likened forced segregation to second-class citizenship. Not all AMEC members translated church doctrine into direct confrontation with the Southern racial hierarchy, but some did, particularly when the black freedom struggle gained momentum. At Mississippi Industrial, too, church doctrine and attitudes influenced college participation in the movement. Unlike its AMEC counterpart, the CMEC was created as a way to maintain segregation. Its doctrines focused not on black equality but on evangelization and racial accommodation. The church's continued affiliation with the MECS—a white denomination, for all intents and purposes, that refused to allow blacks to worship at its churches—also negatively influenced CMEC participation in the movement. In the case of Campbell, alignment with the AMEC's doctrine and mission made it an enemy of the state. In the case of Mississippi Industrial, alignment with CMEC doctrine and mission dissuaded activism and soothed the Sovereignty Commission's concerns.

Tougaloo, on the other hand, was in a stronger position to resist Sovereignty Commission efforts. The nature of philanthropic support buffered it. The AMA, a group of white and black religious philanthropists, supported Tougaloo, and AMA colleges received funding from a nationwide network, not individual districts. Equally important was that the AMA was a nonsectarian organization that received money from religious and secular sources to support its projects. Also, the organization maintained its headquarters in New York, another factor that marked it as different from Campbell and Mississippi Industrial and provided an important degree of autonomy, since philanthropic agencies with headquarters and donors outside the South were less susceptible to state pressure. Tougaloo's financial scaffold provided it with more security, though it was far from wealthy.

Tougaloo and Campbell were located a mere six miles from each other near the seat of government in Jackson, and students often coordinated civil rights activities and visited one another's campus as well as other movement centers like Medgar Evers's NAACP office and COFO headquarters. What marked Tougaloo as different was the level of campus participation in the black freedom struggle. Tougaloo students, faculty, and staff participated in some of the most public and most disruptive assaults on Mississippi's racial hierarchy. Tougaloo also had more extensive campus facilities than Campbell College, which made Tougaloo more attractive for off-campus activists seeking a meeting place in Jackson. On-campus events and off-campus demonstrations garnered the college and the movement increasing publicity in national and local media outlets. These factors combined made Tougaloo the Sovereignty Commission's biggest college target. Commission director Erle Johnston Jr. associated his own career advancement with his ability to quash the activism at Tougaloo.[3] Tougaloo was stronger than Campbell, but it was also a bigger threat to Mississippi laws and customs. Accordingly, the Sovereignty Commission more aggressively harassed the institution and focused its energies on finding an entrée to exploit. A fortuitous fund-raising campaign and a unique charter controversy provided the commission with the fodder needed to undermine Tougaloo's role in the movement and make civil rights activism a campus liability.

Like their Jackson-based counterparts, Rust College and Mississippi Industrial College were in close proximity—they were located across the street from each other in Holly Springs. A few students from Mississippi Industrial participated in the movement, but students at Rust College far outnumbered them and received most of the Sovereignty Commission's attention. However, Rust College was the least influenced of all the private colleges by external pressure and was able to protect itself from punitive measures for a variety of reasons. Like Tougaloo, it was funded by biracial, nonsectarian, and Northern philanthropy, maintained a board of trustees' headquarters outside Mississippi, and was supported by a nationwide financial network. The fact that Rust did not have any peculiar vulnerabilities, like Tougaloo, or extreme financial trouble, like Campbell, frustrated the Sovereignty Commission's agenda. Also, the commission reserved much of its energy for events in Jackson. Sit-ins, demonstrations, and boycotts in the capital embarrassed the state and drew much of the commission's attention. The commission monitored the Rust campus, particularly when activist students became more aggressive and volunteers for the 1964 Freedom Summer used the campus as a pit stop on their way to movement projects across the state, but Rust's geographic location made it a secondary target. Even the Mississippi media ignored much of the movement in northern Mississippi, as Rust students and their allies received little noteworthy press.[4] Last, the Sovereignty Commission learned from its mistakes in Jackson. Local and national newspapers repeatedly carried pictures of Jackson activists, including some from Tougaloo and Campbell, being attacked by hostile whites and chased by police dogs. The commission resented the bad publicity, particularly since one of its missions was to soften Mississippi's image and convince the American populace that Mississippi blacks were content with the existing social structure. Commission representatives put their hard lessons to use in Holly Springs and at Rust, but the campus withstood the pressure.

It is important to remember that the battle between the state and black colleges took place against an international Cold War against communism and African liberation movements, national debate over the 1964 Civil Rights Act and proposals regarding what would become the 1965 Voting Rights Act, South-wide civil disobedience geared toward desegregation and voting rights, and Mississippi-wide protests and legal action to desegregate the state's public schools and facilities and for voting rights. White supremacists at all levels of government promised that Mississippi would never capitulate to the black freedom struggle's agenda and used beatings, jailings, bombings, murders, economic harassment, and other forms of physical and psychological harassment to intimidate activists. The intense media attention focused on Mississippi and the escalating pace of the movement sent racists into a state of panic. The Sovereignty Commission and its allies were charged with getting the movement under control. Colleges were primary targets, but they were only one set of movement centers targeted for disruption.

THE DILEMMA OF BLACK PHILANTHROPY
AND RACIAL RADICALISM

Fueled by fears of the burgeoning black freedom struggle and the demand for desegregation in the immediate post-*Brown* era, the Sovereignty Commission began scrutinizing organizations and institutions that held race-liberal notions. Campbell College's radical theological roots put it in direct conflict with Mississippi's racial hierarchy. In December 1957, an investigator reported that a bishop admonished members attending a regional conference, "I warn you here and now, in the presence of God and this audience, that if any one of you permit any person, white or black, to advocate segregation in any form, your appointment will be immediately revoked. Further, you will be brought to trial for violation of the honor and traditions of this great denomination." AMEC publications in the early 1960s also articulated an overtly political agenda for AMEC schools: "The basic concern of the A.M.E. Church in education is training Christian leaders for the struggle of the Negro to secure by his own efforts full rights, privileges and benefits of citizenship and respect for the worth and dignity of human personality without regard to race, creed or nationality—for realization of Christian and democratic ideals of liberty and justice."[5]

Black Radicals, Black Conservatives, and White Racists

In 1959, the commission, emboldened by federal-level witch hunts for communists in race-liberal organizations, drew links between two Campbell College administrators and SCEF, one of the organizations, according to HUAC and SISS, that "the Communist Party has infiltrated or is using as fronts to create racial unrest in the state." Bishop Sherman L. Greene, who was member of the SCEF board of directors, had been a Campbell trustee, and William R. Wright, a SCEF member, served as chancellor during the 1956–57 school session. The press bolstered the commission's smear campaign by listing the men along with several others (including Pulitzer Prize–winning Mississippi newspaper editor Hodding Carter) under the headline, "MISSISSIPPIANS ARE LISTED IN RED 'INFILTRATED' GROUPS." Without commenting on the nature of the charges against them, President Robert Stevens reminded the public that neither man was affiliated with Campbell since Greene left his position in 1948, and Wright's tenure ended with the 1956–57 school year.[6] The commission's attempt to associate Campbell with communists neither weakened the institution nor tarnished its name, but the mounting attacks presaged trouble for the institution.

The commission also kept tabs on activist black churches, including Pearl Street AME Church, which many Campbell students attended. Its pastor, Reverend G. R. Haughton, who also served on the Campbell board of trustees, used the pulpit to preach about brotherhood and equality and allowed the church to be used for various mass meetings. He also led by example. Between 1956 and 1960, he served as president of the Jackson branch of the Progressive Voters League, a statewide organization that prepared blacks to take the exams necessary to become registered voters; state NAACP Church Work chairman; assistant secretary of the Ministerial Improvement Association, an organization working toward "first class citizenship for all the people of Mississippi regardless of race, color or creed [and] integration in the areas of public transportation, including bus and railroad stations"; and member of the Ministers' Conference of the RCNL.[7]

Not everyone in Haughton's congregation agreed with his political proclivities or his use of church space for movement ends. Percy Greene, the conservative editor of the black newspaper in Jackson, the *Jackson Advocate,* rescinded his church membership to demonstrate his antipathy for Haughton's actions. Haughton could hardly have been surprised, since Greene was well known in the black Jackson community as an informant for the

Sovereignty Commission and an enemy of the movement. Greene focused most of his energy on the NAACP, SNCC, and SCLC but also took aim at black colleges and their students. According to Greene, student demonstrations were a "Communist inspired technique" and "one of the worst things that has happened to us as a race in the struggle for first-class citizenship." Further, he admonished Dr. Martin Luther King Jr. that the greatest service he could provide would be to "advise Negro students to make their schools no longer centers of agitation and demonstration, but places where they put forth the greatest effort towards the attainment of knowledge, wisdom, and understanding." T. S. J. Pendleton, the presiding elder at Pearl Street AME and a Campbell trustee, also objected to Haughton's use of church space for movement projects. His concurrent job as principal of a public black elementary and secondary school, which received an increase in state funds to stall school desegregation, certainly could have influenced his actions and reticence in being linked to activism.[8]

Activism and Reaction

Campbell College's inaugural role in the direct action phase of the movement was as a host for several events centered on the economic boycott of white Jackson stores during Easter 1960. Its proximity to downtown made the location ideal for canvassing and distribution of material to potential shoppers. Chaplain and dean of religion Charles Jones became heavily involved in the boycott and invited the NAACP to use the campus for organizing sessions and press conferences by Medgar Evers, and campus activists posted a sign on college property advertising the boycott. President Stevens was, again, called on the carpet regarding the behavior and associations of campus constituents. When asked about Campbell's role in the movement President Stevens told a local newspaper that the college, as an institution, did not officially sponsor the boycott but that it—and he—was not opposed to it.[9]

The enrollment of almost one hundred black high school students expelled from Burgland High School in McComb, Mississippi, in October 1961 drew the campus deeper into the movement and, in turn, increased Campbell's visibility in the state. The previous summer, a large group of Burgland students participated in a voter registration drive and sit-ins, and 116 had been arrested. Fifteen-year-old Brenda Travis was singled out and sentenced to one year at a school for juvenile delinquents. Jacqueline Byrd (now Byrd Martin), a student at the time, remembered that her Burgland classmates quizzed the principal about Travis's return at an assembly the following fall. He hedged his answer, and the students initiated an impromptu march through downtown McComb. Police arrested them as they prayed on the steps of City Hall. According to Byrd Martin, "After that the students went to school. That's when we were told we would have to sign some papers saying we would not ever participate in anything like that again. We refused. Some agreed and did sign the paper. Those of us who refused were put out of school and suspended." Soon thereafter, President Stevens extended them offers of enrollment at Campbell.[10] This was not the first time Campbell had opened its doors (in 1957 it welcomed the students expelled from Alcorn), but the pairing of the Easter boycott and the arrival of Burgland students put Campbell in the news.

The Sovereignty Commission watched in horror as Campbell constituents joined demonstrations against the state and used the college facilities to plan direct action tactics. President Stevens did not join any demonstrations or participate in the planning of civil disobedience, but he allowed these activities to occur on-campus and refused to curtail the involvement of either students or staff. The commission reserved some of its harshest criticism for Charles Jones and treated him as a primary cause for concern. His membership in the NAACP and close association with Medgar Evers marked him as an enemy of the state. Jones made headlines with an attempt (by himself) to integrate the Jackson Trailways Bus Terminal the same day the Interstate Commerce Commission ordered segregated signage to be removed, and with his participation in an interracial ministerial pray-in at the Jackson Federal Post Office to protest police brutality. Jackson police arrested him and a court convicted him of breach of the peace after both demonstrations. His active involvement in the movement and the support of President Stevens led a commission agent to remark, "The names of Robert Stevens and Dean Charles Jones should be added to our 'trouble-makers list.'"[11]

As Campbell's role in the movement increased, so, too, did commission efforts to destabilize the institution. In 1960, an agent sent a list of Campbell trustees to Jackson police, asking, "If you come up with any ideas regarding the above, please let me know." That the police regularly employed violence and other forms of intimidation did not bode well for the trustees. In January 1962, the commission paid Percy Greene and T. S. J. Pendleton, the disgruntled Pearl Street AME members, two hundred dollars under the auspices of supporting the AMEC.[12] Why the men received payment is unknown, but it is a safe assumption that the money was not to support Pastor Haughton, the Pearl Street AME Church, or AMEC radical theological positions on racial equality. Pendleton, a Campbell trustee, was very likely motivated by the issue of job security as a public school principal as well as personal attitudes about the path and pace of reform. The commission understood that he could be a powerful tool against the militancy of certain AMEC ministers and congregants on or off the Campbell campus.

Sabotage from the Inside Out

Campbell officials gave the commission the opening it could exploit. Conservative AMEC ministers and trustees held gradualist attitudes toward the pace of societal reform and admonished students and staff that a college should focus on academics, not political education. Fearing the campus had spun out of control, one member of the board of trustees and three AMEC ministers, including T. S. J. Pendleton, requested an injunction preventing President Robert Stevens, Dean Charles Jones, and other Campbell College administrators and trustees from performing their campus duties in February 1962, less than one month after Pendleton received a check from the Sovereignty Commission. Reverend Haughton had left his position at Pearl Street AME by the time of the injunction and was therefore not included in it. The state did not act as a plaintiff, but the ends sought by the plaintiffs certainly buoyed the commission's cause. The plaintiffs linked their aversion to campus-based civil rights agitation with accusations that Campbell College officials abused its charter, the laws of the state of Mississippi, and financial donations. The Sovereignty Commission kept a record of the court proceedings and watched the situation carefully.[13]

The plaintiffs focused part of their argument on Charles Jones. They charged that Jones's election as dean of religion was "for the express purpose of preaching to, and disseminating among the students of the college, the radical and unorthodox views held by him, and in order to create dissention among students of the college and to agitate and incite them into a violation of the laws of the State of Mississippi." Jones's aggressive attacks on white supremacy colored the campus atmosphere, they charged. He and other activists transformed Campbell from a respected private institution into a hotbed for political activism. The plaintiffs argued, "He invited and encouraged the so-called 'freedom riders' to congregate on the campus of the College, and he undertook to persuade the students of the college to join in the movement, and to violate the laws of the State of Mississippi; and he himself did, in fact, join in said movement and for his willful violation of the laws of the State of Mississippi, he was arrested by the Police of the City of Jackson, and was tried and convicted, and is now out on bond."[14] His actions, according to the plaintiffs, jeopardized the institution.

Campbell's admission of the ousted Burgland High School students aggravated the situation. Plaintiffs complained that their enrollment flouted the laws of Mississippi and unnecessarily politicized the campus. Campbell had been involved in the movement prior to their arrival, but few people outside Jackson had paid any attention to the college. Their enrollment brought the campus unwanted and negative attention in the white press, a fact that made the plaintiffs very wary. Plaintiffs also attacked the students' right to attend. Their suit argued that the students took the spots of deserving and qualified children of AMEC members. President Stevens admitted the high school students "without any regard whatsoever to their educational and scholastic qualifications or good character, and without requiring them to pay the usual enrollment and tuition fees."[15] Complainants considered these actions a violation of the charter agreement to educate the children of AMEC congregants and evidence of bad judgment.

The injunction also illuminated a split in the board of trustees. The plaintiffs accused chairman Frederick Jordan and Dean Jones of mismanaging large sums of money. They complained that the men diverted donations, church assessments, and rent from college-owned property in Mound Bayou, Mississippi, for personal gain. Jordan, the suit declared, practiced duplicitous behavior on a regular basis. The plaintiffs offered the example of the purchase and sale of property located near the campus. According to the suit, R. A. Scott, one of the plaintiffs and former president of the college, owned land adjoining the campus. Jordan persuaded individual AMEC members that Campbell should purchase the land for educational purposes and raised the necessary funds. The college bought the land, but Jordan immediately sold it to the state for $2,500. The plaintiffs accused Jordan of keeping the funds for himself rather than depositing the money in the college's accounts. The final insult came when Jordan, Jones, and President Stevens conspired to solicit funds under the guise of the Burglund High School student episode. The accused not only wrongly enrolled the students, they did so "as a publicity 'gimmick' to raise money for their personal gain."[16]

Three weeks after the plaintiffs filed their plea, the Chancery Court ordered that the board of trustees be reconstituted and demanded that the Council of Bishops remove Jordan as presiding bishop of the Eighth Episcopal District. But the court allowed Charles Jones to continue as chaplain and dean of religion until the board's election, and it did not object to President Stevens's reinstatement by the new board if it so desired. Four months later, AMEC members reelected fifty percent of the former board of trustees and reinstated President Stevens and Dean Jones.[17] The AMEC effectively reasserted its authority over Campbell and demonstrated the broader AMEC's support for the administration. It is unknown if the court or the Sovereignty Commission expected the trustees to reinstate President Stevens and Dean Jones. It is possible that commission officials miscalculated the broad base of support for the administrators and, by extension, the black freedom struggle. Regardless, Campbell regained an important degree of autonomy in its tug-of-war with the Sovereignty Commission.

The Death of a Black College

Campbell College looked very much the same before and after the litigation. The staff remained largely intact, the Burgland High School students left the college at the end of the academic year, the student body remained active in the movement after 1962, and the campus continued to host civil rights events. The difference was that the Eighth Episcopal District of the AMEC and Campbell grew poorer in the process. The court injunction cost the church money, particularly since it pitted campus officials against each other. Campbell never maintained a large endowment and had been underfunded for years. Neither the court nor the plaintiffs offered incontrovertible evidence that trustee Jordan, President Stevens, or Dean Jones mismanaged money, but the validity of the claim was irrelevant as far as the court was concerned. The claims of financial mismanagement and impropriety provided a perfect opportunity to exploit institutional weakness. The state stepped in, and this time it sealed the college's fate.

In 1964, the state of Mississippi seized the Campbell property by right of eminent domain. The campus had deteriorated and gone into debt, and the legislature wrestled control from the trustees. Legislators never called it an act of retribution, but Campbell's place in the Jackson movement clearly influenced the decision. Campbell administrators planned to move the campus to church-owned land in Mound Bayou but needed time to do so. They applied to the all-white Board of Trustees of Institutions of Higher Learning, which chartered the creation of any new private or public college, for two separate extensions before vacating the premises. The new presiding bishop even used the removal of President Stevens as a bargaining chip: more time to build a college in Mound Bayou for Stevens's forced retirement. The board refused to be swayed, particularly since "the take-over of the property automatically will remove Dr. Stevens." The state clearly never supported a rebuilding campaign and did all in its power to prevent it from succeeding. The state purchased the Campbell property and deeded it to Jackson State College. A new campus was never constructed due to lack of funds.[18]

A combination of radical theological roots, strong presidential leadership, and the dedication of some activist-minded constituents transformed Campbell into a movement center. The fact that all of Campbell's records have been lost or destroyed makes a close examination of the personalities of the trustees, President Stevens, and Dean Jones impossible, but it is doubtful that the campus could have played the role it assumed in the movement if such men (and women) did not support the use of campus space for movement ends. What damned Campbell were its structural vulnerabilities. In particular, its financial situation provided an opportunity the state refused to ignore. The nature of its philanthropic support made the campus susceptible to external pressure. Colleges supported by black philanthropy were notoriously underfunded. Tuition, church assessments, and donations rarely yielded enough for basic operating costs. Their racial makeup made funding agencies wary, and Northern foundations preferred institutions with, if not a white president, a predominantly white board of trustees.[19] The intense internal dissension also facilitated the commission's efforts. Campbell trustees unwittingly primed the institution for the state's successful intervention. Mississippi racists not only halted its role in the movement but helped kill Campbell College.

ACTIVISM VERSUS ACADEMICS

Tougaloo's structural protections, theological grounding in notions of racial equality, and activist students, faculty, and chaplains transformed the campus into the most important college movement center in the state. Still, administrators worried about the movement's impact on the college from an early stage. In 1955, before Tougaloo constituents assumed an active role in the black freedom struggle, Tougaloo trustees applauded the *Brown* decision but openly worried that the desegregation battle would focus unwanted and angry attention on Tougaloo, since it was the only desegregated institution in the state. Two years later, President Samuel C. Kincheloe addressed the increasing racial tension in Mississippi and warned, "These situations mean that [Tougaloo] has a difficult time in relating itself to the white citizens of Mississippi. The college is pursuing a policy of acquaintance and of the development of understanding as to what our objectives are and how we are proceeding."[20]

An Activist President versus a Cautious Board of Trustees

Into this context stepped Reverend Dr. Adam D. Beittel, who assumed the presidency in 1960 when Kincheloe retired. Under Beittel, Kincheloe's policy of acquaintance was replaced by a full frontal assault on white supremacy. According to Beittel, "We have no reason for existing unless we can shake away some of the shackles." Born of Quaker roots, he nurtured his liberal philosophies at progressive institutions like Oberlin and the University of Chicago, where he received a master's and doctoral degree, respectively. Beittel brought with him an aggressive liberalism cultivated while serving as president of Talladega College, a private college in Alabama and a sister institution under the AMA, between 1945 and 1952. While there, Beittel allowed students to host interracial meetings, wrote the governor condemning racial discrimination, tried to attract white students to Talladega (his own son received a degree from the college in 1950), and closed the primary and secondary schools on campus in an attempt to force the city of Talladega to build an academic high school for black youth. The interracial faculty supported him, for the most part, until he closed the schools. At that point, he alienated the black faculty, who had nowhere to send their children. With opposition mounting to Beittel, the trustees reluctantly dismissed him along with other key administrators in 1952.[21] Eight years later Beittel became the president of Tougaloo.

Overt activism at Tougaloo accelerated in the early 1960s and coincided with Beittel's arrival. The March 1961 sit-in at the Jackson Municipal Library became a major public relations crisis because it garnered national attention. Tougaloo administrators, who disavowed prior knowledge of the sit-in, refused to punish the students for their involvement, a fact that infuriated the local press, which reported that students admitted that they intended "to create a racial incident" and that "the 'read-in' was planned [at a] NAACP Youth Council meeting and was conducted with the knowledge of Tougaloo officials." Away at a conference in Atlanta, President Beittel hurried home, visited the Tougaloo Nine in jail, and assured them they could make up their midterm exams. Interviewed on a local television show, Beittel expressed his support for the students: "There is a difference between going to jail for stealing something and going to jail for a conviction. I should respect them for being willing to pay the price for what they believe to be right."[22]

The trustees, on the other hand, debated the issue. One trustee argued that "This incident tore down the image of Tougaloo being built up in Jackson and in the State of Mississippi" and went on record against sit-ins in general. Another offered that he was pleased and impressed with the students' actions. The entire discussion occurred under severe external pressures to curtail student activism. The white First Christian Church in Jackson even suggested that the trustees fire Beittel: "This demonstration, while not being specifically planned by the administration of said College, apparently has its support as does a general program of so-called non-violent agitation, and said administration has refused to consider any disciplinary action whatsoever against said students."[23]

The attention to the sit-in forced trustees to respond and defend the college. To the First Christian Church trustees explained,

> We have given careful consideration to the document and wish to reaffirm our confidence in the administration of President Beittel and the faculty, staff and student body of Tougaloo. We also wish to reaffirm our commitment to the basic principles upon which our nation and Tougaloo were founded, namely, that all men are created equal and are endowed by their creator with certain

inalienable rights. We affirm the right of the students to protest peacefully any customs or laws which they believe to be a denial of their rights as members of our democracy.

S. C. Meisberg, a trustee and member of the First Christian Church, resigned in protest.[24]

From the sit-in onward, Tougaloo constituents participated in the movement. Beittel himself helped reorganize the Mississippi Council of Human Relations, an organization considered "a transmission belt of communist infiltration in the South" by the Sovereignty Commission; spoke out about the evils of racism and segregation; sanctioned student involvement in the movement as long as they also dedicated themselves to their studies; was pictured in national media outlets with students, John Salter, and Ed King at the 1963 Woolworth's sit-in; and was the only white man on the dais at Medgar Evers's funeral.[25]

The escalating involvement of all manner of Tougaloo constituents and the constant bad press worried trustees, who attempted to dispel the notion that Tougaloo, as an institution, supported the movement. The belief in academic freedom, a founding philosophy based on racial equality, and the presence of liberal administrators facilitated campus activism, and the trustees supported the aims of the black freedom struggle. But trustees announced that the promotion of social activism was not the purpose of Tougaloo College, and the board tempered its support for aggressive confrontation of the Southern racial hierarchy through direct action tactics. Rather, they argued that the college sought social change through the education of the black middle and upper classes, who would lift the black masses as they climbed. Wesley Hotchkiss, a Tougaloo trustee, clarified the issue in an editorial in a newsletter published by an arm of the AMA:

All six of the AMA colleges are participating in some way in the revolutionary struggle now taking place for human rights. Perhaps we should say the *people* [emphasis in original] from these campuses are participating, because none of these colleges, as an organization, is directly engaged in action. This is an important distinction. Even in the midst of a revolution these colleges continue to see their role as academic communities. We are proud of the fact that the free exchange of great ideas on these campuses probably has formed the basis for the present revolution, but the prime purpose of the college continues to be education.[26]

Enter the Sovereignty Commission

The Sovereignty Commission escalated its attacks on the campus as years passed and employed some of the same tactics it used to destabilize Campbell

College. In June 1963, the Sovereignty Commission sponsored a court order naming President Beittel, Chaplain King, Professor Salter, and student Bette Anne Poole along with other individuals, the NAACP, CORE, Tougaloo trustees, and "their agents, members, employees, attorneys, successors, and all other persons in active concert with them" in a writ of temporary injunction preventing them from demonstrating in any way, shape, or form.[27]

The point of the injunction, ending civil rights activism, paralleled the mission of the injunction at Campbell, but it was different in important respects. First, the impetus for the Tougaloo injunction came from an external source, not campus officials. The Campbell injunction revealed a serious ideological split and created an opportunity the Sovereignty Commission happily manipulated. The commission attempted to create a similarly exploitative situation at Tougaloo but failed. Second, the injunction against Tougaloo requested a halt to demonstrations, not the termination of employment for individual staff members. The Campbell injunction pitted campus officials against one another and split the campus, while the Tougaloo injunction, by the sheer number and variety of campus constituents named in the court order, unified the campus by pitting it against the state. The plaintiffs in neither injunction succeeded in ending campus activism, but they did weaken the institutions by draining scant resources away from other campus projects. At Campbell, the plaintiffs unintentionally weakened the institution beyond financial recovery. The Commission attempted to create dire financial consequences at Tougaloo, but Tougaloo's national financial network was less rocked by the immediate fiscal requirements of defending itself against a court order.

Enemies of the movement were not convinced by trustee admonitions. Neither was the Sovereignty Commission, which tried another tactic employed at Campbell by attempting to capitalize on the fact that some Tougaloo constituents resented the college's involvement in the black freedom struggle. Dr. John Held, chairman of Tougaloo's Department of Philosophy and Religion, volunteered to become an informant in early April 1964. Held accused Beittel and others of appropriating the college for civil rights aims and transforming Tougaloo into a center for political activity. He also had designs on the presidency. While on a secret visit to the commission's office, Held informed Director Johnston about "the dissension among faculty and students" regarding the policies of President Beittel and Chaplain King (Professor Salter had resigned by this time), threatened to resign if Beittel was not removed, and offered to identify documents linking Beittel to a communist organization. Johnston, grateful for the assistance, requested a list of students and faculty opposed to and in support of Beittel and King, as well as the names of trustees who might be open to commission concerns. According to Johnston, he and Held "worked out a code system for communication and relaying information which would not involve Dr. Held with those at Tougaloo who would be opposed to his contact with the Sovereignty Commission." Days later, "Mr. Zero" submitted a list of trustees considered "most vital and influential" (all of whom were white) and those "probably more easily influenced by pressure" (all of whom were black). The communication also included a list of notable students and a Tougaloo College catalog in which Mr. Zero categorized the faculty.[28]

Concessions in the Name of Philanthropy

Meanwhile, Tougaloo's trustees were attempting to broaden the campus financial base. Annual expenses jumped when Tougaloo experienced a rapid increase in student attendance that forced the college to institute a major new facilities campaign in the late 1950s. President Beittel worked hard to solicit funds from individual donors and philanthropic agencies and was in large part successful, but increasing college costs made the task a daunting one. Also, certain financial sources turned away from Tougaloo. The Mississippi branch of the Christian Churches (Disciples of Christ) withdrew its financial support after Tougaloo activists targeted its segregated churches for pray-ins in 1963.[29] It was not a large financial loss, but it represented the antipathy with which Mississippi whites held Tougaloo and the difficulties Tougaloo experienced in raising local funds. Trustees looked to the Ford Foundation's Fund for the Advancement of Education for financial assistance. The Fund supported partnerships between black colleges and predominantly white Northern colleges. Tougaloo and Brown University already shared a friendly relationship, and both institutions desired a more formal association. In fall 1963, Tougaloo and Brown began the application process for Ford funds.

Tougaloo trustees hinged their financial hopes on the Ford grant and attempted to clear a path for a speedy decision. Tougaloo's public role in the movement became a point of concern. Brown University president Barnaby Keeney warned the Tougaloo trustees that the Ford Foundation was wary of donating the money for the partnership because of the constant state harassment. Brown University shared the same set of concerns. Keeney then targeted Tougaloo's President Beittel, a vocal supporter of the black freedom struggle, and urged that the Tougaloo trustees fire him. Keeney believed that Beittel's refusal to curb campus activism was irresponsible and that Beittel's actions unnecessarily politicized the campus and brought it unwanted scrutiny. He warned the trustees that Beittel's firing was imperative to secure Ford funding: "They will not do much, if anything, until they have this assurance." Certain Tougaloo trustees agreed with Keeney's assessment and set about undermining Beittel's presidency. A self-selected group of trustees, the same individuals Mr. Zero identified as most vital and influential, arranged a special meeting with Beittel at Tougaloo's board of trustees headquarters in New York in January 1964. They explained to Beittel that the partnership program funded by the Ford Foundation needed consistent leadership for at least ten years, an impossibility for him because he was sixty-five. They then requested his resignation. Their next task was to convince the other trustees, a racially mixed group, that their actions were appropriate and necessary. A few of the trustees expressed anger at the subcommittee's unilateral decision, but they presented a united front in public.[30] Rather than announce the decision immediately, the trustees decided to wait for the official board meeting in April.

Racists Claim Another Victim

Beittel fought the decision. The board hired him in 1960, and was fully aware of his liberal leanings since Beittel had been equally involved in civil rights issues while president at Talladega. One of his conditions for employment at Tougaloo had been that the board assured him of job security until age seventy, provided he remained healthy, with the option to continue on a yearly basis after age sixty-five. Beittel found the board's violation of his contract highly suspicious and accused the trustees of using him as a bargaining tool: "It was indicated that Brown University would not continue our promising cooperative relationship unless I am replaced, and that without Brown University the Ford Foundation will provide no support, and without Ford support other Foundations will not respond, and without foundation support the future of Tougaloo College is very uncertain." The board resented the implication that an external source prompted their actions, discounted Beittel's claims in a variety of forums, and refused to alter their decision to fire him.[31]

At the same time, the Mississippi legislature employed measures to punish Tougaloo for its role in the black freedom struggle. Legislators used materials gathered by the Sovereignty Commission to devise two bills meant to cripple the institution and never pretended otherwise. On 17 February 1964, Lieutenant Governor Gartin called for an investigation of the college's role in demonstrations and civil rights activities. Other state leaders joined his cause, and three days later, three senators introduced a bill to revoke Tougaloo's ninety-four-year-old charter in the name of "public interest." The argument was twofold. First, Tougaloo's original charter restricted the campus to five hundred thousand dollars worth of assets, a figure Tougaloo had passed years earlier with no repercussions. Second, and more to the heart of the matter, Gartin and others accused the college of neglecting its charter all together: "The big question to be decided is whether the school has substituted civil disobedience instruction for the curriculum it was authorized to have under its charter." The legislature also contemplated a bill that allowed discretionary powers to the Commission on College Accreditation.[32] Passage of the bill revoked Tougaloo's reciprocal accreditation between the state and SACS, the organization that had been a thorn in the side of the legislature since the James Meredith debacle at Ole Miss two years earlier. The loss of state accreditation prevented education students from receiving state teacher's licenses. Mississippi officials hoped the loss of accreditation would tarnish Tougaloo's reputation, limit attendance, and force those teachers who received their degrees from Tougaloo to leave Mississippi.

Tougaloo mounted an aggressive publicity campaign to call attention to the situation and embarrass Governor Paul Johnson into either vetoing or limiting the influence of each legislative bill. President Beittel, at the same time he was fighting for his own job, aggressively protected Tougaloo from the state's onslaught. He enlisted the assistance of the AAUP, the United Church of Christ, Tougaloo's sister institutions under the AMA, SACS, and other institutions and organizations with a vested interest in protecting higher educational autonomy. Tougaloo's allies wrote the legislature and the governor expressing their horror at such a public and offensive disrespect for institutional integrity.[33] Tougaloo's efforts were successful. The bill to revoke Tougaloo's charter died in the Judiciary Committee. The bill separating accreditation passed but held no teeth. The legislature was increasingly disturbed by the bad press created by the situation and did not use the act against Tougaloo.

The Sovereignty Commission took matters into its own hands in April 1964, months prior to the resolution of the legislative bills. Harassing Tougaloo became a top priority for Director Johnston. With the list of powerful and influential trustees provided by Mr. Zero, Johnston requested a private meeting with a group of trustees to plead his case:

> At the meeting it was our purpose to show that the image of Tougaloo as represented by the President, Dr. A. D. Beittel and [Reverend Ed King], had inspired such resentment on the part of state officials and legislators that a show-down clash appeared imminent. We suggested that if Tougaloo had a good man as president and a good man as [chaplain], the institution could be restored to its former status as a respected private college. We also suggested that if such a move could be made by the trustees, the college would have ample time to prove good faith and a change of attitude and possibly avoid punitive action from the Legislature.[34]

Johnston and Shelby Rogers, a Jackson attorney and commission confidant, flew to board headquarters in New York. They met with a subcommittee of trustees—the same trustees who, unbeknown to the commission, already requested and spearheaded Beittel's forced resignation in January.[35]

Trustees announced Beittel's retirement at their annual meeting only days after the subcommittee's appointment with the Sovereignty Commission. The timing could not have been worse. The subgroup of powerful trustees delayed the announcement of Beittel's resignation until the April board meeting to avoid having his resignation associated with Brown University or the Ford Foundation. Meanwhile, the Sovereignty Commission visit became public knowledge and turned into a public relations fiasco. Off-campus agencies wrote the trustees to express their dismay over Beittel's firing and to inquire about the rumors of Sovereignty Commission involvement. In a particularly damning letter, three Mississippi religious leaders blasted the trustees, "A change in the Presidency at this juncture will so complicate current critical issues about Tougaloo and race relations that the advances of the past few years will be seriously endangered. The reaction of the enemies of Tougaloo has already been made obvious in the press: Dr. Beittel's leaving is a victory for them and the first step in the control which must be exercised by the racists of Mississippi on the campus. Tougaloo is finally surrendering to intimidation."[36]

Trustees initiated a campaign to squash rumors they fired Beittel—they said he accepted the suggestion he retire but changed his mind—or that Beittel's support of the black freedom struggle hastened the board's decision. The board explained that Beittel reached retirement age and that his lack of interest in and commitment to the Brown–Tougaloo partnership necessitated new leadership. A friend and colleague of the trustees alluded to the fact that Beittel's support for civil rights activities influenced their decision: "One of the behavior patterns of some civil rights enthusiasts which I find myself resenting is their easy assumption that every institution and every available person can justifiably be used as a tool in the service of this cause."[37] In communications with their critics and friends, however, trustees resented such an implication.

Johnston, whose career aspirations hinged on the Sovereignty Commission's ability to disrupt the movement, took credit for Beittel's firing and was buoyed by the trustees' explanation of events. "Our pipeline of information from Tougaloo says the trustees gave as their reason for dismissal of Dr. Beittel that he was 'inefficient.' This will certainly work to our advantage. Had Dr. Beittel been asked to resign because of racial agitation or collaboration with communist front organizations, he could have made a martyr out of himself."[38] The self-congratulation was misplaced. The commission's visit with the Tougaloo trustees did not prompt the board's decision, which had been made months earlier, but Tougaloo's involvement in the black freedom struggle did. The legislative bills, court injunctions, and constant harassment became costly. The trustees spent time and money needed to improve the college on defending it instead. Tougaloo's role in the black freedom struggle became a liability. Trustees made a decision they believed would protect the college and ensure its financial future and future existence.

Many of the factors that saved Tougaloo from Campbell's fate became a double-edged sword. Tougaloo's prestige and private status made it the most important black college in the entire state but also made it the commission's number-one college target. President Beittel, like Campbell's President Stevens, supported the movement and the use of the campus space for movement ends, thereby making himself a target. Tougaloo's ability to garner national support and media attention prevented the legislature from closing the campus, but the state merely turned to other tactics to rein it in. Internal dissention did not reach a level at which the campus disintegrated from the inside out, but it did provide fodder for commission aims in the guise of informants and conservative trustees. Tougaloo's relative financial security, made possible by a national network and a unique funding opportunity, prevented an immediate fiscal catastrophe. At the same time, the funding opportunity and desire for increased donations made Tougaloo vulnerable and the college's role in the movement highly problematic. The Sovereignty Commission did not precipitate Beittel's firing or have an immediate effect on daily campus life and activism, but the immense amount of energy, time, and money spent on destabilizing Tougaloo was not in vain. The commission and its allies made it costly for Tougaloo to remain in the movement and forced the trustees to take a particular course of action, one they might not have considered without constant harassment by the state of Mississippi.

MODERATING WHITE SUPREMACY

The Sovereignty Commission focused much of its attention on activities in Jackson but did see cause for concern in the northern part of the state. An investigator warned, "Holly Springs, in my thinking, is one of the most explosive spots in Mississippi for racial trouble due to the fact that Rust College is located there." Rust College's geographical location in northern Mississippi made campus facilities particularly important for the movement in that part of the state. In 1962, the campus played a tangential role in James Meredith's enrollment at the University of Mississippi. The Mississippi press reported that Meredith and his legal team drove from Oxford, Mississippi, to Memphis, Tennessee, during his repeated attempts to enroll at the University of Mississippi, but Meredith sometimes spent the night at Rust College instead. Holly Springs was closer to Oxford, and the Rust College campus offered a friendly and secret space to recuperate from the white racist reaction to his enrollment. Two years later, SNCC's Freedom Summer project made the campus invaluable. Northern student volunteers often traveled through Holly Springs and spent time at Rust before heading to their respective assignments in voter registration throughout the state. The campus also became a clearinghouse for Freedom School materials as books poured in from Northern states and found their way to Rust, where students and staff sorted them for distribution.[39]

Student Activism and Presidential Support

Rust students also used the campus to launch their own attack on Mississippi's racial caste system with boycotts, demonstrations, and voter registration campaigns. Leslie Burl McLemore chose the institution because of its private status. "I wanted to go to a place where I knew I wouldn't have any difficulty with my political activity. I was conscious enough to know that if I went to a state school I wouldn't have lasted." He and other students participated in SNCC, the MFDP, and various direct action initiatives in Marshall County and other surrounding counties. As students devised a plan of action, so, too, did the Sovereignty Commission. When students initiated the 1962 boycott against local druggists who refused to serve black patrons, the commission swung into action. The commission counseled the Holly Springs police to return the students to campus rather than transport them to jail. According to an agent, "This was the best procedure in view of the fact that we know there are a number of racial agitators at Rust College and further . . . [it] would put the college at a disadvantage in any future agitating stemming from Rust College students." The commission learned valuable lessons from the Jackson police, who found pictures of themselves in local and national media brutalizing students with billy clubs and attack dogs. "Newsmen and perhaps television cameras on the grounds [taking] pictures of any incident which might occur from their attempt to integrate the drug stores," the agent suggested, should instead find little newsworthy behavior. The agent also advised the police to warn Rust College president Earnest Smith about continued activism and remind him "that good relationships between Holly Springs and the negro colleges had always been maintained in the past." This type of reaction, the commission believed, would be a "tremendous set-back" and "psychological defeat for Rust College as well as Rust College students."[40] The students, however, were not deterred, and activism continued.

　　Like his counterparts at Campbell and Tougaloo, President Smith did not participate in direct action but refused to punish campus constituents for their involvement. When the National Guard convoy escorted James Meredith from Memphis to the University of Mississippi, according to Smith, "Our kids made a parade out of it. That vexed the whites in Holly Springs a great deal." Smith was pressured to discipline the students, particularly after such a public display of disrespect for Mississippi laws and customs. He refused. He also assisted activist students by calling special faculty meetings to solicit money for bail and demonstrated by example through his membership in the NAACP. Smith's actions angered local whites. The mayor of Holly Springs, Sam Coopwood, stayed in constant contact with the Sovereignty Commission regarding activities at Rust and wrote the Mississippi branch of the Methodist Church to encourage an investigation of the college and the president. He was particularly alarmed by the fact that "white boys and girls are living together with the colored" during the 1964 Freedom Summer project. A commission investigator wrote, "I am sure if the white Methodists of this state, who are supporting this institution, knew these facts they would certainly no longer make contributions for the support of Rust College."[41]

Both the mayor and the investigator wrongly assumed that Rust received substantial money from the MECS, an all-white organization, and their pleas for financial sanction went unheard. Senator George Yarbrough, from Marshall County, also attempted and failed to pressure trustees into taking action against Smith. The continuing boycott strained the already tense racial situation in the area, and Smith was part of the problem. "It was the general consensus of everyone that evidently not just one racial agitator was busy agitating out at Rust College, but there were quite a few agitators out there," the Commission reported.[42] President Smith's refusal to curtail the movement at Rust turned him and the institution from a nuisance into a target.

Building a Case Against a College . . . and Failing

The commission began identifying allies in its fight against Rust and President Smith as early as the late 1950s, and considered two black trustees potential informants since both publicly opposed the NAACP. The commission hoped to capitalize on the delicate situation of trustee Robert E. Hunt. Like T. S. J. Pendleton, the Campbell College trustee and public school principal, Hunt found himself a trustee at an activist institution but employed by the state as the principal of a black public school in Columbus, Mississippi. Like Pendleton, Hunt became "a reliable informant." There is no evidence that Hunt provided the commission with information regarding Rust College in particular, though there is little doubt that the commission encouraged him to voice his conservative attitudes about racial relationships at trustee meetings. A white trustee and Holly Springs bank president, Glen Fant, also maintained close contact with the commission. In 1961, Fant offered information to the commission, persuaded fellow trustees to take particular actions, and promised his resignation before he would become a party to "spawning an integration crew at Rust College." Rust students continued to agitate, and Fant resigned his trusteeship when his term expired in 1963.[43] The commission made little headway in destabilizing the college in part because it misunderstood Rust's financial support and because it focused most of its time and energy on black colleges in Jackson and the black churches and protest organizations that played a large role in the movement in Marshall County. But SNCC's 1964 Freedom Summer project and Rust's geographic importance to it brought the campus under increasing scrutiny.

The commission and its allies attempted to marshal their forces to compel the trustees to take action during the summer of 1964. The commission, buoyed by its "success" at ousting the leadership at Tougaloo, set its sights on Rust and President Smith: "We have put into action a plan for Rust College similar to the plan we used at Tougaloo College. . . . [An agent] has developed pipelines into the college which indicate that President Smith, like Dr. Beittel at Tougaloo, is the cause of all the agitation. It is hoped that the case against President Smith will be ready to present to trustees at Rust College within a short time with the recommendation that the president be removed and a new administration return the college to the educational purposes for which it was established." A commission employee and a member of the Rust board of trustees traveled to Holly Springs to reason with Smith and discern what was happening on the campus, but Smith refused to meet with them and ordered them off the campus. Undeterred, the commission interviewed campus informants who accused Smith of employing a large number of "suspected homosexuals" as faculty, impregnating a young girl, refusing to discipline a white male and black female "caught in the act," and employing a "bunch of white beatniks" to teach summer courses. The local newspaper broadcast the baseless accusations and exploited two of the deepest fears of white racists: interracial sex and communism. In an article entitled "NO ROOM FOR COMMUNISTS," the Holly Springs *South Reporter* testified, "These sloppy so-called Civil Rights workers . . . stress the point that they do not wish to see intermarriage between the races but the social behavior of the workers here obviously reflects their approval of it. . . . Their dress alone is enough to convince all right-thinking people, white or colored, that they will be unable to teach anyone higher ideas or morals." Together, the state and local media worked to poison attitudes toward the college and its president.[44]

The commission returned to the board of trustees with their evidence, hoping to get Smith fired, but their attempts to oust President Smith failed. He remained president until 1966, when he retired of his own volition. Beyond their misunderstanding of Rust's finances, a series of miscalculations frustrated the commission's efforts. The commission's assessment of the board of trustees was somewhat accurate. Several trustees wanted to insulate Rust from the black freedom struggle, and the board's lukewarm support of civil rights activism frustrated President Smith and contributed to his voluntary departure. In Smith's words, "They weren't supportive, hardly at all. . . . I was getting more and more disgusted with the board of trustees." But the Commission miscalculated the level of the board's antipathy toward the movement. Many of the white board members from the Mississippi branch of the church were angry about the campus's place in the movement, but Rust received most of its financial sustenance from the national church, so financial threats from the Mississippi branch carried little weight. The commission also overestimated the level of dissension between the board and President Smith. Board members may have tempered their support for the campus-based movement, but they found the commission's morals charges against Smith distasteful and obvious. The commission's crass attempts offended the board, which refused to take any action.

The Commission also misjudged its power over private black colleges. It did not by itself precipitate the president's firing at Tougaloo or the demise of Campbell. Tougaloo's charter and fund-raising crisis and Campbell's financial situation provided the Commission with a rare opportunity. Though it was not wealthy, Rust's financial situation was not as dire as that at Campbell. Nor was Rust in the middle of a charter controversy or a funding campaign like that at Tougaloo. The Commission considered Rust a threat to the state, but it could not capitalize on fortuitous vulnerabilities. Rust was able to withstand state pressure in part because it received less concerted attention from the Commission but also because it did not provide the Commission with a particularly exploitable opportunity.

MODERATING BLACK RADICALISM

The CMEC began to shed its conservative roots in the 1950s. Some laity became activists; certain pastors disobeyed church law, which forbade the use of church property for political purposes; and the 1954 name change to the Christian Methodist Episcopal Church reflected the concern that "Colored" carried negative connotations, particularly in the segregated South, and a desire to practice racial inclusiveness. Still, the CMEC remained more conservative than its AMEC counterpart. CMEC youth leaders attending a National Youth Conference in Chicago in 1960 issued a statement that "to be silent in the face of injustice, need and exploitation would be denying [Christ]," but CMEC leaders counseled patience and accommodation with regard to racial relationships. The church considered racism a moral evil that needed to be eradicated, but founding church doctrine that eschewed involvement in political and social concerns influenced the church's place in the black freedom struggle. Church bishops refused to condone the direct action tactics employed by SNCC, CORE, or SCLC and encouraged blacks to use moral suasion and the legal system to remedy their grievances.[45]

The Paine College Ideal

This sentiment influenced the ethos at CMEC colleges. The "Paine College Ideal," a philosophy named after a prominent CMEC college, promoted racial accommodation. Church leaders, who also acted as college trustees, admonished campus constituents to focus on the power of academic and moral training as a vehicle for racial uplift rather than direct participation in voter registration, sit-ins, or boycotts. Trustees picked presidents accordingly, and Mississippi Industrial's president Edgar Everett Rankin Jr., who served between 1957 and 1978, was no exception. Rankin, who had been born and raised in Holly Springs, maintained a close relationship with local whites. In part, such associations were born of financial and political necessity, though former students speculated that the relationships were also fueled by the fact that he had white relatives in Holly Springs, because of his light complexion. Much like the presidents of the public institutions discussed in the next chapter, President Rankin sought to keep the doors of the college open by discouraging student activism.[46]

Mississippi Industrial was the least active of all the private colleges in the state. A handful of students participated in off-campus protest activities, but the campus never became an important movement center. In fact, the Sovereignty Commission took comfort in the fact that

> M.I. students have never given any trouble and when one is involved in any kind of brush with the law, he is immediately expelled from M.I. College. President Rankin lets it be known to all students attending M.I. that he is interested only in giving them the opportunity to gain an education for themselves, thereby better qualifying them for their future places in life. He does not back any student, who does not comply with the school's rules and regulations.[47]

The commission never identified Rankin as an informant, but it did consider him an ally. It was particularly gratified by Rankin's stance because President Smith at nearby Rust College refused to punish activist students and allowed the campus to be used for movement ends. Smith's actions angered racist whites, including the mayor of Holly Springs, who asked why President Smith refused to punish activist students the way President Rankin did: "President Rankin made it crystal clear to all students attending M.I. that the institution was a place of learning in which those who would take advantage of it could better qualify themselves for any vocation in life; whereas, Rust College appears to defend those who violated the law."[48]

Understanding a Lack of Activism

Why did Mississippi Industrial students and faculty participate at such a low rate? Some scholars on the movement looked to personal characteristics like social class, parental attitudes, gender, and home–community demographics to explain differential rates of participation.[49] The problem with this argument is that it assumes that students at any particular college were entirely monolithic. In the case of Mississippi Industrial, most students were from Mississippi, but an overwhelming percentage of students at Mississippi's other black colleges were in-state residents also. It may have drawn more students from the rural and predominantly black counties in the northern part of the state because of its location, but Rust College drew from the same constituency and had a more active student body. Also, Mississippi Industrial enrolled students from a variety of religious backgrounds, so individual CMEC affiliation did not play an influential role in curtailing activism.[50] Though data do not exist, there is no reason to believe that students at Mississippi Industrial came from economic or social backgrounds very different from those of their counterparts at Mississippi's other private black colleges or that their personal histories were so similar that the entire Mississippi Industrial student body opted out of activism.

Rather, a combination of church history, financial support, and administrative attitudes hindered student activism and prevented the campus from becoming a movement center. Three of Mississippi's black colleges were affiliated with the Methodist Episcopal Church: the AMEC supported Campbell, the Northern and biracial branch supported Rust, and the CMEC supported Mississippi Industrial. The AMEC, predictably, practiced the most radical form of Christianity, in which members were expected to work toward racial equality and agitate for freedom. Their financial autonomy from whites and the appointment of liberal college presidents allowed Campbell to become an important movement center despite the fact that some constituents, trustees, and church members advocated a more conservative course. The biracial Northern Methodists also used Christianity to advocate racial equality and chartered Rust College for that purpose. Though their theological position was not as inherently political as that of the AMEC, they refused to fire President Smith during the apex of the movement or withdraw funding to punish the college. The CMEC represented the most conservative theological position on the role of the church in social change. Founding doctrines explicitly focused on personal redemption, amity between the races, and evangelization. Unlike the AMEC, which emerged as a protest against segregation in the North, the CMEC evolved out of the conditions of a Jim Crow South. The CMEC advocated an end to racism and discrimination, but its history and continued relationship with Southern white Methodists influenced its attitude toward student involvement in direct action and the use of college space for movement ends. President Rankin supported a gradualist and amicable resolution to racial strife and ensured that Mississippi Industrial did not stray too far from that model of social change. Activist students participated in the movement under the dual threat of state and college sanction.

CONCLUSION

The experiences of these private institutions add a new dimension to the conceptualization of philanthropy in higher education and of college involvement in the movement. First, they make explicit the porous relationship between private institutions and the state. In its 1819 *Dartmouth College* decision, the Supreme Court addressed the issue of state influence on private colleges and found that a privately funded college should not be subjected to legislative whims, public opinion, or the rise and fall of political parties. Education was a public matter, but the faculty and philanthropic interests had the right to act as a private entity. The decision had nothing to do with private black colleges; none existed at the time. But missionary philanthropists set up private black colleges with the same assumption: financial and political autonomy from the state and the right to develop curricula, campus policies, and other matters without the fear of state intervention. In the 1960s, when Southern state interests collided with constitutionally protected freedoms, private institutions provided a forum for dissent and became oases of freedom in an oppressive state. However, philanthropic support only buffered the colleges from state influence; it did not immunize them. The state violated the autonomy of private colleges after they became involved in the black freedom struggle. It overestimated its influence on college affairs, but it did create a climate of fear and precipitate crises on campuses that forced administrators and trustees to make certain concessions. Private institutions, as Rust's President Smith put it, "were not as free as everyone thought we were."[51]

Also, the experiences of Mississippi's private black colleges allow for a reexamination of philanthropy in black higher education. Denominational philanthropy is juxtaposed against industrial philanthropy to draw a distinction between liberal and conservative ideas on black racial advancement in the late nineteenth and early twentieth centuries.[52] But the global characterization of religious philanthropy as liberal does not hold by the 1960s. As many black college constituents sought to participate in the movement, some denominations were more tolerant than others in their attitudes toward mixing academics and activism. The point is that white *and* black *religious* philanthropists could be so conservative that their colleges closely resembled the state's public institutions in their hostile attitudes toward campus involvement in the movement. Also, *liberal* money could be used for *conservative* purposes and negatively impact institutional autonomy. Beholden to grant-makers in a way many white colleges were not, these poor black colleges sought money that sometimes came with strings attached. In this way, liberal money became a bargaining chip against institutions and their involvement in the movement.

Last, their experiences complicate the assumptions regarding college participation in the movement. Social movement literature portrays private colleges as inevitably involved in the black freedom struggle because of their ties to black churches.[53] That was true in the case of Campbell, but it was exactly the opposite at Mississippi Industrial. Also, Tougaloo and Rust had very active campus constituents, though both maintained very loose denominational affiliations. Religious philanthropists supported racial equality, but it is important to remember that none of the philanthropic agencies understood activism as a primary component of the college mission. Instead, they argued for the dismantling of white supremacy through higher education. Their students, the future leaders of the race, would lift the black community out of moral and intellectual deprivation to prove their worth to whites. When students and campuses began to morph into activists and movement centers, presidents and trustees worried about the mix of academics and activism in part because they were concerned about the educative mission of the colleges becoming secondary and also because of the financial and political cost of constant state harassment. These private college administrators faced the delicate task of striking a balance between keeping the doors of the college open and a frontal attack on the Southern racial hierarchy. Structural protections and personal proclivities influenced their choices and their colleges' particular role in the movement.

Chapter Six

Foes or Allies:
The Battle on Public College Campuses

Alcorn Agricultural and Mechanical College, Jackson State College, and Mississippi Vocational College, Mississippi's public black institutions, had some of the features of movement centers. They drew a motivated student constituency into an environment where they learned, lived, and socialized together. The campus space provided opportunities for private gatherings without supervision. And students created communication networks, participated in student organizations meant to develop leadership potential, and enrolled in classes with professors who encouraged intellectual growth and curiosity. The colleges' relationship to the state, however, made their becoming movement centers virtually impossible. Public institutions relied on appropriations and goodwill from a state legislature determined to protect the Southern racial order.

The attitudes of the public college presidents also played a pivotal role in constraining on-campus activism and participation in off-campus ventures. The all-white Board of Trustees of Institutions of Higher Learning appointed public black college presidents less for their credentials than for their conservative and gradualist ideas on the pace and direction of the black freedom struggle. The board expected full compliance on the part of the presidents and threatened to fire them if they faltered in their mission to quash the movement. Caught between an increasingly aggressive student body and the escalating black freedom struggle off-campus on one hand, and their role as public employees and college presidents on the other, Presidents John D. Boyd, Jacob Reddix, and James H. White chose to follow the directives of their employers—the board of trustees—out of a combination of the desire for job security, severe duress, and their conservative attitudes on social reform. They were not completely successful, but their positions as college presidents made them important allies in the Mississippi government's battle to preserve white supremacy.

THE PRECARIOUS POSITION OF PUBLIC COLLEGES
AND THEIR STUDENTS

The 1954 *Brown v. Board of Education* decision and the 1955 mandate to desegregate public schools with all deliberate speed put black educational institutions, including colleges, in a delicate situation. Legislators and governors across the South promised to defy the Supreme Court and enlisted the assistance of black conservatives. Mississippi Governor Hugh L. White called black leaders to a meeting to discuss the decision and, ultimately, to issue a statement in support of segregated schools. The group included Percy Greene, the conservative editor of the *Jackson Advocate* and Sovereignty Commission informant, James H. White, the president of Mississippi Vocational College, and John D. Boyd, then president of Utica Normal and Industrial Institute, a black public and junior college focused on industrial education and teacher training, and future president of Alcorn A&M College (Alcorn's actual president, Jesse R. Otis, was noticeably absent). Functioning in a climate in which many Americans believed in the inevitability of a race war and aware of massive and violent white antipathy toward desegregation, the school leaders demurred in their demands for racial equality. The fact that the governor and legislature dangled the carrot of increased funding for segregated schools certainly influenced their position. These men interpreted their role not as race traitors but as racial pragmatists working to alleviate racial tension. In Percy Greene's words, "The greatest need in Jackson, in Mississippi, and in the rest of the South is more and more 'Uncle Toms'." The white power structure never sincerely supported black education, much less black higher education, and black presidents believed the monetary windfall for black schools in the post-*Brown* era could transform them into first-rate institutions. Whether that education would afford blacks the ability to participate equally in the existing social structure or in a segregated black society was a matter left unaddressed.[1]

Public college campuses became contested terrain as students began to play a pivotal role in the black freedom struggle. Legislators and boards of trustees across the South argued that students entered into a contract with an institution when they enrolled and that their enrollment signified their willingness to abide by institutional rules. In defying the regulations by participating in activism, according to white officials, the students forfeited their right to attend. Students and their allies, on the other hand, argued that a student's citizenship status preempted any contractual obligations or in *loco parentis* institutional mandates and provided the student with constitutional protections. In 1961, the United States Court of Appeals, in *Dixon v. Alabama*, sided with student activists expelled without a hearing from Alabama

State College after participating in a sit-in at the state capitol and found that students had the right to due process and equal protection guaranteed under the Fourteenth Amendment. Legal scholars credit the decision with altering the relationship between students and institutions and providing precedent for cases involving student activists in the later part of the decade.[2]

Student freedoms were not absolute, however. The *Dixon* litigation required only that public institutions grant students a hearing before dismissal. It did not prohibit administrators from disciplining or expelling students *in toto*. Administrators retained the right to curtail student speech and activities when they disrupted the educational environment and violated campus rules and regulations. Activist students found less friendly courts when institutions fulfilled their due process obligations. As with the tension between academic freedom and freedom of speech for faculty, students found themselves vulnerable in the space between constitutional protections and a college's right to protect itself.

Colleges, as institutions, also were in a vulnerable position. The interference of the board of trustees and the governor with the University of Mississippi chancellor's attempt to handle James Meredith's enrollment and James Silver's radical comments in *Mississippi: The Closed Society* demonstrated that white colleges and their leaders were not immune from direct state intervention. Public black colleges were even more prone, since they housed black youth who heavily populated the freedom struggle, and the abuses at black colleges often went unnoticed and unchallenged by the national press or academic community. One example of the lengths to which the trustees and Sovereignty Commission went was the demand that Presidents White, Boyd, and Reddix invite Reverend Uriah Fields, a black anticommunist speaker, to each campus in 1963. Fields served as secretary of the Montgomery Improvement Association, the organization that spearheaded the 1955 Montgomery Bus Boycott, but left the association after accusing it of accepting financial contributions from suspected communists. His message coincided with what the commission wanted black students to hear: "He'll speak in defense of America, of *American* not socialist or Communist solutions for American problems. In doing so, he stands firmly for the purpose of 'less government, more responsibility and a better world'" (emphasis in original). Rather than issue the invitation itself, the commission "decided that the invitation should originate with the schools without any connection with the Sovereignty Commission." This way, the colleges and the presidents appeared to condone Fields's interpretation of the movement and discourage student participation in it.[3]

The Mississippi government's enmity toward the black freedom struggle made constitutional provisions, court rulings, and federal protections null and void. The legislature, governor, board of trustees, Sovereignty Commission, and other white officials vowed to undermine any initiatives that smacked of racial equality and made the possibility of black public institutions acting as movement centers virtually impossible. The board, in particular, had been warned by SACS and the AAUP against interfering in campus business after the Meredith crisis at Ole Miss, but trustees merely attempted to remedy the situation there while offering perfunctory statements when challenged about their interference with black public colleges. At times, trustees did not actually need to intervene, since they appointed presidents who could predict their wishes and act in their stead. Whether under the directives of the board or the presidents, activist constituents at Mississippi's black public colleges remained prone to the whims of racists.

THE COLLEGE PRESIDENTS: POWERFUL BUT PRONE

Jacob L. Reddix, president of Jackson State College from 1940 to 1967, became the first president to head Jackson State under state control. Born in North Carolina and raised in Alabama and Mississippi, Reddix received a teaching degree from Miller's Ferry Normal and Industrial Institute in Alabama, spent two years in the army, taught high school, and spent one year of graduate study at the University of Chicago prior to coming to Jackson State. His lack of administrative experience was irrelevant, since the legislature and the trustees were not committed to creating a strong black higher educational institution. State financial support for the institution grew in the 1950s as the Mississippi legislature attempted to stall desegregation and deemed Jackson State the state's flagship black public college, but the state remained apathetic in its support for black higher education.[4] With the state's mission clear—to equip blacks with minimum skills and perpetuate the racial hierarchy—Reddix struggled to make a reputable institution within the confines of Mississippi laws and customs.

John D. Boyd, president of Alcorn from 1957 to 1969, was a native of Mississippi and held a bachelor's degree from Alcorn, a master's degree from the University of Illinois, and took additional coursework at Harvard University. Prior to becoming Alcorn's fourteenth president he was a classroom teacher, school principal, and instructor in Alcorn's agronomy program. He left his position at Alcorn to become president of Utica Normal and Industrial Institute. He returned to Alcorn when the board of trustees appointed him president after the 1957 student boycott and subsequent firing of President Jesse R. Otis. Alcorn's land-grant status meant little for college funding or growth, particularly since trustees purposely isolated the college in a remote location. The only road to and from campus, a seven-mile stretch, remained unpaved until the late 1940s. Also, trustees selected Jackson State, not Alcorn, as the flagship black public institution in the state.[5] Boyd's mission at Alcorn was as clear as that of President Reddix at Jackson State: follow the directives of the board of trustees and the Mississippi legislature or meet the same fate as President Otis.

James H. White became the first president of Mississippi Vocational College in 1950 and served in that capacity until 1971. Born and raised in Tennessee, White received a bachelor's degree from Tennessee A&I and a master's degree from Columbia University. He returned to Tennessee and eventually became a school principal, a county superintendent of black schools, and the president of Lane College in Jackson, Tennessee, one of the CMEC's flagship institutions. When White assumed control of Mississippi Vocational in 1950, he found 450 acres of cotton land with no buildings, lights, roads, students, or faculty. White struggled to build the college, since the legislature left it underfunded. The campus resorted to earning extra money for its building campaign by leasing land to farmers and selling crops grown by students. The legislature and trustees considered Mississippi Vocational the least important of the three public black colleges. Despite the lack of support and attention from the state, the trustees were deliberate in their choice of president. President White was particularly conservative in his approach to the pace and direction of the black freedom struggle. He remained steadfast in his support of state aims and worked closely with the Sovereignty Commission to kill the movement on or near the Mississippi Vocational campus.[6]

Although the presidents at each of the state's five white public institutions held doctoral degrees, none of the black public college presidents earned more than a master's (though each had an honorary doctorate).[7] Academic credentials, as far as the board was concerned, were secondary in selecting a black college president. Further, the board held the black colleges and the presidents in such low esteem that they treated the three public black colleges as tangential to their central concerns, rarely allowed the presidents to address the board, created an all-white Negro Education Committee to handle black college issues, and worked toward accreditation of black colleges only after pressure from SACS. The trustees worked in collusion with the Sovereignty Commission to ensure that each president toed the line. Presidents Reddix, Boyd, and White assumed their posts prior to the creation of the Sovereignty Commission, but the commission eventually gave its blessing and expressed "considerable confidence" that each would thwart campus activism and report any suspicious behavior and agitation against Mississippi laws and customs.[8]

The presidents did not categorically oppose equal rights, but they disagreed with the pace and tactics of the movement and with the use of the campus space for movement ends. They were particularly averse to direct action tactics like boycotts, sit-ins, and marches and favored legal maneuvers and less disruptive measures.[9] Beyond their personal proclivities, the fact that the trustees had a history of firing presidents and punishing colleges further constrained any vocal support for campus-based activism. Wholly dependent on state appropriations for everything from routine building maintenance to the creation of new academic programs, public college presidents could not afford—politically or financially—to alienate legislators, the governor, or trustees. The level of white hostility toward the movement forced the presidents to accept the conditional promise of increased funding for public black colleges if they remained outside the movement. Each president, then, vowed to keep his college open at any cost and used harsh punishment to dissuade activists from turning the campuses into movement centers.

The presidents and other administrators employed a variety of measures to intimidate students at Alcorn, Mississippi Vocational, and Jackson State into compliance. Curfews; mandatory attendance at class, vespers, and chapel; and prohibitions regarding vehicles kept students close to campus. These sorts of paternalistic regulations had existed since the colleges were founded, and Mississippi's private black institutions maintained similar policies. But the regulations became a useful instrument wielded at some private and all public institutions to discourage student participation in the movement in the early 1960s. The public colleges developed even more elaborate rules, including barring civil rights groups from campus, as the black freedom struggle gained momentum.

DIFFERENCES IN ACTIVISM BETWEEN THE COLLEGES

At Alcorn and Mississippi Vocational, their geographical locations made student participation in the movement difficult. Alcorn was in a remote site at the end of a road that became impassible in bad weather. The campus was an entirely self-contained community, with students and many faculty living, working, and socializing on-site. Participation in activities off-campus was very difficult. Significant movement centers existed in Natchez and Vicksburg, the closest sizable cities, but they were more than thirty miles away. Mississippi Vocational was located near sizable cities with important movement centers like the RCNL, SNCC, NAACP, and activist churches, but it was in the Delta, the part of the state where white repression was the most intense. It was also, to a large degree, a commuter campus that enrolled a considerable number of part-time students who spent little time on campus except to attend classes.[10]

Jackson State was in a different situation. It did not become an important movement center, but its students found ways to participate in the movement and use the campus space for movement aims. Its location in the capital city and urban center of the state facilitated student involvement. National and regional civil rights organizations like the NAACP and COFO maintained headquarters within walking distance, it was located near private black colleges with highly active student bodies, and Jackson State students blended in so that white officials (and even some black students) could not tell if a student attended Jackson State, Tougaloo College, or Campbell College.[11] In short, Jackson State students were in good company.

It is plausible that other factors fueled the off-campus activism of Jackson State students versus those at Mississippi Vocational or Alcorn. Studies on black student participation in the movement found that those at the most prestigious institutions participated at a higher rate than those at less reputable colleges. Of the three public black colleges, Jackson State enjoyed the highest rank, attracted students from across the state as opposed to the immediate region, and employed the highest number of faculty with doctoral degrees. Also, Jackson State was located in a county in which the ratio of blacks to whites was relatively equal, where black autonomy from whites in terms of home and business ownership outpaced that in more rural counties, and where black educational levels exceeded those in the rest of the state. Such an environment, sociologists and political scientists posit, attracted liberal-leaning students who were more likely to become movement activists and contributed to a climate in which activism flourished.[12] The combination of structural characteristics and clientele personalities, including those of the presidents, influenced the ability of campus constituents to organize and mobilize against white supremacy.

Despite state and administrative pressure to the contrary, the campuses did not escape turmoil. Students at Mississippi Vocational initiated the first massive student boycott of the civil rights era; Alcorn students executed several disruptive demonstrations throughout the late 1950s and 1960s; and Jackson State students participated in direct action campaigns sponsored by off-campus movement centers and used the Student Government Association to plan others. The public colleges did not become hotbeds of activism, but student activists understood their on-campus fight as analogous to the off-campus battle and refused to accept second-class status. The responsibility of reining them in was left to the presidents.

REPRESSION AS PROGRESS

President White's particularly active role in repressing the movement earned him the title of "our enemy #1" from an NAACP official. The activities surrounding college campuses were of primary interest for him, and White became involved in a higher education desegregation battle involving Clyde Kennard, a decorated veteran who applied for admission to Mississippi Southern College, a white institution. President White helped dissuade Kennard from filing his initial application in 1955, but Kennard followed through on his application for enrollment in September 1959. The board of trustees and Sovereignty Commission swung into action and turned to President White, who volunteered his services. The trustees trusted White but "were somewhat apprehensive that White could harm himself more than any good he could [do because] White had some very bitter enemies both among the white and colored races." The board gave the commission permission to use White provided he worked "behind the scenes" and "merely counseled and advised as to the steps to be taken." Days later, White visited Kennard to pressure him into revoking his application. He warned Kennard that trustees might close the state's black colleges if Kennard persisted and that "this responsibility would be entirely on him." President White's efforts failed, and the state employed more aggressive measures to discredit Kennard, who was arrested, convicted on false charges of accessory to burglary, and sentenced to prison. Kennard never enrolled at Mississippi Southern and died of intestinal cancer shortly after the entire episode.[13]

White exerted more control at his own institution and with his own students. The campus, except for the 1957 boycott to demand a Student Government Association, remained the quietest in terms of organized student participation in the movement, whether because of White's leadership, the structural characteristics of the college, the particularities of the clientele, or some combination of each. Individual students, however, did participate. In 1962, Dewey Greene Jr., a student activist involved in SNCC voter registration projects during the 1961–62 academic year, applied to the University of Mississippi—the same year as James Meredith. President White promised the Sovereignty Commission that he would reprimand Greene when the 1962 academic year resumed "for his activities in agitating Negroes to go register to vote in various parts of Mississippi." Instead, Greene terminated his affiliation with Mississippi Vocational and continued his movement work. The following year, President White helped the commission identify five Mississippi Vocational students involved in an altercation with white youth days after the shooting of Jimmy Travis, a local civil rights worker.[14]

President White's association with the Sovereignty Commission was well known. He made no apologies for his actions and believed that he furthered the cause of black education, and therefore black liberation, by keeping the doors of Mississippi Vocational open throughout the turbulent years of the black freedom struggle. In a 1956 convocation address to the Mississippi Vocational student body White stated, "I have been called by many Negroes in the State of Mississippi as a 'compromiser.'" Blacks deserved fair treatment, he told the audience, but they had certain shortcomings that must be addressed and should focus on character-building rather than overt political agitation. Two years later his message remained the same as he admonished black Mississippians to focus on the privileges of American citizenship rather than the unfulfilled promises of the Constitution. Invoking the Cold War rhetoric of the time, White explained, "I have seen doors of opportunity opened before my eyes. The progressive improvement in race relationships and the economic rise of the Negro in America is an example of democracy in action. The most 'exploited' Negroes in America are more fortunate than the citizens of Russia or her satellites." White's attitudes remained firm even when reflecting back on his career and his place in history. In his autobiography, published in 1979, he recalled, "I was called an Uncle Tom—though buses brought students from their doors to the College. Yes, I was called a *House Nigger,* 'too far behind the times, too slow, too conservative.'" But, he stated, the words of the Urban League's Whitney Young rang true: "You can holler, protest, march, picket and demonstrate, but after all this, somebody must be able to sit in on the strategy conference and plot a course."[15] President White fancied himself at the table.

President White's attitudes toward the black freedom struggle were not atypical. A segment of the black community favored a gradualist approach, believing that slow and steady work toward racial equality, through legal channels and the courts, could positively influence white community attitudes toward black political participation. Conservative black leaders worried that aggressive civil disobedience was counterproductive, aggravated the racial situation in the South, and alienated potential white allies by appearing to fulfill the then-popular myth that blacks were determined to turn the tables and oppress whites. Such fears were compounded by the anticommunist scare, in which any person who criticized the United States was considered anti-American. Fueled by HUAC and SISS hearings on the communist infiltration of minority groups and civil rights organizations, black Americans, as a whole, found their loyalties questioned. There is little doubt that each of the presidents, like the black conservatives paraded in front of HUAC and SISS promising to ferret out communists, perceived themselves as friends to blacks and uniquely patriotic.[16]

The pressures on President White, as well as the other public college presidents, cannot be overestimated. Though White acted out of his own beliefs regarding black advancement, the coercion of the board of trustees, Sovereignty Commission, and legislature was both intense and constant. Campus activism threatened his job security and the institutional viability of Mississippi Vocational. Also, White's heavy-handed tactics and *in loco parentis* ideals can be construed as ensuring student safety. White-on-black violence escalated after the 1954 *Brown* decision; the Delta (in which Mississippi Vocational was located) held the honor of being the birthplace of the White Citizens' Council; the immediate area around the college housed a vibrant Ku Klux Klan chapter; and Emmett Till had been lynched less than twenty miles from campus merely for whistling at a white woman. Keeping students on-site literally protected their lives. Last, White's warning that trustees would close the state's public black colleges as a retaliatory strike was not exaggerated. In hindsight, history tells us that no colleges were closed, but their safety was not so clear at the time. Racists bastardized the *Brown* decision as fodder for an attack on black colleges, declaring that they should be shut down as desegregationists demanded of black primary and secondary schools. The promise of more funding for black schools, for many public employees, became an attractive option and a bid for self- and institutional preservation.[17]

AUTOCRACY VERSUS DEMOCRACY

The board of trustees' expulsion of the Alcorn student body and firing of President Jesse R. Otis after the 1957 boycott regarding professor Clennon King's inflammatory articles in the *State Times* garnered nationwide press. Whites and blacks registered opinions, recognizing that the battle represented something larger than a tug-of-war between trustees and school officials or students; instead, it represented an early battle over the proper path and pace of the movement and the place of blacks in society. Some white supporters described the firing of the president and the expulsion of students as necessary steps to ensure that blacks remembered their appropriate place in the racial hierarchy and that public black colleges were not drawn into political causes. One white reporter heralded Clennon King as a hero: "It may be that the Negro named King who is to stand highest in the race history of these unhappy times will not be Martin Luther but Clennon."[18]

The black community, on the other hand, considered King a pariah and lauded President Otis and the students for their brave actions. The RCNL presented Otis with its award of the year. Otis was unable to attend the ceremony, and Medgar Evers accepted the honor on his behalf by stating, "Thank you and I am glad to be able to accept this award for a man who did not [compromise] the college student body, and himself." Though the trustees succeeded in purging the campus of the most vocal supporters of democratic rights, the black press considered the boycott a major blow to institutionalized racism: "It was this mass act of defiance by Negro students against the symbol of Mississippi power and authority—the all white board of directors—that shook the very foundations of white supremacy and the jim-crow system in that state."[19]

Desperate to be rid of Otis, the trustees allowed John D. Boyd to be president of Utica Institute and Alcorn until his term at Utica expired at the end of the academic year. Trustees did not mince words when explaining his duties. As E. R. Jobe, the executive secretary, told an AAUP official, "The Board had appointed Boyd as president of Alcorn A&M to 'keep control of the situation and keep things quiet'—maintain the status quo." Jobe also recalled that Boyd crafted the idea to have students sign a statement promising no further involvement in disruptive actions. By doing so, Boyd anticipated trustees' desires and earned their trust.[20]

During the 1960s, Alcorn students continued to demonstrate against the campus's strict rules and regulations, the low quality of the faculty, and poor facilities, and focused their grievances and anger at President Boyd, who, as far as students were concerned, was a puppet of white racists. In 1966, their activism coincided with a highly effective NAACP-sponsored boycott in Claiborne County centered in Port Gibson, the town nearest to Alcorn. Charles Evers, the Mississippi field secretary for the NAACP since his brother's murder in 1963, local resident, and alumnus of the institution, married the boycott with campus concerns by helping create a list of demands that addressed student and employee grievances, including freedom of speech on campus, due process, and relaxed social restrictions for students; competitive salary and public notice of tenure procedures for the faculty; and improved work conditions and pay for the staff. He, like students, took aim at President Boyd. In early March 1966, Evers led a thousand demonstrators, including a handful of students, to the gates of the campus, where they were stopped by Alcorn security officers and highway patrolmen who tear-gassed, beat, and arrested them. Released with help from the Lawyers' Committee for Civil Rights Under Law, Evers organized a second march to campus during which he submitted the list of grievances to President Boyd.[21]

Though Alcorn students were only peripherally involved in the marches, Boyd suspended all those who participated. In response, concerned students created on-campus organizations to register their frustrations with the administration. Boyd's attitude that "we are not going to sympathize with any student who is trying to get up a disturbance in support of some outside agitators who are trying to injure the school. In my opinion, if a student is not satisfied at Alcorn College, he is free to leave and seek his education elsewhere," did not help the situation. The Student Movement at Alcorn College, an organization formed to coordinate student actions, explained to the student body, "Our purpose is to eradicate some of the pathetic rules and regulations of the administration here at the college. Our chief objective is not to destroy the college, but to make it a more conducive place for higher learning." Activist students created a second organization, United Student Movement, in the same spirit. Together, the organizations sponsored a boycott of the campus union that mirrored the boycott in Claiborne County and Port Gibson.[22]

The constant demonstrations and Evers's involvement infuriated Boyd and the trustees, who filed injunctions to prevent the marches and future disturbances. Evers and his supporters filed their own injunctions to prevent the police from interfering with their right to peacefully protest and with students' rights to freedom of speech and assembly. A judge banned all demonstrations pending the outcome of *Evers v. Birdsong*, the case filed in support of Evers, the NAACP, and Alcorn students. When a federal district court finally decided the case two years later in 1968 it found in favor of the state. In the decision, the court weighed First Amendment rights against administrative responsibilities to maintain order and protect public property and concluded, "The right of free speech, assembly or protest has never been so judicially enlarged as to permit disruption of a school and destruction of its property." The fact that a wood-frame building had been set ablaze during the March 1966 disturbances meant students forfeited constitutional protection. The court also issued an injunction against further demonstrations on or near the campus, an injunction that remains in place in 2007.[23]

Evers, the NAACP, and students met with limited success in gaining major concessions from the white power structure, though campus administrators made some cosmetic changes consistent with court rulings on due process. The failure reflected the trustees' sovereignty in the face of external pressure and Evers's lack of long-term planning. It also testified to Boyd's success at keeping Alcorn estranged from the off-campus black freedom struggle. Though students regularly protested during the late 1950s and 1960s and were inspired by the movement, they remained isolated from it. That changed, very briefly, in 1966, when Evers's antipathy for Boyd motivated the pairing of student and nonstudent concerns. But white supremacist repression curbed activists' ability to affect local or campus reform. The state's on-campus agent, President Boyd, made no apologies for his actions. Instead, he positioned himself and others like him as important tools for racial progress:

> It is time our state wakes up and recognizes the fact that our relationship is fast approaching the breaking point in that we are giving all the recognition in the world to irresponsible leadership and none to those persons who have given, are giving, and will continue to give their best to the welfare of Mississippi. The answer lies in finding ways of bringing these problems to the conference table and there, before the face of public opinion, thrashing them out in an atmosphere of calmness and trust.[24]

Boyd believed that boycotts, marches, and protests did not profit the black freedom struggle but created unnecessary hostility between the races. Patience and compromise, not civil disobedience, brought about true change.

He was not alone in his admonitions, but his attitude toward the movement and his actions to thwart it earned him the enmity of many Alcorn students and other black Mississippians, which followed him until 1969 when he became Alcorn's first officially retired president—all others had quit or been fired by the board of trustees.[25]

An unintended consequence of the battle at Alcorn was that it confirmed to black activists that whites and their black allies would take all legal and extralegal steps to maintain the racial hierarchy. The arrests and brutality faced by activists—many of whom were high school students protesting conditions at their schools as well as at Alcorn—further radicalized blacks in Claiborne County. Following the March 1966 demonstrations, several black men created an armed self-defense group in the image of the Deacons for Defense in Louisiana, the Lowndes County Freedom Organization in Alabama, and Robert Williams of the NAACP chapter in Monroe, North Carolina.[26] As far as local blacks were concerned, the failure of the legal system, the presence of a strong local Ku Klux Klan chapter, and white-on-black violence precipitated the need for arms, and the continued intransigence of Alcorn officials and white businesses in Port Gibson necessitated aggressive tactics. Increasing assertiveness became a natural and necessary next step in the black freedom struggle, a position fortified by the Black Power Movement, which was launched in Mississippi later that year.

NEGOTIATING THE MIDDLE GROUND

Trustees and the Sovereignty Commission expected President Reddix, like his counterparts at Mississippi Vocational and Alcorn, to maintain order on campus and dissuade activism. Jackson State's proximity to highly effective college movement centers made that task difficult. Jackson State students began their participation in the Jackson phase of the struggle with the 1960 Easter boycott of local white stores. Trustees and the Sovereignty Commission expressed alarm at student participation and questioned Reddix, who explained, "We have no part in it. Insofar as I know Jackson State is not in any way participating either officially or unofficially. No faculty member or student is co-operating either officially or unofficially." The presidents of Campbell College and Tougaloo College made similar statements disavowing institutional support. The difference was that the all-white board of trustees controlled Jackson State, employed Reddix, and was in collusion with the Sovereignty Commission. Reddix promised to punish student participants, particularly those who attended the boycott planning meetings at Campbell College, but he was not wholly successful in terminating Jackson State student involvement in the off-campus movement or in student use of campus space for movement ends.[27]

The 1960 boycott, which by all accounts was a failure, was followed by two events that put Jackson State and President Reddix back in the news. First was the Jackson State student demonstration in support of the nine Tougaloo College students arrested at the whites-only library in 1961. The Jackson State student march to the city jail and subsequent tear-gassing and use of police dogs by local law enforcement garnered national attention. Infuriated by the bad press and by the aggressive nature of student protest, the trustees and Sovereignty Commission demanded that Reddix take immediate action. Reddix dissolved the Student Government Association, expelled a student activist, and created new rules and penalties regarding student conduct. All clubs, classes, and groups met only with the consent of the dean of students and the physical presence of a faculty sponsor. The president himself cleared requests for meeting space. The new campus regulations even barred off-campus meetings without the dean's consent. A coded reference to the black freedom struggle warned, "No student or student organization shall participate in any controversial activities or issues on or off the campus unless he has been duly authorized by the college administration."[28]

While attempting to allay trustee and Sovereignty Commission fears, Reddix earned the enmity of a national audience. *Jet*, a popular black weekly magazine, covered the incident and sent a reporter to interview Reddix. The article portrayed Reddix as power hungry and backward in his ideas on black liberation. Though a simplification of the situation, the article did offer a glimpse of the middle ground Reddix attempted to strike. For instance, Reddix told the reporter who challenged his decision to disband the Student Government Association, "I'm not against student government. . . . After all, I organized it here 21 years ago. But it's like a President's cabinet. If any cabinet member disagreed with the President's basic philosophy he would have to go." Similarly, according to the reporter, he argued "that student 'idealists' must first acquire an education and then and only then go out and 'save the world.' His major concern, he continued, was to keep open his college, which incidentally is unaccredited."[29]

Reddix's actions also alienated much of the student body. The rumor that he pushed a female student to the ground during the Tougaloo Nine demonstration damaged his reputation, and his collusion with the white power structure infuriated students. Two students, sisters Dorie Ladner and Joyce Ladner, transferred to Tougaloo after growing frustrated with Reddix's admonitions to focus on academics at the expense of civil rights agitation. According to Joyce Ladner, Reddix "called us in and he told us, 'I know you girls have been behind this mess that's been going on,' and he even told us that he knew we'd been going to Medgar Evers's office. . . . Talk about being in a straitjacket." When Reddix expelled former Student Government Association president Walter Williams in the fall of the 1961–62 academic year, the second student expelled for participating in the post-Tougaloo Nine activism, students held a demonstration in protest. MIAS, the clandestine organization dominated by Jackson State students, empathized with Reddix's delicate situation but used their anonymity to chastise Reddix for his role in suppressing activism on campus:

> MIAS does not look upon the administration and staff of Jackson State College as foes, but as allies, and we seek their support in accomplishing our goal. However, we realize that it is literally against the law for Negroes to actively seek to change the social and political structure for their betterment in the state of Mississippi. Jackson State College is a state supported and controlled institution; and if the administration of any State supported school follows the politics as handed down by the state officials, it will naturally conflict with the aims of MIAS.[30]

The second major incident to garner national attention was James Meredith's application to transfer from Jackson State to the University of Mississippi. Meredith's application threw the state into a frenzy. Governor Ross Barnett declared, "No school will be integrated in Mississippi while I am your governor," prepared to close the University of Mississippi rather than desegregate the institution, and vowed to go to jail in defiance of the federal court order to admit Meredith. The Sovereignty Commission sought evidence to bar Meredith's enrollment on voting irregularities and moral grounds. And the trustees attempted to use Jackson State's unaccredited status as a barrier. The Sovereignty Commission and trustees also pressured President Reddix to find some grounds on which to nullify Meredith's ability to transfer. According to Meredith, trustees "used pressure including the threat of firing him to force him to expel me from Jackson College after I applied to the University of Mississippi in order to disqualify me as a transfer student. He was very proud of the fact that he had successfully resisted the Mississippi College Board."[31] Reddix's actions did not, by themselves, allow Meredith to enroll at the University of Mississippi in 1962, but Reddix could have sabotaged the application at any time. His refusal to do so facilitated Meredith's transfer and struck a major blow against white supremacy in Mississippi.

President Reddix was not a closet radical. He fully believed that Jackson State should educate the black leaders of the future but held conservative attitudes toward black advancement—attitudes that clashed with student ideas on the issue. Despite his objections to overt student activism, Reddix believed his contributions to the movement were valuable. His autobiographical portrayal of his role in the movement closely matched that of Presidents White and Boyd,

> I have never personally participated in an organized protest. Undoubtedly, I have been criticized for not doing so. For more than fifty years, I have devoted my life to the education and enlightenment of young people. By using whatever means I have had at my disposal, I believe that I have contributed to the training of young people for full participation as responsible citizens in a democracy. During my twenty-seven-year tenure as president of Jackson State College, the institution has granted upward of 5,000 degrees to its students. I believe this contribution is as important as participating in organized protest.[32]

CONCLUSION

Anecdotal evidence regarding presidential defiance of the trustees and the Sovereignty Commission exists. Reddix's successor at Jackson State, John A. Peoples, recalled instances when Reddix protected campus constituents from the state's wrath and speculated that Reddix was a life member of the NAACP. And it is possible that Presidents White and Boyd found clandestine ways to buck the system. But individual acts do not an undercover militant make. These men were racial conservatives who fully believed that containing campus-based activism furthered black advancement and liberation. They were not as extreme as their caricature counterparts, described in E. Franklin Frazier's *Black Bourgeoisie* as having "no real interest in social questions," or in Ralph Ellison's *Invisible Man* as so power hungry as to declare, "I'll have every Negro in the country hanging on tree limbs by morning if it means staying where I am." But the public black college presidents argued that they did the bidding of the all-white board of trustees and uplifted the race at the same time.[33]

Many of their presidential contemporaries were highly critical of their role in thwarting the movement on campuses but recognized their vulnerability as public employees. As Benjamin Mays, president of Morehouse College (private) stated, "If you knew that the legislature, with no Negroes in it at all, have got to decide on what you get, how [do] you expect a bunch of radicalism to come out of that?" Also, it is important to remember that the presidents were not alone in their opinions on the movement, as members of the black community debated how best to ensure equal opportunity and racial uplift. That they counseled patience and explained their actions as a necessary compromise that secured the future of black higher education made sense to some blacks but angered others, including many of their own students, who considered them white racists in blackface.[34]

Beyond the layer of race, what lay at the heart of the matter was a particular conception of "public." As far as white Mississippians were concerned, the state-supported colleges necessarily fortified the existing social and political structure. When institutions, black or white, ventured too far from this aim and educated students or supported faculty who challenged the contemporary order, they violated the public interest and necessarily triggered government intervention. Government interference in Mississippi higher education began in 1930 with Governor Theodore Bilbo's purge of the state's public white colleges, and the pattern repeated itself during Meredith's attempted enrollment at Ole Miss with Governor Ross Barnett being named registrar and trustees divesting authority in campus officials regarding Meredith's application. In theory at least, trustees enjoyed autonomous status from the government. But the interests of elected officials and trustees converged during the black freedom struggle era and blurred the line between them.

The relationship between the government and state-supported colleges in white Mississippi's understanding of "public" mirrored that of the late nineteenth century in which a court found that public employees did not enjoy First Amendment protections. To paraphrase the words of a Massachusetts Supreme Court justice, a public college employee may have a constitutional right to talk politics, but he or she had no constitutional right to be a public college employee.[35] Such precedent came under attack with a series of middle–twentieth century cases that extended First and Fourteenth Amendment rights to the faculty (provided they were not communists), but college presidents did not receive similar protections. Racists also blurred the lines between the government and universities by arguing that the Tenth Amendment (which declared that the powers not delegated to the United States by the Constitution were reserved for the states) provided the state legislature with the power to participate in the business of any corporation chartered under state laws. The race issue placed their co-optation of the Tenth Amendment for state's rights purposes in direct conflict with the Fourteenth Amendment, but the argument remained: as far as white supremacists were concerned, the state's public institutions served state and thus the white power structure's interests.

Chapter Seven

Making Black Campuses Black: Activism and Response in the Black Power Era

The philosophy of nonviolence and the goal of integration lost favor with a large segment of the black community during the middle to late 1960s. After decades of attempting to force their way into the existing social order only to meet intense white resistance and repression, many blacks, including youth, became disillusioned with integration to the point of disdain. The murders of Louis Allen, James Cheney, Andrew Goodman, and Michael Schwerner in 1964, the murders of Jimmy Lee Jackson, James Reeb, and Viola Luizzo in 1965, the infamous beating marchers received on their walk from Selma to Montgomery in 1965, and the murder of Sammy Younge in early 1966 added fuel to the fire. Some redefined integration as a philosophy that ignored questions of power and usurped the black community of the skills and energies of its most productive members, rather than being the answer to black America's problems. Doubtful of the federal government's dedication to improving the conditions of blacks, suspicious regarding the extent to which white liberals could be considered true allies, and aware of the large discrepancy between expected results and actual achievements, a shift in ideas on the proper tactics and means to gain black liberation occurred. Many youth grew frustrated with the slow pace of change and demanded more power, real power, Black Power.

Media attention on the black freedom struggle turned northward as black urban areas from Watts to Detroit to Newark exploded in response to persistent and unaddressed racism, police brutality, and political disenfranchisement. Similarly, Northern black and white college students garnered intense press as they dramatized their accusations of institutional dehumanization and powerlessness with building takeovers, threats of violence, and millennial rhetoric. The black freedom struggle continued in the Southern context also. Though coverage remained scant in national media outlets, Southern blacks continued to push for societal reform, human dignity, self-determination, and racial uplift. Like their predecessors and Northern counterparts, they created movement centers to organize and mobilize against the white power structure. Students, too, created on-campus movement centers to close the gap between democratic rhetoric and a democratic reality both on- and off-campus. This chapter charts the rise of the Black Power movement in Mississippi, patterns of black college student activism and the legal conflicts that arose as a result of it, and the obstacles activists faced in translating Black Power ideology into an institutional reality.

THE RISE OF BLACK POWER:
THE MOVEMENT TURNS A CORNER

In June 1966, Stokely Carmichael, an SNCC worker, inaugurated the Black Power movement during a demonstration in Greenwood, Mississippi. Infuriated by persistent white racism and black degradation, he told the audience assembled to finish James Meredith's March Against Fear—Meredith had been shot on the second day on his way from the northern Mississippi border to Jackson—that blacks should focus their energies on "Black Power," not desegregation, on self-defense, not nonviolent resistance. As the Black Power movement gained momentum, young ideologues such as H. Rap Brown, Imamu Amiri Baraka, Ron Karenga, and Julius Lester rushed to define the amorphous phrase and popularize its concepts and principles, as did new organizations like the Black Panther Party for Self-Defense, the Republic of New Africa, United Slaves, Revolutionary Action Movement, and the newly radicalized and racially monolithic SNCC and CORE. Carmichael and Charles V. Hamilton, a political scientist, authored the seminal text on the topic, *Black Power: The Politics of Liberation in America*, a year after Carmichael's speech in Greenwood. In the book, they described Black Power as "pride rather than shame in blackness, and an attitude of brotherly, communal responsibility among all black people for one another." It became a call for blacks to recognize and be proud of their heritage, build a sense of community, define their own goals, and control their own organizations. To successfully accomplish the above tasks and therefore attain Black Power, blacks were called to unite: "Before a group can enter the open society, it must first close ranks. By this we mean that group solidarity is necessary before a group can operate effectively from a bargaining position of strength in a pluralistic society." Under the banner of blackness, they would be able to address their grievances and demand their share of the American Dream.[1]

Not all activists embraced Black Power. Some damned it as a dangerous slogan that set the black freedom struggle back through its appeals to racial separatism. Though they did so in different degrees, Martin Luther King Jr., Bayard Rustin (a lifelong activist and associate of King), Roy Wilkins (NAACP executive director), disillusioned SNCC members, and other prominent freedom fighters issued statements opposing the concept. In a particularly inflammatory speech, Wilkins warned, "No matter how endlessly they try to explain it, the term 'black power' means anti-white power." According to him, all that separatism offered impoverished black communities was "a chance to shrivel and die." Wilkins drove the point home by putting Black Power advocates in horrific company: "It is a reverse Mississippi, a reverse Hitler, a reverse Ku Klux Klan."[2] Black Power's critics chafed under the slow pace of societal reform and vowed to continue the battle, but they diverged with Black Power adherents regarding both the means to liberation and the desired end.

Dr. Martin Luther King Jr.'s 4 April 1968 assassination not only seemed to validate the call for Black Power and closing ranks, it further radicalized the Black Power movement. Warning what King's murder would mean for the black rights struggle, Carmichael, at a news conference soon after King's death, announced, "I think white America made its biggest mistake because she killed the one man of our race that this country's older generations, the militants and the revolutionaries and the masses of black people would still listen to."[3] Northern cities went up in flames as blacks vented their rage in their segregated communities and clashed with police. Black students at predominantly white institutions and historically black institutions were a part of this growing movement and experienced the same sort of anger and frustration. Like their nonstudent counterparts, college activists sought to make Black Power real at institutions of higher education. Activists at Columbia University, Cornell University, Howard University (a black college), Duke University, Southern University (a black college), and other institutions across the nation used incendiary rhetoric and hyperbole to dramatize their grievances and frustrations with the slow pace of change in society and on their respective campuses. The most sensational demonstrations—like the one at Cornell in which students emerged from a building fully armed—made national news and shocked the American public.

Black student activism at white colleges emerged alongside intense white student protest against the Vietnam War. Chapters of Students for a Democratic Society, the most popular white leftist organization, appeared on campuses across the nation and sponsored monthly antiwar moratorium marches, demonstrations, and building takeovers, which sometimes turned violent. A more radical group, the Weathermen, advocated the destruction of university property as a way to prohibit university complicity in the war effort. Like blacks, militant whites garnered intense and often negative press. However, black and white students at predominantly white institutions rarely worked in concert, since their priorities differed: black students demanded race-based campus reforms like black studies, black cultural centers, and increased black enrollment, while white students engaged in symbolic attacks on the war in Vietnam. The demands of black students at black colleges mirrored the spirit of black students at white institutions in that a general appreciation for blackness was paramount and antiwar demonstrations were few. But black students at black colleges also heavily focused on student power and quality of life issues, particularly because the authoritarian ethos at black colleges strangled student freedoms.[4]

BLACK POWER MISSISSIPPI STYLE

Try as the white power structure might, Mississippi did not escape the Black Power movement. In fact, the racial reality in the state fed it. Blacks continued to press for the *Brown* mandates amid extreme white intransigence, violence, and legal maneuvers. Not until 1970 did the primary schools in the capital city of Jackson desegregate, and even then it was under a court order and against the backdrop of massive resistance. White businesses persisted in their refusal to serve black patrons despite the 1964 Civil Rights Act. White government officials continued in their attempts to stem black voting potential despite the 1965 Voting Rights Act and to obstruct the MFDP from making headway on a national level. And whites continued to murder blacks with impunity, the most contemporaneous being voting rights activist Vernon Dahmer, killed by a Ku Klux Klan firebomb in January 1966. The June 1966 assault on James Meredith during his March Against Fear—an act intended to prove that a black man could walk safely through the state of Mississippi— became the last straw. According to Joyce Ladner, one-time Tougaloo student turned sociologist,

> Since many of the efforts Mississippi Negroes made to change the social structure— through integration—were futile, they began to reconceptualize their fight for equality from a different perspective, one designed to acquire long-sought goals through building bases of power. The black-power concept was, then, successfully communicated to Mississippi Negroes because of the failure of integration. But it was also communicated to them by the shooting of James Meredith on his march through Mississippi. This act of violence made Negro activists feel justified in calling for audacious black power. For only with black power, they contended, would black people be able to prevent events like the shooting.[5]

Meredith's shooting affected blacks (and liberal whites) nationwide, but it hit Mississippi blacks particularly hard because he was a resident, a local hero, and a freedom fighter in their struggle against white supremacy in the state. As with the 1963 murder of Medgar Evers, the assault represented one link in a long chain of murders and attempted murders of activists and provided a vivid reminder that the racial hierarchy bred not only segregation but rabid hate and violence. Adding insult to literal injury, the white press's treatment of the incident further inflamed racial tensions. The *Jackson Daily News*, for instance, dismissed the shooting as part of a conspiracy to tarnish Mississippi's reputation, implicated Dr. King for precipitating the event in a cartoon titled "An incident . . . an incident . . . my kingdom for an incident!," and shifted the blame from racist whites to civil rights activists by pleading, "When will the great American people wake up to the fact racial agitation is the vehicle on which sinister forces are taking this nation to enslavement and destruction?"[6]

The condition of Mississippi politics provided yet another source of anger and disappointment. By 1966, black Mississippians had begun to register to vote in record numbers (by 1969, they were registered at a higher rate than blacks in any other Southern state). Some even made it onto local tickets. A few white politicians, who as a whole completely ignored blacks until after passage of the 1965 Voting Rights Act, now fretted over how to deal with the new constituency. Some carefully courted them. Still, race-baiting had been a popular tactic prior to black voting rights, and racist politicians relied on the strategy even after blacks could punish them for dong so. William Forrest Winter, a moderate white candidate in the 1967 gubernatorial Democratic primary, found himself a target of the White Citizens' Council, the Ku Klux Klan, and several elected officials. A picture of Winter addressing a racially mixed crowd with blacks standing in the front row graced the front page of the *Commercial Appeal*. The caption read, "Are these front row sitters going to determine the destiny of Mississippi? For the first time in our history we are faced with a large NEGRO MINORITY BLOC VOTE— William Winter's election will insure negro domination of Mississippi elections for generations to come. WHITE MISSISSIPPI AWAKE."[7] The rabidly racist rhetoric, relentless and unchecked violence against black citizens, and glacial pace of change in the state frustrated and infuriated black Mississippians. Black activists turned to more militant forms of activism and redefined their ultimate liberatory goals as a result.

Black students at Mississippi colleges participated in the campus-based version of the Black Power movement sweeping the nation.[8] They, like their Northern counterparts, focused heavily on campus issues, but the dichotomy drawn in the literature—that students of the early 1960s focused on *off-campus* societal issues while those of the late-1960s focused on *campus-based* concerns—does not resonate with the black college experience. Students at *black* colleges, including those in Mississippi, had complained for years about conditions on campus, and student government candidates routinely ran on platforms promising campus changes. The emergence of the black freedom struggle in the 1950s and early 1960s only diversified their targets, and the shift toward more radical ideology in the later 1960s simply made their on-campus demands more aggressive. In short, the late-1960s activism at black colleges was informed by a tradition of campus-based attacks on white supremacy and attempts to make democratic rhetoric a reality. That students focused most of their attention inward did not change the underlying purpose of their activism: increased power, self-determination, and autonomy.

SYNCHRONIZED AGITATION: CROSS-FERTILIZATION BETWEEN MOVEMENT CENTERS AND CAMPUSES

Students appropriated a variety of organizations to attack the vestiges of white supremacy on their campuses. Student Government Associations played a particularly important role in organizing and mobilizing for change. Students also created other organizations for the same purpose. At times the organizations were informal and existed without university sanction either because the university refused to recognize the organization, the organization was too short-lived to seek sanction, or the students considered administrative recognition irrelevant for their purposes. At other times, radical student organizations sought university recognition for the funds and privileges that came with such status. Separate media accompanied the new radicalized spirit. Campus-sanctioned newspapers remained important conduits of information and included an increasing amount of aggressive language and content, but students created separate newspapers with names like *Harambee,* the *Nitty Gritty,* and the *Gadfly* to attack the administration and chastise their fellow students into participating in activism.[9]

A Reversal of Roles: The Pairing of a Private and a Public College

Black student organizations at different campuses remained in close contact with one another, a fact that marked them as different from white student groups and in which black student activists reveled, since it lent an aura of unity to their independent struggles.[10] Jackson State and Tougaloo, though in a reversal of roles, remained paired in their aggressive attacks on white supremacy in Jackson. The first bicampus activism between them occurred in 1961 when Jackson State students demonstrated in sympathy with the Tougaloo students arrested at the whites-only public library. Subsequent pairings were facilitated by the fact that the campuses were only nine miles apart and that students from both campuses participated in the citywide NAACP Youth Councils, not to mention the fact that they dated each other and frequented the same social spaces in downtown Jackson. They saw themselves as natural allies, though they recognized the privileged situation at

Tougaloo and lamented conditions at Jackson State. As Anne Moody, a Tougaloo student, remembered, "Jackson State, like most of the state-supported Negro schools, was an 'Uncle Tom' school. The students could be expelled for almost anything. When I found this out, I really appreciated Tougaloo." Tougaloo students supported the Jackson State student-inspired MIAS by printing its literature; sisters Joyce Ladner and Dorie Ladner transferred from Jackson State to Tougaloo shortly after the library sit-in and subsequent demonstrations; and Dorie Ladner and Anne Moody traveled to Jackson State immediately after Medgar Evers's assassination to incite students to demonstrate (they were summarily ejected by President Reddix not long after arriving on campus).[11] In 1967, however, Tougaloo students found themselves in a secondary role to Jackson State students who struck out against white supremacy in a way they had not done previously.

Jackson State student anger regarding campus conditions and grievances against the administration subsided after President Reddix's retirement in 1967 and his successor, Dr. John A. Peoples, took significant steps to assuage student concerns with the quality of campus life by reinstating an autonomous Student Government Association and relaxing stiff regulations governing student conduct. Still, Jackson State students, like black students and nonstudents elsewhere, remained bitter about the slow pace of change to the Southern racial order and grew increasingly frustrated with the fact that "years of protest—by turns vigorous and muted—have not brought white Mississippians to respect the full human dignity of black people."[12] Lynch Street, a popular thruway from white neighborhoods to downtown Jackson that bisected the campus, provided Jackson State students with an immediate reminder of the fact that, as former student Charles Beard put it, "We had no respect or rights where whites were concerned."

Beginning in 1965 when a white motorist struck a black female student (she suffered a broken leg), disturbances centered on Lynch Street each spring. White motorists routinely sped through the campus, putting students in jeopardy, but Jackson State security officers had no authority, since the street was city property. Each spring students and local youth threw rocks and bottles at white motorists, and police responded with tear gas, bullets, and an armored riot control vehicle. Violence escalated in May 1967 when police chased a male student onto campus and attempted to arrest him for a traffic violation. He escaped into a dormitory, and angry students pelted the squad car with rocks. During a peaceful protest by students and nonstudents the next day police shot into the crowd, killing Benjamin Brown, a well-known local activist, and wounding at least three others. According to President Peoples, "It was in this initial disturbance that I first perceived the deep seated anger in the students who had suffered racial discrimination and suppression. When the white policemen invaded the campus and emptied shotguns and tear gas at students who were doing no more than peacefully protesting, all the repressed anger, rage and aggression came forth."[13]

Several Tougaloo students were present the night police murdered Brown. Hermel Johnson, president of the Jackson State student body, had contacted Constance Slaughter (now Slaughter Harvey), president of the Tougaloo student body, and asked her to bring Tougaloo students to the Jackson State campus to protest the police presence. According to Slaughter, she enlisted the help of white faculty to make several trips to Jackson State. But

> when [police] put out the curfew that you had to be off the streets by six o'clock, I realized there was no way to get the kids back to campus since they came there in shifts. I called the campus and asked to speak to [an administrator] who was over the physical plant. I told him my dilemma and asked if we could use the bus. He asked, "Well, how did you get there?" I told him we went in shifts. He was one of the ones who wouldn't support anything. I tried to twist his arm, but he wouldn't yield. So, I called Bennie Thompson. He was a bus driver. . . . I asked if he would help us, [and] he said yes.

Thompson, a junior, took the bus without administrative permission.[14]

Slaughter and Thompson, identified as the ringleaders, argued that seizing the bus was necessary to demonstrate solidarity with Jackson State students and the black community in general, particularly since racist whites behaved similarly when the police killed Brown and prosecutors refused to investigate or charge anyone with the murder. Slaughter, Thompson, and their allies believed that theirs was an obligatory act on behalf of black humanity. They argued that this, and the fact that students returned to campus without violating the curfew and without damage to the bus, outweighed their violation of campus regulations. When the president and a disciplinary committee voted to punish Slaughter by not allowing her to participate in graduation and Thompson by placing him on probation, the campus exploded. Students boycotted classes and final exams, and several faculty wrote a letter to the president in solidarity with Slaughter: "As I am as guilty as those students charged in the case involving the protest of the murder of Benjamin Brown and the use of the Tougaloo bus, I will accept the restrictions meted out as long as they stand and consider myself excluded from the Commencement ceremonies."[15]

Back at Jackson State, the Student Government Association and a newly formed black citizens' committee drew up a list of demands and presented them to Mayor Allen Thompson, who refused to believe the grievances were indigenously inspired and blamed "those agitators like Stokely Carmichael and his Black Power movement, which is not only anti-white, but almost all that is anti-American." Though Jackson State was the center of the disturbances, none of the demands focused on campus conditions. Instead, they

reflected the black community's frustrations with the city of Jackson's refusal to move beyond its racist roots: a fifteen-mile-per-hour speed limit on
Lynch Street through the campus; more black police officers; punishment of
the officers who killed Brown; opening of the city's swimming pools, closed
since the mid-1950s to prevent desegregation; hiring of black workers at local
white businesses; and the creation of a biracial employment commission and
housing authority. The mayor met with the committee and promised to work
toward racial amity, but conditions in Jackson, and Mississippi in general,
continued to improve at a fitful pace.[16]

For students, marrying on- and off-campus concerns made complete
sense. The relative deprivation of their campus situations reeked of white
paternalism, and the heavy *in loco parentis* ethos was reminiscent of the racial
hierarchy off-campus. That they would use Student Government Associations to organize was not surprising, since the organizations drew politically
minded students. At Jackson State, such students had no other campus-based
outlets, since trustees barred civil rights organizations from public institutions (students did not form a campus chapter of the NAACP until 1972).
At Tougaloo, the student government most frequently focused on campus
issues but had linked its concerns with the off-campus black freedom struggle
since the early 1960s. The purpose of a Student Government Association,
according to Thomas Jefferson, who first advocated the concept, was to imbue
students with democratic habits that would serve them postgraduation.[17] At
black colleges in the 1960s and 1970s, students appropriated the organizations to extend that democratic reality to *all* American citizens, and the newly
radicalized organizations became a training ground for on- and off-campus
pursuits.

Blackening a White and a Black Institution

Activists at black colleges and newly admitted black students at white institutions also worked in concert, though the possibility had only recently
emerged because of the state's segregation laws. Such was the case at Mississippi Vocational College, renamed Mississippi Valley State in 1964, and
the University of Mississippi, where personal connections and what sociologists call contagion—where students at one campus emulate those at
another—played a role in the pairing.[18] The 1966 Meredith March provided
a temporary jolt to both student bodies. Black Ole Miss students were infuriated that Meredith, their idol and pathbreaker, had been shot. Students at
Mississippi Valley were only ten miles west of Greenwood, the town in which
Stokely Carmichael delivered the speech that inaugurated the Black Power
movement. Wilhelm Joseph Jr., a student from Trinidad, remembered, "That
radicalized me and made me say, 'I'm going to do something about this.'"

Joseph agreed when Carmichael, also from Trinidad, asked him to approach President White about the possibility of marchers using college facilities to change clothes, shower, and rest. According to Joseph, "The response I got was that Mr. White called out the National Guard. He called the National Guard to guard the campus to prevent the marchers from having anything to do with the college. I said, 'But it's a *black* college! Something is wrong here.'"

It was not until the later part of the decade, however, that the colleges experienced sustained activism that eventually merged across the campuses. It began when the Mississippi Valley campus exploded in 1969 and 1970. The Student Government Association, the same organization President White and the board of trustees feared would entertain aggressive politics in 1957, spearheaded the protests against the administration. Joseph, who was elected president of the student body, ran on a ticket that boasted, "We are going to move this place! This is a *black* college. We are going to use this opportunity to teach folks about black independence. We are going to broaden the vision." Student activists attacked the vestiges of second-class status and echoed the complaints of their counterparts at other black colleges across the nation: paternalistic campus rules, the complete absence of student representation on campus committees, and the low quality of faculty and facilities. Their demands also reflected the burgeoning black nationalism of the late 1960s and included an expanded library and course offerings on black America and the right to wear African-inspired clothes and Afro hairstyles. After a peaceful demonstration in February 1969, police and campus security officers forcibly transported 196 students to Jackson, incarcerated 12 others at the Leflore County jail, and issued warrants for 4 protest leaders, including the president of the student government, Wilhelm Joseph Jr. President White expelled all of the offending students, though he allowed most to reenroll after hearings before the Administrative Council.[19]

In early 1970, the Student Government Association and its new president, Tyrone Gettis, issued another list of demands and filed a complaint against the administration in U.S. District Court for violating the students' right to dissent and due process. President White threatened, "If the students are desirous of remaining in school, you will have to abide by the rules of the institution or withdraw from the institution. Faculty are asked to support the administration or resign." Students refused to budge. A February 1970 on-campus speech by Fannie Lou Hamer, a highly respected Mississippi activist, exacerbated the situation when she relentlessly attacked White's attitude toward student grievances; told students "if your education is not better than making you do things that you know is wrong, you are no better than President White"; admonished President White, who was present, that it was time for him to retire, "go home, and be quiet"; and told the audience, "I've seen some of the world's greatest Toms in service, but this man must be a Nuclear Tom." Students met at the Student Center the evening after the speech to plan a boycott of classes. The Sovereignty Commission, with President White's consent, used recording equipment to eavesdrop on the meeting and was fully aware of their plans.[20]

Days later, police arrested almost nine hundred students during a protest march—the largest arrest in the history of higher education in the United States—and President White closed the campus for a week. Offending students were expelled and two faculty members were fired for participating in the boycott, a situation precipitated by the fact that public black colleges continued to violate the tenure regulations outlined by the board of trustees (with board sanction, of course). Many students transferred to other institutions, including Tyrone Gettis, who went to Tougaloo, and enrollment plummeted by 60 percent. Rather than reprimand White for violating board policy and federal rulings regarding students' rights to due process and freedom of speech, trustees applauded White's "superior judgment in dealing with the student boycott of classes" and passed a resolution commending him for his actions. President White made no apologies for his actions and remained president with the board's blessing until he retired of his own volition in 1971. At his retirement dinner, President White told his audience, "I have gone through various tests of my allegiance to our State of Mississippi and my record is clear; I have never been found lacking."[21]

The activism at Mississippi Valley State spilled onto the University of Mississippi by way of a personal connection: Wilhelm Joseph Jr., student body president during the 1969 demonstrations at Mississippi Valley, enrolled at the University of Mississippi School of Law the next academic year. At that time, fewer than two hundred black undergraduate and graduate students attended the University of Mississippi, comprising 2.5 percent of the student body. Under the banner of the newly formed Black Student Union, of which Joseph was a member, the students devised a set of demands and attempted to present them to the chancellor, the highest-ranking official on campus. Black student actions highlighted the lack of support and alienation they experienced on campus and demonstrated sympathy for student activists at Mississippi Valley State, particularly since Joseph and Tyrone Gettis, Mississippi Valley student body president in the 1969–70 academic year, maintained a friendship. When rebuffed, the Black Student Union employed direct action tactics to draw attention to their cause. In February 1970, at the height of the demonstrations at Mississippi Valley, sixty-one black Ole Miss students interrupted a concert by sitting on the stage and were arrested for breach of the peace. Within forty-eight hours, twenty-eight more were arrested during demonstrations outside the chancellor's home and at the YMCA.[22]

The arrest of almost half the black student body sent the campus into a state of shock. Racial tension, never absent at Ole Miss, escalated. As student hearings proceeded, the entire campus debated the validity of black student concerns and tactics. Some administrators advised dropping the criminal charges against the students, though they were outnumbered by those who felt that harsh action was justified in order to ensure that the violence at Columbia, Cornell, Duke, Howard, and Southern would not be revisited on the Ole Miss campus. Faculty were similarly conflicted. The Ole Miss AAUP chapter criticized the black students for some of their behavior but argued that the criminal charges should be dropped and condemned the institution's "general indifference" to the "well being of the black student at this university," who were treated as "an unwelcome guest." Students in the Young Democrats Club, a left-wing organization, attempted to mend black and white student relationships while others attacked the black students for biting the hand that fed them and used the racist newspaper *The Rebel Underground* to attack them. Black students defended themselves against their critics, including the lieutenant governor, who used the crisis to fortify his run for governor the following year. In the words of the Black Student Union president, John Donald, black students would not "succumb to the racist practices of the administration. We feel that our needs are of such urgency that we cannot sit idly by and be apathetic and complacent any longer." In the end, all but eight black students were allowed to reenroll.[23]

The Persistent Specter of White Supremacist Defiance

The board of trustees watched the public campuses in horror. Only a small percentage of black and white students participated in activism, but they succeeded in garnering nationwide media attention, thereby embarrassing the trustees, already highly sensitive to negative press since the riot after Meredith's enrollment at Ole Miss and the 1964 Freedom Summer. White students in the Young Democrats invited Charles Evers, Aaron Henry (state president of the NAACP), Fannie Lou Hamer, and other *personae non gratae* to speak on campuses, and other white liberal groups organized antiwar demonstrations; all three black public institutions experienced activism to the point where they had to be closed; and all of the state's white public institutions except the Mississippi University for Women experienced periodic unrest, some of it spearheaded by newly admitted black students. The combination of antiwar sentiment and Black Power sentiment smacked of communism, as far as trustees were concerned, and the fact that it infiltrated Mississippi's institutions of higher education infuriated them.

M. M. Roberts, member of the board between 1959 and 1972, represented the face of massive resistance. In a 1969 address to the AAUP chapter at the University of Southern Mississippi, Roberts focused his comments on the racial issue and explained, "As I've gone along through the years and looked back I've said to myself really that I am a racist. Every time I read a definition I say, 'Well, that's me. I have no apologies for it though. It's me.'" He also expressed his admiration for Governor Theodore Bilbo, the unabashedly racist governor who precipitated sanctions against all of Mississippi's colleges in 1930; called anyone suggesting the University of Southern Mississippi hire a large number of black faculty a "stupid idiot" who "ought to get out of here . . . because you don't belong in our society if you think that is necessary"; and made his attitudes about the importance of accreditation—a constant source of tension since the battle to desegregate Ole Miss—clear: "Somebody said, 'If we don't do this we'll lose our accreditation,' and I always said, 'To hell with it,' you know, because what do we have? Do we have education for accreditation, or do we have it to educate boys and girls? Are the schools run for the students, or are the students run for a university complex?"[24] Such attitudes meant the board had little sympathy for student demands and supported college presidents who punished those who disrupted campus life.

FROM THE STREETS TO THE COURTS:
EXPANDING STUDENT RIGHTS

The fact that students refused to terminate activism forced college administrators into legal battles regarding the difference between constitutionally protected speech and behavior and the right of a college campus to control its property and constituents. The *Dixon* ruling, which extended Fourteenth Amendment protections to students in 1961, became the precedent for subsequent cases in which administrators attempted to discipline students without due process. Other cases dealt with First Amendment protections. In 1967, a district court ruled that a college administration could not prohibit parades or demonstrations in *Hammond v. South Carolina*. Two years later, the Supreme Court's *Tinker v. Des Moines* decision bolstered a student's right to free speech as long as that speech did not disrupt campus business or the rights of others to participate in the educational enterprise. In 1970, in *Jones v. State Board of Education of Tennessee*, and in 1972, in *Healy v. James*, the Court reified *Tinker*, though it cautioned future petitioners that "the critical line for First Amendment purposes must be drawn between advocacy, which is entitled to full protection, and action, which is not. Petitioners may, if they so choose, preach the propriety of amending or even doing away with any or all campus regulations. They may not, however, undertake to flout these rules."[25]

The Mississippi government's refusal to follow federal mandates without force, intransigence of the board of trustees, equation of freedom of speech with leniency for communists, and persistent animus toward the black freedom struggle meant that the Supreme Court's admonition that free speech "best serves its high purpose when it induces a condition of unrest, creates dissatisfaction with conditions as they are, or even stirs people to anger" did not sit well with white officials and their allies in the state's attempt to quell campus unrest. From Alcorn to Mississippi Valley to the University of Mississippi, courts reprimanded university officials who violated *Dixon*. At Mississippi Valley, they had to do so in 1968, 1969, and again in 1970. Reinstatement, however, did not necessarily mean that students had their records wiped clean or were allowed to permanently reenroll.[26]

Testing the Fourteenth Amendment

The first test of the line between student-as-citizen and student-as-campus-constituent came with *Brandon v. Alcorn*, a case that grew directly out of the March 1966 Alcorn demonstrations and subsequent student suspensions and ran parallel to the *Evers v. Birdsong* litigation regarding the right to demonstrate on public property. Three days after the first demonstration, a dean requested that seven student participants appear before the Disciplinary Committee but did not inform the students of the nature of the request or that a formal hearing was to take place. The students refused to meet individually with the committee and were suspended without a hearing or knowledge of the charges against them. With the help of the Lawyers' Committee for Civil Rights Under Law, Nettie Ruth Brandon and her sister, Dorothy Mae, along with the other suspended students, filed suit against Alcorn, President Boyd, and the board of trustees for violating their free speech, assembly, and due process rights as afforded by the First and Fourteenth Amendments and reified by *Dixon*.[27]

A court agreed with the Alcorn students, at least with their due process claims, and forced Boyd to reinstate the students and hold a proper hearing. In the formal hearing, held 1 June 1966, the Disciplinary Committee questioned the students about the demonstration, accused them of violating class attendance requirements and regulations that required students to sign out prior to leaving campus, resuspended the students (two of whom, including Nettie Ruth, expected to graduate), and told them to reapply for admission the following academic year. The students appealed but lost. Each of the student litigants reenrolled at Alcorn, though one filed a second suit in order to do so.[28]

The litigation had several consequences. It fortified *Dixon's* admonition that attendance at a public institution was of significant interest to individuals, and as such, those individuals deserved the right to defend themselves when the institution or the state attempted to prohibit that privilege. At the same time, the *Brandon v. Alcorn* decision reified the *in loco parentis* rights of colleges. Though each of the student litigants resided off-campus, Boyd and his counsel argued that residential status was immaterial—when students checked in on-campus they became subject to the rules of the institution, and when they left to participate in the demonstration they violated those regulations by not signing out. In essence, the ruling helped Boyd curb the movement and keep the campus isolated from the off-campus movement.

An unintended outcome of the litigation was the radicalization of many Alcorn students. Despite (or perhaps because of) the authoritarian manner in which Boyd ruled the campus and the administration's attempts to crush activism, Alcorn students like the Brandons became more aggressive in their demands and tactics. Some students focused their attention on Boyd with the assistance of on-campus organizations like the Student Movement at Alcorn College and the United Student Movement, while others translated their energies into off-campus activism after graduation through organizations like the NAACP.[29]

Testing the First Amendment

Student litigants in Mississippi also broadened the First Amendment rights of campus constituents. The 1964 speaker ban barred controversial speakers from public campuses with a particular eye toward race liberals advocating desegregation and racial equality and, as far as the board of trustees was concerned, communism and the overthrow of the American government. The following year, trustees expanded their oversight by creating measures to investigate faculty "who are troublemakers and to scrutinize efforts at granting of tenure" and sought to limit the number of out-of-state students to prevent the "possible creation of on-campus disturbances and to avoid trends toward ultra-liberalism in our state by outside infiltration."[30] The policy demonstrated the sentiments popular with enemies of the black freedom struggle: that student activism and the movement in general were not organic phenomena arising from local communities and organizations but from national organizations with communist sympathies bent on destroying America.

In 1966, the board adopted a policy that completely stripped speaker's committees and presidents of the right to even invite speakers to campus. It also prohibited speakers who had been charged with a crime (which barred hundreds of civil rights activists arrested for their activism), any person who advocated "a philosophy of the overthrow of the United States" (which covered any activist who had not been arrested), political or sectarian meetings sponsored by any outside organization on campus (which included organizations like SNCC, the NAACP, and Students for a Democratic Society), and any speech on a political topic (which barred race liberals and racists alike). The trustees hoped the revised speaker ban would sanitize and depoliticize Mississippi's college campuses in the wake of massive student activism across the country.[31]

Students chafed under the newly crafted speaker ban. At Mississippi State University, eight hundred students demonstrated against it in 1969, though one scholar posits that the demonstration drew such a large crowd because the stringent ban barred segregationists from speaking engagements. Liberal students and the AAUP applauded a three-judge panel that forced the board of trustees to alter the speaker ban by lifting the restrictions on who could address the student body and investing the college president and speaker's committees with the authority to approve speakers in 1969. In the decision, *Stacy v. Williams*, the court recognized a college's right to make and enforce reasonable rules but explained that it took up the case to parse out "the sensitive area of speech control [where] the university's power ends and students' rights begin."[32]

Activist students tested the ruling almost immediately. In early 1970, white University of Mississippi students in the Young Democrats Club invited Tyrone Gettis, the student body president at Mississippi Valley State who helped organize the demonstrations on his campus that year, to speak on the Ole Miss campus. The Mississippi Valley campus, by the time of the invitation, had experienced two months of almost constant demonstrations, and half of Ole Miss's black students had been arrested for their own demonstrations. The University of Mississippi chancellor refused to grant permission on the grounds that Gettis's speech presented "a clear and present danger" to campus safety in that it would inflame student activists already demonstrating and disrupting campus life. The Young Democrats filed suit, and in *Molpus v. Fortune* a court ruled against the chancellor using *Stacy v. Williams* as precedent. The court explained that registered student organizations could invite and host a speaker when that speaker promised to limit his or her speech to a discussion of the crisis at a different institution and refrained from advocating disorder or violence. Gettis's participation in the demonstrations at Mississippi Valley State was not enough to prevent University of Mississippi students from enjoying their First Amendment rights to hear controversial speech.[33]

The board of trustees and campus administrators in Mississippi were not alone in their bid to control their campuses by regulating speech and in their attempt to purge their campuses of radicals. Southern and Northern trustees and administrators faced student and faculty constituents in court over the breadth of First and Fourteenth Amendment rights throughout the late 1960s and early 1970s. Activism accelerated to a point at which students participated in more than nine thousand demonstrations involving almost two-thirds of all college campuses during the 1969–70 academic year, and the rate of litigation similarly increased as students sued administrators and administrators sued students.[34] Though scholarly attention focuses most heavily on the battle between administrators and students at Northern institutions like Berkeley, Wisconsin, Cornell, and Columbia, the battle was no less fierce in the South or Mississippi. Fueled by the Southern black freedom struggle and its racist countermovement, campus constituents pitted themselves against each other for the power to control the campus space and over the role of a college in society.

A COMMUNITY DIVIDED: WHAT IS A *BLACK* COLLEGE?

Black colleges faced a separate set of *intra*-institutional debates regarding the responsibilities of a *black* college in society. The Black Power movement forced black colleges to confront the questions, what makes an institution *black*, and who and to what end does a *black* institution serve? As far as many activists were concerned, no longer were constituent demographics or historic purpose enough to qualify an institution as a black college. Now colleges, like individuals, had to be black on the "inside" as well as the "outside." In other words, the institutions were expected to adopt an overtly political and ideological framework that encouraged students to use the campus for liberatory purposes before and after graduation. Black colleges had been similarly prodded by scholars like Carter G. Woodson, W. E. B. DuBois, E. Franklin Frazier, and Harold Cruse, who argued that black colleges should train students for an active role in battling the racial hierarchy rather than simply training the black bourgeoisie to become, in Frantz Fanon's words, "black skin in white masks."[35] Such radicalized visions of black colleges found new adherents in the Black Power era.

Students became the most vocal supporters of a politicized black college campus and routinely positioned themselves as the vanguard of the new blackness by juxtaposing themselves against the civil rights generation, a popular rhetorical strategy at the time not necessarily based in fact, since many adult activists, like Fannie Lou Hamer, and scholars, like Vincent Harding, embraced Black Power. Still, across the South, black students harshly judged their colleges and administrators for their timid approach in confronting white supremacy and pushed the movement forward on and off their campuses. As one scholar described them, "Today's black students are in a race to build a sense of black community before a racial Armageddon overtakes them. This sense of urgency must be grasped if one is to understand the powerful forces which are motivating them."[36]

Mississippi was no exception. Hermel Johnson, the Jackson State student body president, spoke openly about his mixed opinions regarding black colleges and President Reddix's legacy at the president's retirement program in 1967. Johnson told the audience,

> In my opinion, all Negro colleges have one flaw in common: they were born into a segregated world and set out to serve us with the view that our separate world would someday be equal. As a result each Negro college has a stake in the status quo. And, needless to say, status quo is now anathema to most Negroes. The Negro revolt required the Negro college president to spend much of his time attempting to soothe the restless Negro students, who are embarrassingly aware that they are receiving an inferior education while being surrounded by all the trappings of segregation. Jacob L. Reddix and other Negro college presidents were the heroes of my father's late youth and early manhood. . . . Men like President Reddix stood between us and the raw nakedness of our educational plight. . . . They went before hard-core segregationist school boards and pleaded for money to build us a library, a chemistry lab, a dormitory, or a football stadium. . . . I do not envy men like President Reddix. Only with reluctance do I sing their praise. Yet praiseworthy they are. They fashioned us into the rebels we are.[37]

No longer would their campuses be pale imitations of white institutions with a white man's puppet at the helm. Instead, students at black colleges hoped, as did Vincent Harding, that "When the final accounting is done, it may be that the new directions forged at Fisk, victories won at Dillard, black control developed at Spelman, or experiments at Tougaloo will prove to be most important of all—if such things ever come."[38]

Should a College Be a Movement Center?

A main point of contention between students and administrators centered around the question of how directly black colleges should be involved in societal reform, a debate reminiscent of the early 1960s. Activist students (and some faculty and administrators) demanded that colleges actively engage in black community uplift and argued that the walls around the ebony tower should be porous. In that spirit, Tougaloo's Political Action Committee (PAC) created and operated the Black and Proud Liberation School for youth in Jackson, Rust College students continued to work in voter registration in Madison County, and Alcorn students campaigned for Charles Evers's election to Congress. Such politically active students, however, were few in number. Jackson State's underground newspaper, the *Gadfly,* chastised the student body for its apathy, Tougaloo's *Harambee* regularly implored students to participate more fully in blackness, and members of the Student Movement at Alcorn College verbally abused and threatened to physically attack students who did not support the 1966 boycott of the campus union asking them, "Are you going to sit back and let WHITE MONKEY'S [*sic*] control you, beat you and make you look like fools?"[39] In short, students did not unanimously participate in political activism. Instead, many simply adopted the cultural forms of Black Power, including growing Afros, wearing dashikis, and choosing Swahili names, while they remained aloof from overt participation in direct action.

Black college presidents sometimes agreed with the need to inculcate pride in blackness and communal responsibility in students. Institutional affiliation with political projects, however, was a different matter. At private institutions, a politicized campus risked alienating funding agencies wary of supporting activist colleges. At public institutions, white trustees continued to attempt to crush any and all dissent. The persistent violence against black activists and negative media attention also haunted college administrators, who argued that black colleges should serve as intellectual training grounds for a productive citizenry rather than as change agents in themselves. As the president of North Carolina Central University stated, "It is the obligation of the college or university to be neutral and to serve as a medium through which ideas are developed, presented, analyzed, evaluated and through which the frontiers of knowledge are expanded." Putting it even more bluntly, he continued, "The need for an enormous increase in the embourgeoisement of the black American population" should be one of the college's primary concerns.[40]

The trustees at Mississippi's most radical institution, Tougaloo, agreed. Scarred by the Sovereignty Commission and legislative campaigns to close the campus in 1964, the trustees were determined to strike a new path for the institution. They took pride in the institution's involvement in black advancement but explained that the "overwhelmingly dominant view on the campus, however, is that Tougaloo must concentrate its energies on the task of making itself a first-rate liberal arts college. This view is based on the conviction that the advances won in the Movement can best be consolidated through significant improvements in the educational opportunities available to Negroes." According to John Dittmer, a historian and faculty member at Tougaloo from 1967 to 1979, trustees passed on several opportunities to align the institution with the off-campus black freedom struggle. In his words, "There were efforts underway to improve our image in the white community and to get some white support for the school, or at least to get the state legislature off our backs." Playing a passive role in black advancement, trustees hoped, would attract funding agencies skittish about overt campus activism but interested in racial equality and higher education.[41]

Do Whites Have a Place in a Black College?

Another point of contention between students and administrators was racial separatism. In Mississippi, separatist sentiment butted up against the raging battle to desegregate the state's primary and secondary schools and the increasing number of black students enrolled at the state's white colleges. Though research on the era focuses on Northern white college administrators battling with black students regarding race-exclusive campus spaces and programs, black college administrators also worried that separatist sentiment would damage their campuses. Like their white counterparts, they were concerned that Black Power–era demands violated the principle of integration and, in turn, would lead to SACS sanctions or a loss of accreditation similar to what occurred at Ole Miss during the Meredith crisis. Similarly, they worried about losing funding by violating Title V of the Civil Rights Act of 1964, the Federal Tax Reform Act of 1969, and the Internal Revenue Code, which denied protection and funds to institutions and groups found to discriminate based on race. Their fears—that federal initiatives to prevent white institutions from discriminating would be transformed into weapons against black colleges—were not unfounded: Southern legislatures threatened to close public black colleges after the *Brown* decision, and racists continued to use legal and extralegal means to stem the black freedom struggle at private institutions.

Of the black colleges in Mississippi, Tougaloo was most impacted by the debate over separatism. Tougaloo's reputation as the most radical college in the state derived from the fact that it was the only voluntarily desegregated institution in Mississippi and that its activist constituents—black *and* white—valiantly battled white supremacy and used the campus as a movement center in the early 1960s. The burgeoning Black Power movement forced campus constituents to examine the college's racial reality in the late 1960s: trustees appointed the institution's first black president, George A. Owens, in 1965, but the faculty remained predominantly white. The presence of a large number of white professors, once a mark of liberalism, now smacked of paternalism and colonial rule to radical students. They, like SNCC and CORE, which ousted whites in 1966, could not fathom how blacks could close ranks and use black colleges as movement centers when whites assumed positions of power.

The 1969 Black Spring Weekend, also called the Black Power Conference, put the issue in stark relief. Organized by the Political Action Committee, the most politically active group on campus, the weekend consisted of a series of speakers on the future of the black freedom struggle. Invited to attend were the local chapter of the Black Panther Party, the Republic of New Africa, SNCC, and Mississippi activists. The administration knew to anticipate separatist and millennial rhetoric, but it was unprepared for the committee's request for university sanction of a meeting that would exclude whites. In a heated faculty meeting, several faculty—black and white—expressed anger and dismay at the request and demanded that "no program involving racial exclusion should be approved by the faculty since it is seriously contrary to the basic traditions of the College." Others offered a compromise, suggesting, "It might be possible to provide the means by which students could hold such meetings off campus." Still others supported the committee's request, explaining that the "desire for an all-black meeting was not motivated by racist sentiments but rather a desire to be alone for reasons of comfort and solidarity." In the end, President Owens and the faculty begrudgingly allowed the Political Action Commitee to exclude whites from the meeting to avoid a student shutdown of the campus.[42]

What Is and Who Should Teach Black Studies?

A related concern was Black Studies. Just as the emerging concept of blackness grew beyond pigment to include cultural and political components, the designers of Black Studies insisted that it have a black ideological and intellectual center. As Nathan Hare, director of Black Studies at San Francisco State, maintained, "If all a black-studies program needs is a professor with a black skin to prattle about Negro subject matter, then our Negro schools would never have failed so painfully as they have." Generally, collegiate Black Studies departments assumed no neutrality in their role in the struggle. Their founders did not view a college education as an instrument by which to socialize young adults into the dominant culture. Instead, they saw the postsecondary experience as serving an openly political purpose and as an instrument with which oppressed peoples could learn to change society.[43]

On the other hand, prominent black scholars and activists heavily critiqued the concept as anti-intellectual and a threat to integration in education. Roy Wilkins, Bayard Rustin, Kenneth Clark (a renowned sociologist), and A. Philip Randolph (a civil rights and labor activist) sympathized with student demands for black subject matter and racial solidarity but warned that Black Studies, particularly at white institutions, would be marginalized. As Wilkins stated, "No person who has watched the halting march of Negro civil rights through the years can fail to sympathize with the frustrations and anger of today's black students. . . . But, in demanding black Jim Crow studies . . . they are opening the doors to a dungeon." Critics also warned students that white college administrators would create Black Studies as a short-term solution to quell activism but that institutions would remain uncommitted to black advancement. Despite their cautions, black students persisted in their demands, and more than five hundred such departments and programs existed across the nation by 1971.[44]

Only recently had Mississippi's white institutions admitted black students when they demanded black faculty and black-oriented courses.[45] Institutions capitulated very slowly and reluctantly, and only Ole Miss created a Black Studies department, though a few black-oriented courses appeared in other colleges' catalogs. At the state's black colleges, students demanded black-oriented courses as a way to make their institutions authentically *black* rather than poor imitations of white institutions. Similarly, activist students believed that hiring more *black* faculty—meaning politically, culturally, and ideologically black rather than simply genetically black—would further transform the institutions into movement centers in which the black community could close ranks and plot a course for societal reform. Limited resources meant that few black institutions could support a coherent program or department, but like white campuses, black colleges began to offer black-oriented courses in the late 1960s and early 1970s.

The issue of who would teach such courses came to a head at Tougaloo because of the sheer number of white faculty. Tentative proposals for an interdisciplinary program circulated as early as 1963, but Black Studies did not become an institutional reality until after a 1969 student strike about the lack of black-oriented classes, texts, and professors. John Dittmer, the historian hired in 1967, helped spearhead the program and suggested that the core faculty should be black while white instructors would teach only if the situation necessitated it. Some faculty chafed under the suggestion "on the grounds that it is discriminatory." Himself a white man, Dittmer attempted to assuage faculty fears in that all students (Tougaloo enrolled a handful of white students at the time) could enroll and that the courses taught by white faculty would count for credit toward the major. Using history as an example to support his case, he explained, "Given the evidence of White historiography in the area of Afro-American history and culture, it is only natural that Black students across the country—and at Tougaloo—are demanding that Black Studies Programs be directed by Black people. This is not 'racism in reverse,' but simply an effort to take the necessary steps to set the record straight."[46]

Black students and their allies pushed white professors to the periphery of Black Studies, but the development of the programs and departments relied heavily on white philanthropy. According to Noliwe Rooks, white philanthropists wanted "to increase the acceptance of the subject's entrance into the academy, but not in a manner that would structurally strengthen and legitimize the actual programs and departments themselves. They certainly did not want Black Studies tied to efforts to promote Black Power."[47] From the available information on Black Studies in Mississippi, her analysis appears correct. At Tougaloo, in particular, Black Studies began as an academic *and* political enterprise but was quickly transformed into a purely academic endeavor much like programs and departments across the nation. Political activism was left to individually interested students, as Black Studies never became the mini–movement center activists hoped for. The dire need for funds and tepid support for the Black Power movement led even liberal administrators to position their institutions as passive supporters of the black freedom struggle.

OLD WINE IN NEW BOTTLES: THE RACIST COUNTERMOVEMENT DURING THE BLACK POWER ERA

In Mississippi, the countermovement remained virulent and highly organized. White racists employed intimidation and misinformation to attack activists and capitalized on federal-level connections and precedent. The local Federal Bureau of Investigation included Tougaloo's Political Action Committee in a list of organizations targeted as a part of J. Edgar Hoover's Counterintelligence Program, a clandestine federal initiative created to "expose, disrupt, misdirect, discredit, or otherwise neutralize the activities of black nationalist, hate-type organizations and groupings, their leadership, spokesmen, membership and supporters, and to counter their propensity for violence and civil disorder." Local agents also employed a tactic popular at the federal level by sending one particularly active Tougaloo student an anonymous fake letter from a campus organization criticizing his "conduct and general demeanor" and advising him to stay away from campus. The student left Mississippi shortly thereafter, believing fellow students threatened his safety. Local agents celebrated, "A black extremist has been cut off from his usual contacts and area of operation by counterintelligence technique."[48]

The Sovereignty Commission turned to friends on the Ole Miss faculty to revoke the scholarship of Wilhelm Joseph Jr., the Mississippi Valley and Ole Miss activist originally from Trinidad. When that did not work—a friendly professor helped Joseph find another scholarship, and he eventually graduated with a law degree—the Commission enlisted the assistance of a senator, a representative, the governor, and the Immigration and Naturalization Service to attack him. In a letter to James Eastland, SISS chair and rabid racist, the commission's director asked that consideration "be given to promotion of legislation which would provide deportation proceeding in any case where a foreign student is found guilty of participation in this undesirable and unlawful activity on the campus of any tax supported institution." In response to further inquiries, the House Subcommittee on Immigration's counsel assured the commission that "Immigration and Naturalization Service is well aware of Mr. Joseph's existence and has him under observation. . . . I have been advised by the Immigration and Naturalization Service that if the subject qualifies for deportation, the Immigration and Naturalization Service will take necessary steps to remove him from the United States."[49] The actions against Joseph, Tougaloo's Political Action Committee, and other activists reveal that the Sovereignty Commission was neither a group of bungling keystone cops nor bounded by local constraints. Instead, they were part of a highly coordinated and interconnected network of white supremacists at all levels of government that worked together to cripple the movement activist by activist, organization by organization.

White racists continued to employ brute force and violence as well. At black colleges from the University of South Carolina at Orangeburg to Texas Southern University to Southern University at Baton Rouge, police injured and killed students with billy clubs, tear gas, and bullets. The white-on-black violence in Mississippi was particularly intense and rarely, if ever, was prosecuted. In 1968, police shot into a crowd of Alcorn students demonstrating against the expulsion of those caught campaigning for Charles Evers and injured three of them. The following year, racists tossed a bomb onto the Tougaloo campus, destroying a dean's on-campus residence. Like the murderers who stalked and killed nonstudent activists, none of the assailants faced legal action.[50]

The deadliest attack on students in Mississippi occurred in 1970, when police fired four hundred rounds of buckshot into a crowd of unarmed Jackson State students and other youth demonstrating against "the historical pattern of racism that substantially affects daily life in Mississippi," the war in Southeast Asia, the draft, and the police murder of four white students at Kent State University during an antiwar protest days earlier. The barrage, which occurred without warning and without an order to fire, killed a Jackson State student and a high school student and wounded a dozen others. A highway patrol investigation and a Hinds County, Mississippi, grand jury absolved the officers of wrongdoing. A federal grand jury also returned no indictments. Instead, they placed the blame squarely on the students and their use of foul language during the protest. One officer was quoted as saying, "We may not have as high a tolerance for insults from Negroes as some Northern policemen do." The press followed suit and bristled at the attention now focused on the state: "Many Southerners simply feel the South has a great edge monopoly on social problems and that local officials should be given the chance to responsibly handle the jobs to which they were elected by their constituents. And the officials should do so without mayhem and public glare that comes with politicians in search of a whipping boy and with their eyes on polls and national attention." The federal-level Commission on Campus Unrest, however, found differently and shifted the blame to Mississippi's white supremacist reality: "A significant cause of the deaths and injuries at Jackson State College is the confidence of white officers that if they fire weapons during a black campus disturbance they will face neither stern departmental discipline nor criminal prosecution or conviction." No one was prosecuted, though the shooting—and the massive school desegregation campaign occurring in Jackson at the exact same time—topped a poll of noteworthy news conducted in Mississippi by the Associated Press.[51]

Black students at white institutions fared better in that they were not fired on by police, but they fared worse than their white counterparts—a fact that did not escape the attention of blacks or liberal whites on the University of Mississippi campus. As two particularly outspoken white members of the Young Democrats Club reminded campus constituents in an editorial in the college paper, when white students rioted over James Meredith's enrollment, the same politician who condemned black students for their nonviolent protest "had no words of condemnation" for white students. Administrators neither punished the white students who physically attacked Tougaloo students visiting the University of Mississippi campus for a literary festival in 1965 nor penalized the one thousand white students rioting over a referendum on the sale of beer, even though "property was destroyed, profane language was abundant, and disrespect for law enforcement officials was not rare." Similarly, police simply slapped twenty white students at the University of Southern Mississippi on the wrist after a panty raid in which hundreds of students tossed rocks, eggs, and bottles at police, damaged a transformer that left the campus dark for several hours, and burned a cross on campus.[52]

On the other hand, police shipped black student activists at both the University of Mississippi and Delta State University to Parchman Penitentiary—the harshest prison work farm in the state—after peaceful though disruptive demonstrations, and administrators took severe action against them. To black students and their white allies, the differential administrative treatment of black and white students reeked of the same racist attitudes that allowed police to fire on blacks with impunity and drew national attention to the murder of white civil rights workers when countless blacks had been assaulted and killed without notoriety. As John Donald stated at the time, "I think it's unfair. I've seen instances where white students have done far worse things. I don't consider what we've done as really being an evil thing. And nothing has ever happened to them. I think it's unfair and the precedent has been set already. And I think now the fact that we, we're getting all the punishment, you know, seems to set another precedent that black students are not equal to white students."[53]

CONCLUSION

Black students and black colleges are at the margins of the story on student activism in the late 1960s and early 1970s. Though they receive little scholarly attention, students at black colleges were highly active and faced the harshest penalties of all students at any type of institution.[54] So, too, were black students at white Southern institutions highly active and harshly punished. Black activism in Northern colleges was no cakewalk, but black Southern students faced not only a fully organized countermovement that was completely integrated into the social, legal, and political fabric of the region but also an intense hatred on the part of whites built during the contentious years of the black freedom struggle. The literature's focus on activism at Northern white institutions fortifies the illusion that the South in general and black colleges in particular were not touched by the Black Power movement. In fact, the Black Power movement was inspired by the Southern black freedom struggle and inaugurated in Mississippi. That the countermovement remained so violent is evidence that the movement itself was strong.

Also, the claim that Northern black students, Northern white students, or Northern black urban riots inspired Southern black college activism comes dangerously close to the assumptions that many Southern whites held of the black freedom struggle: that Southern black activism (of the early or late 1960s) was not an indigenous phenomenon but inspired and spearheaded by Northern forces.[55] Students at black colleges certainly were invigorated by Northern youth protest, but such an analysis divorces them from the previous generation of black college activists and ignores a history of campus activism. As Clayborne Carson says of the broader black freedom struggle, "Rather than claiming that a black power movement displaced the civil rights movement, [local activists] would argue that a black freedom movement seeking generalized racial advancement evolved into a black power movement toward the unachieved goals of the earlier movement."[56] So, too, did Black Power–era students build on an activist tradition in which they appropriated campus space, organizations, and media in a battle against white supremacy and for human dignity. Theirs was but a new phase in an older war.

The fascination with the activism at white campuses derives in part from the intense media attention heaped on black and white students at those institutions and the dramatic nature of their activism. Indeed, they helped shape higher education in a way that remains present in contemporary times. However, the overwhelming focus on those campuses means that the historiography on student activism resembles a Columbus Discovered America narrative in which, as Charles Payne puts it, "History is something that happens when the White Folks show up and stops when they leave."[57] When

white students left the South after the 1964 Freedom Summer, media attention followed them to their campuses, where they were joined by black student activists in their attacks on white college administrators and policies.
Activism at black colleges, though no less extreme, was virtually ignored;
the differential media attention given to the murder of students at Kent State
versus Jackson State is a case in point. As an American Civil Liberties Union
official stated, "Let's face the terrible fact! If only the two at Jackson had
been killed, there would probably have been [no federal-level investigation].
Kent was special because the victims were *white* students"[58] (emphasis in
original). The consequence of such a one-sided treatment is not only that the
literature draws incorrect generalizations about student protest, it becomes
another way of writing blacks out of history.

Chapter Eight

Conclusion

The 1970 demonstrations at Jackson State in which police murdered two black youth marked the end of large-scale college-based activism in Mississippi. Students at individual campuses continued to press for campus reform, and some continued to participate in the bid to improve the quality of life for the black community off-campus. But the number of widely disruptive acts that brought colleges or their surrounding communities to a grinding halt dwindled. The disintegration of Mississippi's black student movement mirrored the decline in activism at black and white colleges throughout the nation and the decline of the Black Power movement in general. The American public grew wary of the war in Vietnam and Northern urban unrest. Press coverage of local black freedom struggle campaigns faded. Radical political and social policy recommendations were co-opted and sanitized. The federal government accelerated its attempt to crush youth activism with its Counterintelligence Program. And activists defected, graduated, fled to exile, or were incarcerated. "Without a regular regimen of angry militants waving lists of non-negotiable demands at reporters," William Van Deburg writes, "the average American couch potato slipped easily into a post-Vietnam-era stupor."[1]

STRUGGLE AND SUCCESS

Did the student movement succeed? It depends on the measure of success. Black college administrators continue to fashion their colleges as places that educate future leaders who should participate in social reform after graduation. On the other hand, students continue to join the NAACP and other on-campus groups that directly tie the colleges to the off-campus black community, and colleges regularly host community meetings and conferences addressing racial concerns with presidential consent. Paternalistic rules regarding dress code and personal conduct remain at many colleges though they have been loosened significantly. Only the University of Mississippi and Tougaloo offer any semblance of a Black Studies major, but all of Mississippi's institutions of higher education offer black-oriented classes. Students and faculty are still subject to rules regarding demonstrations and acceptable speech, but the proscriptions fit AAUP guidelines regarding First and Fourteenth Amendment protections. Students and other activist campus constituents may not have received all the concessions they demanded, but research demonstrates that black students were more effective than white students in gaining compromises from their administrations.[2]

At the state level, success is more concretely measured. Governor William Waller appointed the first black member to the board of trustees in 1972. In 1973, the same year as the first Medgar Evers Memorial Day celebration in Jackson, the Sovereignty Commission disbanded when Governor Waller vetoed its appropriations. The following year, black activists filed suit on behalf of Jackson State and Alcorn students, accusing the governor and trustees of maintaining a segregated and unequal system of higher education, thereby violating the Fourteenth Amendment. The litigation dragged on for almost twenty years and trustees vowed not to capitulate, but the Supreme Court finally decided *United States v. Fordice* in 1992, and forced reluctant state agents to increase funding for public black colleges and to improve their academic programs.[3] Ole Miss, though far from the most diverse institution in the nation, enrolls a student body made up of 18 percent students of color as of 2007, a far cry from the racially monolithic student body of the past. Such changes were a long time coming. The black freedom struggle's demand for racial equality and the prominent role played by activist campus constituents helped fuel the shifts in higher education in Mississippi and ensured that the changes were not simply cosmetic.

The movement's successes are evident in less easily quantified ways as well. In particular, the black freedom struggle increased black students' expectations and acted as a psychological and cultural boost on which to build. As William Van Deburg says of the late 1960s in general, "By decolonizing their minds, cultivating feelings of racial solidarity, and contrasting their world with that of the oppressor, black Americans came to understand themselves better. In developing a greater pride in blackness than had any generation before them, the sixties activists discovered a deep well of untapped energy which enabled ordinary people to do extraordinary things." The spirit of the movement remains in contemporary times. Black Student Unions are fixture on Mississippi's white college campuses. Tougaloo hosts "Freedom Now!," an archival research project staffed by Tougaloo and Brown University students in which they learn about the Mississippi black freedom struggle and upload pertinent documents to the World Wide Web. And the University of Mississippi's William Winter Institute for Racial Reconciliation, established in 1999, seeks to "foster reconciliation and civic renewal wherever people suffer as a result of racial discrimination or alienation, and promote scholarly research, study and teaching on race and the impact of race and racism."[4] The demand that Mississippi face its bloody and horrific past is alive and well on Mississippi's college campuses. So, too, is the demand that it become an increasingly open and democratic society.

Also, the movement became a springboard for several former activists with regard to their future careers. Bennie Thompson, the Tougaloo student disciplined for commandeering the campus bus to transport students from a Jackson rally back to Tougaloo in 1967, was elected mayor of Bolton, Mississippi, in 1973, and later became a United States representative. Constance Slaughter Harvey, the Tougaloo student body president who enlisted Thompson's assistance, graduated from the University of Mississippi School of Law and later joined the Lawyers' Committee for Civil Rights Under Law and the Southern Legal Rights Foundation. Wilhelm Joseph Jr., the Mississippi Valley and Ole Miss student whom the Sovereignty Commission hoped to deport, became the executive director of the Legal Aid Bureau in Baltimore. Leslie Burl McLemore, a Rust activist involved in a variety of campaigns, became heavily involved in the MFDP and later became a professor at Jackson State and director of the Fannie Lou Hamer National Institute for Citizenship and Democracy. Nettie Ruth and Dorothy Brandon, two of the Alcorn students suspended after the off-campus demonstrations in 1966, became heavily involved in the NAACP and local activism. Though these students' attempts to enlist the campus space as a movement center were sometimes thwarted, they and other former students used their experiences in the black freedom struggle to fuel a lifelong pursuit of justice, dignity, and humanity for the black community.

LESSONS LEARNED FROM THE BLACK COLLEGE EXPERIENCE

This book has sought to provide a more complicated picture of the black freedom struggle and one of its most important movement centers. But the lens of the black college experience does more than illuminate the intimate details of campus life during the 1960s and 1970s. It forces a re-visioning of the role of philanthropy in black education, the global picture of student activism, current stressors on institutional sovereignty and academic freedom, and the growth of American conservatism.

Rethinking the Role of Philanthropy in Black and White

A persistent theme in the literature on black higher education is that of white control. Much of the scholarly work focuses on the role of white philanthropy in the late nineteenth and early twentieth centuries as educational reformers battled over how to integrate nearly four million freedmen and freedwomen into American society. While early literature portrayed religious philanthropy as unequivocally radical, more recent scholarship provides nuance to the description by documenting how liberal white philanthropists refused to allow blacks to run their own institutions, believed in white cultural superiority, and counseled that racial uplift depended on slow and steady work rather than revolution.[5] As this book demonstrates, white philanthropists continued to play a major role in directing the path of black education in the 1960s and 1970s. And, as with their predecessors, there were limits to their liberalism. Whether through constraining the political possibilities of Black Studies or having a hand in curbing campus connections to the black freedom struggle, white philanthropic agents had significant power in dictating the colleges' relationship to society. The white trustees on the Tougaloo board and at Alcorn were vastly different, but they were not polar opposites: both refused to grant campus administrators wide-ranging power, took action against radical presidents, and described their decisions as necessary to further the cause of black education.

The Mississippi black college experience is a reminder that white philanthropists were not alone in their bid to keep campuses estranged from the race-based questions of the time. Just as Booker T. Washington sought to create amity between the races by encouraging blacks to eschew political and social issues during the late nineteenth and early twentieth centuries, black college presidents and others believed that black colleges should remain aloof from the black freedom struggle during the 1960s and 1970s. Washington's actions fit neatly into the story that positions industrial philanthropy against religious philanthropy, but the Mississippi experience demonstrates that black religious philanthropists acted similarly. The AMEC and CMEC diverged widely in their attitudes toward activism, although both denominations were exclusively black, and the CMEC's Mississippi Industrial College closely resembled the state's public institutions in its hostile attitudes toward campus involvement in the movement. Yet even members of the racially radical AMEC wanted to disassociate Campbell College from the Jackson movement and blasted their activist colleagues for allowing the campus to be used for political purposes. As such, the story of philanthropy is more complicated than the traditional industrial philanthropy versus missionary philanthropy dichotomy or the black philanthropy versus white philanthropy dichotomy. Instead, philanthropic attitudes toward the proper role of a black college were situation-specific and influenced not only by race but by the layers of funding patterns, organizational history, and the particularities of the countermovement poised against them.

Radicalizing an Understanding of Student Protest

Also, the portrait of student protest changes when we examine black colleges. As previous research demonstrated, the generalizations drawn from white students—that activists came from homes with a permissive, child-centered, and nonreligious environment—do not facilitate a complete understanding of black student activism. Similarly, the claim that protest occurred in large, selective institutions must be revised if black colleges are included in the analysis. In fact, one scholar found that among black colleges, small campuses were more likely to have higher rates of student engagement because "the cohesive and intimate elements in small college life outweigh the obstacles of protest." The examination of Mississippi's black colleges also reveals that the traditional divide between public and private institutions was more nuanced than is typically portrayed in the literature. And though research on white students reports that alienation and a search for authenticity motivated them to participate, it was black students who were *integrated* into on- and off-campus movement centers—not those reporting a sense of estrangement—who became the most active.[6]

The radical nature of black college activism is lost when it is subsumed under the umbrella of white student protest. Take, for example, the stark contrast between white and black activism and response at the University of California, Berkeley, and Alcorn in 1964 as both sets of students sought to liberalize their respective campuses. At Alcorn, students held a demonstration on the football field to register their grievances with the administration and demand an autonomous student government, a relaxed dress code, more highly trained faculty, and longer library hours. Though students had demonstrated against the president since his installation in 1958, the 1964 protest was a one-night affair. A handful of Berkeley students had spent time in Mississippi and other parts of the South with the Freedom Rides and 1964 Mississippi's Freedom Summer project, earning them the moniker of "modern-day grasshopper hordes of Egypt . . . at that big ol' university at Berkeley" in the Mississippi press. After returning to campus for the 1964–65 academic year, liberal students attempted to solicit support for the black freedom struggle, a direct violation of university regulations that prohibited advocacy of political causes or candidates. Students protested, organized a group called the Free Speech Movement, and were joined by other liberal *and* conservative student groups in sit-ins and demonstrations that stretched over three months.[7]

The basic nature of the Alcorn grievances seems mundane against the Berkeley demand that administrators acknowledge the students' right to freedom of speech and academic freedom. However, it was the context in which Alcorn students agitated that made their activism both radical and dangerous. Berkeley's faculty passed a resolution in favor of the (white) student strike for freedom of speech, while Alcorn's President Boyd fired faculty and expelled students for exercising such rights. The Free Speech Movement received nationwide and even international press, while Alcorn students barely made the local newspapers. Berkeley students received assistance from the American Civil Liberties Union while Alcorn students remained isolated, unsupported, and unprotected. The academic community rallied behind the Berkeley students and their faculty supporters while it largely ignored the abuses at Alcorn, and the AAUP was forced to admit there was nothing it could do because of the intransigence of the president and board of trustees. Police arrested and detained Berkeley students after months of disruptive protests, a building takeover, and the commandeering of a police car, while police arrested Alcorn students after a peaceful demonstration on the football field and shipped them almost 180 miles to the harshest prison work farm in the state. Their differential experiences highlight what SNCC members said of the attention given to the three civil rights workers killed during Freedom Summer 1964: "Before the summer project last year we watched five Negroes murdered in two counties in Mississippi with no reaction from the country. We couldn't get the news out. Then we saw that when three civil rights workers were killed, and two of them were white, the whole country reacted, went into motion."[8] Under such conditions, that Alcorn students even organized is a miracle considering the fact that they faced severe bodily harm and intense pressure from administrators, the Sovereignty Commission, police, trustees, and even parents to remain aloof from protest. By omitting black colleges and their students, the historical record on student activism is distinctly whitewashed, distorted, and incomplete.

The Southernization of America and the Rise of Modern Conservatism

Using the black college as a lens also lends itself to a deeper understanding of the growth of American conservatism in the second half of the twentieth century. Recent scholarship charts how "the state"—meaning the federal government, through HUAC, SISS, and the Federal Bureau of Investigation—intimidated liberal-leaning activists and created a climate hostile to political dissent and social liberalism in the middle of the century. But state-level harassment—meaning state governments and entities—furthered the white conservative cause into the latter part of the century in a way that was different from federal initiatives. In Mississippi, the massive network of racist whites in the legislature, board of trustees, police and highway patrol, Sovereignty Commission, and other public and private groups shared a unanimity of purpose unmatched at the federal level. Similarly, the federal-level system of checks and balances between branches of government and the presence of race liberals in federal positions could mediate against the most heinous constitutional violations, but state-level officials consistently protected white supremacy and created safeguards to shelter their allies. Whereas the Cold War seemed ephemeral to most Americans, with talk of espionage and military secrets, white Southerners had their daily lives impacted by sit-ins, protests, and demonstrations. Such real-life experiences created a sense of urgency that fortified the countermovement's dedication to preserving the racial hierarchy and contributed to an environment in which political and social conservatism flourished.

The white South's battle against the movement actually fed the national mood. As recent scholarship has noted, the entirety of the United States experienced "Southernization" during the 1960s and 1970s as Southern racists nurtured and capitalized on the growing fear of liberalism run amok. Congressional approval of the 1964 Civil Rights Act and the 1965 Voting Rights Act, the executive branch's progressive racial policies, and the Supreme Court's support for desegregation and busing (not to mention its ousting of prayer from schools) smacked of liberal excess, according to white Southerners. Such an agenda, along with a leftist antiwar movement, stoked white resentment in the South *and* the North as many whites wondered if the mission to eradicate racism had translated into entitlement programs and social decay. Though couched in the language of individual rights, freedom of choice, and a reduction of government regulation rather than the racist rhetoric of white supremacy, whites in the North began to look more like their Southern counterparts in terms of their voting patterns and opinions on social policy. The overt strategy and ideology of Mississippi's countermovement faded, but it helped push America to the right in the coming decades as massive resistance morphed into modern conservatism and became a nationwide phenomenon.[9]

National Security and Academic Freedom in Contemporary Times

So, too, are the heated battles over academic freedom part of the contemporary reality. The 11 September 2001 terrorist attacks on American soil created an atmosphere of fear, suspicion, and hyperpatriotism and have created a political climate reminiscent of the Cold War era of the 1940s and 1950s and the black freedom struggle of the 1960s and early 1970s. The need to protect the integrity of the nation, contemporary conservatives argue, necessitates wider latitude in the government's ability to root out enemies of the state. Moderate and liberal philanthropic organizations have since placed restrictions on the sharing of information between American grant-holders and foreign academics and placed other restrictions on colleges accepting philanthropic funds. Provisions in the USA PATRIOT Act allow federal agents to gather information about the materials individuals borrow from libraries and purchase from bookstores in order to "protect against international terrorism or clandestine intelligence activities." Private conservative groups like the Center for the Study of Popular Culture and Students for Academic Freedom consider themselves watchdog groups and seek to expose liberal (in their words, "anti-American") faculty and get them sanctioned. The Bruin Alumni Association (which is not affiliated or sanctioned by the University of California, Los Angeles) offered $100 to students enrolled in courses taught by suspected radicals if they provided "full tape recordings of every class session, companion notes highlighting audience questions and reactions, and copies of all professor-distributed materials." Once compiled, the organization ranks the professors on a scale of one to five "power fists" on a list called the "dirty thirty," and even selects a "radical of the week."[10] Such federal mandates, government interference, harassment from private entities, and philanthropic agendas require that colleges and universities sacrifice institutional autonomy for the sake of national security. It is the same argument that Southern states employed to restrict free speech and punish offending students and faculty in the name of national security during other volatile times in our nation's history.

The AAUP, a watchdog group itself, established the Special Committee on Academic Freedom and National Security in a Time of Crisis on the first anniversary of the terrorist attacks. To the AAUP, the alarmist calls to limit constitutional freedoms in the name of national security sounded eerily like those that provoked the organization to issue statements, devise policies, and file litigation during the 1940s, 1950s, and 1960s. According to its report, "There may be points where some of our freedoms will have to yield to the manifest imperatives of security. What we should not accept is that we must yield those freedoms whenever the alarm of security is sounded. Given the extensive historical record of governmental overreaching and abuse in the name of security, we are right to be skeptical." The AAUP and other organizations filed a brief arguing that the latitude given to law enforcement agents through the USA PATRIOT Act was overbroad, and they continue to press for constitutional protections. The report also found that state legislators and angry citizens have attempted to pressure college administrators to fire particular faculty. Though many institutions withstood the challenges to institutional sovereignty, some capitulated, and a separate study found that a significant number of faculty in the social sciences believe their academic freedom is threatened in the current political climate. The Supreme Court, in a case involving a professor's right not to answer questions about the content of his lectures in 1957, wrote, "To impose any strait jacket upon the intellectual leaders in our colleges and universities would imperil the future of our Nation."[11] Apparently, many government representatives have yet to learn that lesson.

CONCLUSION

The focus on campus constituents is not meant to convey that they were the only or the most important actors in the black freedom struggle. Nor does the focus on the college campus mean that constituents should be analyzed as if the campus context were the only environment that shaped them and their ideas on social reform. Still, black colleges merit attention, since they are consistently labeled as one of the pivotal movement centers in the Southern black freedom struggle. Though often relegated to the role of foot soldier in another movement center's campaign, activist black college constituents *chose* to become involved and *worked* to transform the college's indigenous resources into weapons against white supremacy. They did so in the face of enormous pressure from administrators, parents, and Mississippi officials to the contrary. At times they were successful, and at others they were not. But all of them forced society to think more deeply about what a college education entailed and the end to which students should be educated. By envisioning the college campus as a fertile environment for racial uplift, social activism, and the pursuit of democracy, they invigorated the educative enterprise. In the words of W. E. B. Du Bois, "The opposition to Negro education in the South was at first bitter, and showed itself in ashes, insult, and blood; for the South believed an educated Negro to be a dangerous Negro. And the South was not wholly wrong; for education among all kinds of men always has had, and always will have, an element of danger and revolution, of dissatisfaction and discontent."[12] Black college constituents as well as racist whites in the 1960s and 1970s well understood the danger of which DuBois spoke. Not only did education raise the expectations and hopes of the black community; black college activists used the college campus as a weapon against the racial hierarchy and amplified both the concept and the reality of education for liberation.

List of Interviewees

Anderson Crouther, Emma Louise,
2 February 2006

Beard, Charles, 28 July 2005

Byrd Martin, Jacqueline,
27 August 2003

Crosby, David, 1 June 2006

Dittmer, John, 22 February 2006

Franklin, Jimmie, 18 July 2005

Guyot, Lawrence, 13 August 2005

Harkless, William Jr., 27 July 2005

Johnson, Henry and Opal,
24 August 2005

Joseph, Wilhelm Jr., 11 May 2007
and 24 July 2007

King, Edwin Jr., 28 August 2003

Ladner, Dorie, 5 February 2006

Ladner, Joyce, 13 July 2005

McLemore, Leslie Burl,
29 August 2003

Meredith, James, 23 August 2003

Owens, George, 25 August 2003

Peoples, John A., 28 August 2003

Slaughter-Harvey, Constance
26 August 2003

Smith, Earnest, 13 February 2004

Ward, Jerry, 29 July 2005

White, Bernard, 19 October 2006

White, Clark, 2 August 2006

Williams, Malvin, 17 July 2006

Williams, Walter,
9 December 2004

Winter, William Forrest,
19 July 2006

Notes

Abbreviations Used in Notes

AAUPP   American Association of University Professors Papers, George Washington University Archives, Washington, D.C.

AAUPA   American Association of University Professors Archives, National Office, Washington, D.C.

AUA   Alcorn University and A&M College Archives, Alcorn State, Mississippi

AMEC   African Methodist Episcopal Church Papers, Nashville, Tennessee

ARC   Amistad Research Center, Tulane University, New Orleans, Louisiana

EKP   Reverend Edwin King Jr. Papers, Mississippi Department of Archives and History

GAOP   George A. Owens Papers, Tougaloo College, Tougaloo, Mississippi

JSUA   Jackson State University Archives, Jackson, Mississippi

MCA   Millsaps College Archives, Jackson, Mississippi

MDAH   Mississippi Department of Archives and History, Jackson, Mississippi

MVSUA   Mississippi Valley State University Archives, Itta Bena, Mississippi

RCA   Rust College Archives, Holly Springs, Mississippi

SCR   Mississippi Sovereignty Commission Records, Mississippi Department of Archives and History, Jackson, Mississippi

SCRLR   Southern Civil Rights Litigation Records, Eudora Welty Library, Jackson, Mississippi

TCA   Tougaloo College Archives, Tougaloo, Mississippi

UMA   Archives and Special Collections, J. D. Williams Library, University of Mississippi, Oxford, Mississippi

Chapter 1

1. Some of the best examinations include William Chafe, *Civilities and Civil Rights: Greensboro, North Carolina, and the Black Struggle for Freedom* (New York: Oxford University Press, 1980); John Dittmer, *Local People: The Struggle for Civil Rights in Mississippi* (Urbana: University of Illinois Press, 1994); Charles M. Payne, *I've Got the Light of Freedom: The Organizing Tradition and the Mississippi Freedom Struggle* (Berkeley: University of California Press, 1995); Doug McAdam,

Political Process and the Development of Black Insurgency, 1930–1970, 2nd ed. (Chicago: University of Chicago Press, 1999).

2. Howard Zinn, *SNCC: The New Abolitionists* (Boston: Beacon Press, 1964); Julius Lester, *Look Out, Whitey! Black Power's Gon' Get Your Mama!* (New York: Dial Press, 1968); James Forman, *The Making of Black Revolutionaries: A Personal Account* (New York: Macmillan, 1972); Cleveland Sellers, *The River of No Return: The Autobiography of a Black Militant and the Life and Death of SNCC* (New York: William Morrow, 1973); Clayborne Carson, *In Struggle: SNCC and the Black Awakening of the 1960s* (Cambridge: Harvard University Press, 1995); Emily Stoper, *The Student Nonviolent Coordinating Committee: The Growth of Radicalism in a Civil Rights Organization* (Brooklyn: Carlson Publishing, 1989); Cynthia Griggs Fleming, *Soon We Will Not Cry: The Liberation of Ruby Doris Smith Robinson* (Lanham, Md.: Rowman and Littlefield, 1998).

3. Aldon Morris, *Origins of the Civil Rights Movement: Black Communities Organizing for Change* (New York: Free Press, 1984); McAdam, *Political Process.*

4. Martin Oppenheimer, "The Genesis of the Southern Negro Student Movement (Sit-In Movement): A Study in Contemporary Negro Protest," Ph.D. diss., University of Pennsylvania, 1963; Donald Matthews and James Prothro, *Negroes and the New Southern Politics* (New York: Harcourt, Brace, and World, 1966); John Orbell, "Protest Participation Among Southern Negro College Students," *American Political Science Review* 61, no. 2 (June 1967): 446–456; Richard Flacks, "The Liberated Generation: An Exploration of the Roots of Student Protest," *Journal of Social Issues* 23 (July 1967): 52, 56–58; Anthony M. Orum, *Black Students in Protest* (Washington, D.C.: American Sociological Association, 1972); Patricia Gurin and Edgar Epps, *Black Consciousness, Identity, and Achievement: A Study of Students in Historically Black Colleges* (New York: John Wiley and Sons, 1975).

5. Morris, *The Origins,* 201.

6. See Martin Luther King Jr., *Stride Toward Freedom: The Montgomery Story* (New York: Harper and Brothers, 1958); Ralph David Abernathy, *And the Walls Came Tumbling Down: An Autobiography* (New York: Harper & Row, 1989); Morris, *The Origins.*

7. John Orbell, "Social Protest and Social Structure: Southern Negro College Student Participation in the Protest Movement," Ph.D. diss., University of North Carolina, Chapel Hill, 1965; Orum, *Black Students;* Matthews and Protho, *Negroes and the New Southern Politics.*

8. Durward Long, "Black Protest," in *Protest! Student Activism in America,* edited by Julian Foster and Durward Long (New York: William Morrow, 1970): 459–482; Henry N. Drewry and Humphrey Doermann, *Stand and Prosper: Private Black Colleges and Their Students* (Princeton: Princeton University Press, 2001).

9. Chafe, *Civilities;* Carson, *In Struggle.*

10. Morris, *Origins;* Orum, *Black Students;* Matthews and Prothro, *Negroes and the New Southern Politics;* Ruth Searles and J. Allen Williams Jr., "College Students' Participation in Sit-ins," *Social Forces* 40 (1962): 215–220; Jacob R. Fishman and Frederic Solomon, "Youth and Social Action: Perspectives on the Student Sit-In Movement," in *Roots of Rebellion,* edited by Ronald P. Young (New York: Harper & Row, 1970): 129–142.

11. A number of studies on black college activism include: Sophia McDowell and Gilbert A. Lowe, "Howard University's Student Protest Movement," *Public Opinion Quarterly* 34, no. 3 (Fall 1970): 383–388; C. A. Higgins, "Paper on Student Unrest at Tuskegee Institute," *Journal of Social and Behavioral Science* 16 (1970): 18–26; Lawrence B. deGraaf, "Howard: The Evolution of a Black Student Revolt," in Foster and Long, *Protest*; Adam Fairclough, *Race and Democracy: The Civil Rights Struggle in Louisiana, 1915–1972* (Athens: University of Georgia Press, 1995); E. C. Harrison, "Student Unrest on the Black College Campus," *Journal of Negro Education* 41, no. 2 (Spring 1972): 113–120; Joel Rosenthal, "Southern Black Student Activism: Assimilation vs. Nationalism," *Journal of Negro Education* 44, no. 2 (Spring 1975): 113–129; Tae Nam, "A Manifesto of Black Student Activism in a Southern Black College under the Integration Order," *Journal of Negro Education* 46, no. 2 (Spring 1977): 168–185. The murders of black college students by local police receive their own treatment in: William W. Winn, *Augusta, Georgia and Jackson State University: Southern Episodes in a National Tragedy* (Atlanta: Southern Regional Council, 1970); President's Commission on Campus Unrest, *The Report of the President's Commission on Campus Unrest; Including Special Reports: The Killings at Jackson State, the Kent State Tragedy* (New York: Arno Press, 1970); Robert M. O'Neil, John P. Morris, and Raymond Mack, *No Heroes, No Villains* (San Francisco: Jossey-Bass, 1972); Attorney General of Louisiana, *Attorney General's Special Commission of Inquiry of the Southern University Tragedy of November 16, 1972* (Baton Rouge: State of Louisiana, 1973); Jack Bass and Jack Nelson, *The Orangeburg Massacre* (Macon: Mercer Press, 1984); Tim Spofford, *Lynch Street: The May 1970 Slayings at Jackson State College* (Kent, Ohio: Kent State University Press, 1988).

12. Urban Research Corporation, *Student Protests 1969: Summary* (Chicago: Urban Research Corporation, 1969).

13. Alexander W. Astin, Helen S. Astin, Alan E. Bayer, and Ann S. Bisconti, "Overview of the Unrest Era," in *The History of Higher Education*, 2nd ed., edited by Lester F. Goodchild and Harold S. Wechsler (New York: Simon & Schuster, 1997): 724–738; Philip Altbach, *Student Politics in America: A Historical Analysis* (New York: McGraw-Hill, 1976). Doug McAdam examines the catalytic importance of the Free Speech Movement but highlights how white students were influenced by the black Southern freedom struggle in *Freedom Summer* (New York: Oxford University Press, 1988).

14. See also Nathan Glazer, "The Aftermath of the Student Revolt," *AGB Reports* 26, no. 6 (November/December 1984): 23–28.

15. Gurin and Epps, *Black Consciousness*, 239.

16. Charles V. Willie and Donald Cunnigen, "Black Students in Higher Education: A Review of Studies, 1965–1980," *Annual Review of Sociology* 7 (1981): 177–198.

17. A small sampling of the most recent include Harry Lefever, *Undaunted by the Fight: Spelman College and the Civil Rights Movement, 1957–1967* (Macon: Mercer University Press), 2005, and several articles in the *Journal of African American History* 88 (Spring 2003): 204–217.

18. Ellen W. Schrecker, *No Ivory Tower: McCarthyism and the Universities* (New York: Oxford University Press, 1986), 341.

19. See "Academic Freedom and Tenure: Allen University and Benedict College," *AAUP Bulletin* 46 (Spring 1960): 87–104; "Academic Freedom and Tenure: Alabama State College," *AAUP Bulletin* 47 (Winter 1961): 303–309; C. Vann Woodward, "The Unreported Crisis in the Southern Colleges," *Harpers Magazine* 225 (October 1962): 82–84, 86, 89.

20. Schrecker, *No Ivory Tower*, 289.

21. V. O. Key Jr., *Southern Politics in State and Nation*, 2nd ed. (Knoxville: University of Tennessee Press, 1984), 229 (first quote), 130 (second quote); Neil R. McMillen, *Dark Journey: Black Mississippians in the Age of Jim Crow* (Urbana: University of Illinois Press, 1989), 73, 155; National Association for the Advancement of Colored People Papers, Boxes C-359, C-360, and C-371, cited in *Ibid.*, 229–230; Margaret Price, *The Negro and the Ballot in the South* (Atlanta: Southern Regional Council, 1959), 9.

22. James W. Silver, *Mississippi: The Closed Society* (New York: Harcourt, Brace, and World, 1964); John R. Salter Jr., *Jackson, Mississippi: An American Chronicle of Struggle and Schism* (Hicksville, N.Y.: Exposition Press, 1979); Andrew Young, quoted in Payne, *I've Got the Light*, 103 (first quote); *The Citizens' Council* 2, no. 2 (November 1956), 1, Citizens' Council Newspapers, 1956–1957, Accession Number 90.25, TCA (second quote); Payne, *I've Got the Light*, 34–35 (third quote); *General Laws of the State of Mississippi*, 1956, Chapter 365, Section 5, 521 (fourth quote); Erle Johnston Jr., "Sovereignty Commission Agency History," summary report included in Sovereignty Commission Records, MDAH; Yasuhiro Katagiri, *The Mississippi State Sovereignty Commission: Civil Rights and States' Rights* (Jackson: University Press of Mississippi, 2001).

23. Payne, *I've Got the Light*; Steven F. Lawson, *Black Ballots: Voting Rights in the South, 1944–1969* (New York: Columbia University Press, 1976), 93 (quote).

24. Dittmer, *Local People*; Fannie Lou Hamer, speech made 22 August 1964, www.americanrhetoric.com/speeches/fannielouhamercredentialscommittee.htm (quote).

25. McAdam, *Political Process*, xxv.

26. E. Franklin Frazier, *The Black Bourgeoisie* (New York: Collier Books, 1962); Louis Lomax, *The Negro Revolt* (New York: Harper & Row, 1963).

27. Dittmer, *Local People*; Kenneth T. Andrews, *Freedom Is a Constant Struggle: The Mississippi Civil Rights Movement and Its Legacy* (Chicago: University of Chicago Press, 2004).

28. Sellers, *The River*, 166.

Chapter 2

1. Anderson, *The Education of Blacks*.

2. Other black junior colleges included publicly supported Coahoma Community College and Utica Junior College, and privately supported Mary Holmes Community College and Okolona Community College.

3. James M. Mcpherson, *Abolitionist Legacy, from Reconstruction to the NAACP* (Princeton: Princeton University Press, 1975), 222, cited in Anderson, *The Education of Blacks*, 243.

4. "An Act to Incorporate the Trustees of Tougaloo University," May 1871, American Missionary Association Archives, Addendum (1869–1991, n.d.), Series A, Subseries Tougaloo Correspondence, Box 112, Folder 11, ARC; Clarice Campbell and Oscar Allan Rogers Jr., *Mississippi: The View from Tougaloo* (Jackson: University Press of Mississippi, 1979).

5. M. E. Strieby, Secretary of the American Missionary Association, unnamed source, and George S. Pope, unnamed source, cited in Campbell and Rogers, *Mississippi*, 117. Tougaloo did have one white student prior to the 1960s. In 1879, the first normal school graduating class included Luella Miner, daughter of Tougaloo's treasurer (Campbell and Rogers, *Mississippi*, 14).

6. *Ibid.*

7. George O. Thomas, "African Methodist Episcopal Church," in *Encyclopedia of Religion in the South*, edited by Samuel S. Hill (Mercer Press, 1984), 3–6; Raymond R. Sommerville Jr., *An Ex-Colored Church: Social Activism in the CME Church, 1870–1970* (Macon: Mercer University Press, 2004).

8. Freedmen's Aid Society, Report, 1893, cited in Ishmell Hendrex Edwards, "History of Rust College, 1866–1967," Ph.D. diss., University of Mississippi, 1982, 43.

9. Freedmen's Aid Society, *Report of the Methodist Episcopal Church, 1875*, Anonymous letter, *The Christian Educator* (October 1894), and R. Watkins, "Reconstruction in Marshall County," *Publications of the Mississippi Historical Society* (1912), cited in Edwards, "History of Rust"; Jay S. Stowell, *Methodist Adventures in Negro Education* (New York: Methodist Book Concern, 1922), 22 (quote).

10. Freedmen's Aid Society, *Report of the Methodist Episcopal Church, 1892*, 23, cited in Edwards, "History of Rust," 51 (quote).

11. Freedmen's Aid Society, *Report of the President McCoy to the Board of Directors, 29 June 1942*, cited in *Ibid.*, 76.

12. Thomas, "African Methodist Episcopal Church."

13. *Journal of the Twenty-Ninth Quadrennial Session of the General Conference of the A. M. E. Church, 1932*, 414–415 (quote), AMEC; Thomas Jesse Jones, *Negro Education: A Study of the Private and Higher Schools for Colored People in the United States, Volume I* (Washington, D.C.: Government Printing Office, 1916), 353.

14. *Journal of the Twenty-Fifth Quadrennial Session of the General Conference of the A. M. E. Church, 1916*, 368, AMEC; Charles Spencer Smith, *A History of the African Methodist Episcopal Church* (Philadelphia: Book Concern of the A. M. E. Church, 1922), 364 (quote); *Journal of the Twenty-Ninth Quadrennial*, 416.

15. Jones, *Negro Education*, 354; Smith, *A History*, 364; *Journal of the Twenty-Eighth Quadrennial Session of the General Conference of the A. M. E. Church, 1928*, 350, AMEC; "Minutes of the General Conference of the A. M. E. Church, 1904," 226, 227, 241, AMEC; *Journal of the Twenty-Ninth Quadrennial*, 415.

16. Methodist Episcopal Church, South, "General Conference Minutes, 1870," cited in Sommerville, *An Ex-Colored Church*, 38 (first quote); *New Orleans Christian Advocate*, 20 July 1870, cited in *Ibid.*, 17 (second quote).

17. William F. Holmes, *The White Chief James K. Vardaman* (Baton Rouge: Louisiana State University Press, 1970); Charles H. Wilson, *Education for Negroes in Mississippi Since 1910* (Boston: Meador Publishing Company, 1947); Booker T. Washington, *Up from Slavery* (New York: Norton, 1901/1996); W. A. Bell, ed., *Missions and Cooperation of the Methodist Episcopal Church, South with the Colored Methodist Episcopal Church* (Nashville: Board of Missions, Methodist Episcopal Church, South, 1923), 91–92, cited in Sommerville, *An Ex-Colored Church*, 54.

18. Glenn T. Eskew, "Black Elitism and the Failure of Paternalism in Postbellum Georgia: The Case of Bishop Lucius Henry Holsey," *Journal of Southern History* 58, no. 4 (November 1992): 637–666, 641 (first quote); Sommerville, *An Ex-Colored Church*, 55 (second quote).

19. *Journal of the General Conference*, 1954, 59, cited in *Ibid.*, 85 (quote).

20. Anderson, *The Education of Blacks*; David Sansing, *Making Haste Slowly: The Troubled History of Higher Education in Mississippi* (Jackson: University Press of Mississippi, 1990).

21. James Lusk Alcorn, "Message to the Mississippi Legislature, 1871," cited in Josephine McCann Posey, *Against Great Odds: The History of Alcorn State University* (Jackson: University Press of Mississippi, 1994); *Washington New National Era*, 4 April and 2 May, 1872, cited in William C. Harris, *The Day of the Carpetbagger: Republican Reconstruction in Mississippi* (Baton Rouge: Louisiana State University Press, 1979), 348 (quote); Edward Mayes, *History of Education in Mississippi* (Washington: Government Printing Office, 1899), 174, cited in Sansing, *Making Haste*, 63.

22. Harris, *The Day*, 350; Melerson Guy Dunham, *The Centennial History of Alcorn Agricultural and Mechanical College* (Hattiesburg: University and College Press of Mississippi, 1971), 13, 14.

23. Act of the Mississippi Legislature, Chapter XIX, Section 1, cited in Posey, *Against Great Odds*, x (first quote); James K. Vardaman, "Inaugural Address, 1904," in Robert E. McArthur, ed., *Inaugural Addresses of the Governors of Mississippi, 1890–1980* (University of Mississippi: Bureau of Governmental Research, 1980), 29–30, cited in Sansing, *Making Haste*, 79 (second quote).

24. Sansing, *Making Haste*, 83; John Hudson, "The Spoils System Enters College: Governor Bilbo and Higher Education in Mississippi," *The New Republic*, (17 September 1930), 123–125, 124 (quote), Higher Education in Mississippi, 1900–1979 Subject File, MDAH; "Leading Mississippi State Schools Are Suspended by S.A.C.," *Commercial Appeal*, 5 December 1930, Higher Education in Mississippi, 1900–1979, Subject File, MDAH; "Schools Again Hit as Result of Bilbo Firing of Educators," unknown newspaper, [1930], Higher Education in Mississippi, 1900–1979, Subject File, MDAH. Sansing offers a much kinder treatment of Governor Bilbo's actions and an alternate interpretation of events in *Making Haste*, 91–110.

25. *Ibid.*, 130.

26. Patrick H. Thompson, *The History of Negro Baptists in Mississippi* (Jackson: W. H. Bailey Printing Company, 1898), 62, cited in Leila Gaston Rhodes, *Jackson State University: The First Hundred Years* (Jackson: University Press of Mississippi, 1978), 8–9.

27. B. Baldwin Dansby interview with Leila Gaston Rhodes, August 1971, cited in *Ibid.* There was one black faculty member in 1877, but he resigned in 1878 (*Ibid.*).

28. *Ibid.;* Jacob L. Reddix, *A Voice Crying in the Wilderness* (Jackson: University Press of Mississippi, 1974).

29. Rhodes, *Jackson State,* 103 (quote); Reddix, *A Voice.*

30. *Ibid;* Board of Trustees, minutes, 18 January 1951, Board of Trustees Biennial Report 1949–1951, 7, cited in Sammy Jay Tinsley, "A History of Mississippi Valley State College." Ph.D. diss., University of Mississippi, 1972, 63–64; Rhodes, *Jackson State,* 116–120; Jackson State College Bulletin, 1961–1963, JSUA.

31. The State of Mississippi, Office of the Secretary of State, *Laws of the State of Mississippi* (Jackson: State of Mississippi, Office of the Secretary of State, 1946), 518–519, cited in Tinsley, "A History," 20 (first quote); Delta Council, *Delta Council History: 1938–1943* (Stoneville, Mississippi: Delta Council, 1943), 33, cited in Tinsley, "A History," 17 (second quote); Mississippi Valley State College Catalogue, 1950, MVSUA (third quote).

32. Tinsley, "A History," 54 (quote).

33. Bureau of the Census, *Statistics on Mississippi, 1960* (Washington, D.C., 1960): Tables 82 and 87; Matthews and Prothro, *Negroes and the New Southern Politics.*

34. Bureau of the Census, 1960.

Chapter 3

1. Morris, *The Origins.*

2. McAdam, *Freedom Summer;* McMillen, *Dark Journey;* Dittmer, *Local People;* Carson, *In Struggle;* Payne, *I've Got the Light;* Salter, *Jackson, Mississippi;* Leslie Burl McLemore, "The Mississippi Freedom Democratic Party: A Case Study of Grass-Roots Politics." Ph.D. diss., University of Massachusetts, 1971; Emilye Crosby, *A Little Taste of Freedom: The Black Freedom Struggle in Claiborne County, Mississippi* (Chapel Hill: University of North Carolina Press, 2005).

3. Bureau of the Census, *Statistics on Mississippi, 1950,* Volume II, 28–29.

4. D. M. Nelson to Tom [no last name], 13 December 1954, in *Conflicting Views on Segregation* (Winona, Mississippi: Association of Citizens' Councils [1955]), 10, H. E. Finger Papers, Box 4, Folder Segregation, MCA.

5. John R. Wright, "Citizens Council Celebrates Seven Years of Segregation," *Clarion-Ledger,* 14 May 1961, 2 (first quote); Percy Greene, no title, *Jackson Advocate,* 3 October 1959, cited in Julius E. Thompson, *The Black Press in Mississippi, 1865–1985* (Gainesville: University Press of Florida, 1993), 46 (second quote).

6. Payne, *I've Got the Light;* J. Michael Butler, "The Mississippi Sovereignty Commission and Beach Integration, 1959–1963: A Cotton-Patch Gestapo?" *Journal of Southern History* 68, no. 1 (February 2002), 107–148.

7. "Edmund Noel, "Thompson Sees No Riots Here," *Clarion-Ledger*, 23 May 1961, 1 (first quote); "State Called No. 1 Target of Civil Rights Groups," *Jackson Daily News*, 2 February 1962, 6 (second quote); William G. Snow Jr., "Genocide is Aim," n.p., January 1964, EKP, Box 4, Folder 166 (third quote).

8. Payne, *I've Got the Light*; Carson, *In Struggle*; Dittmer, *Local People*.

9. Thomas Jefferson, "Report of the Commissioners Appointed to Fix the Site of the University of Virginia" (Richmond: Virginia Senate, 1818), 12 (quote); Raymond Wolters, *The New Negro on Campus: Black College Rebellions in the 1920s* (Princeton: Princeton University Press, 1975).

10. "Negro Students Stage Boycott," *Greenwood Commonwealth*, 22 February 1957; "Negro Student Boycott Settled," *Greenwood Commonwealth*, 23 February 1957; James H. White, *Up from a Cotton Patch: J. H. White and the Development of Mississippi Valley State College* (Itta Bena, n.p., 1979).

11. Clennon King, "Negro Writer Hits America Race Myths," *State Times*, 3 March 1957, "Adam Powell Called 'Dupe' to Northern Race Trickery," *State Times*, 4 March 1957, 14, and "Real Uncle Toms May Come from North, Be College Bred," *State Times*, 6 March 1957; Jerry Proctor, "King Tries to Stop Student Walk-Outs," *State Times*, 8 March 1957.

12. Board of Trustees, minutes, 9 March 1957, MDAH; Verner S. Holmes and Euclid R. Jobe interview, 24 July through 20 November 1978, Jackson, Mississippi, 58, Verner Smith Holmes Collection, Bound Volume 5, UMA.

13. "Alcorn A&M College, March 1957," MP 1980.01: WLBT Newsfilm Collection, Reel D03, Item 0018. The number of students arrested varies in different sources, but all cite the overwhelming participation of students in the boycott.

14. Board of Trustees, minutes, 9 March 1957, MDAH (first quote); "The End of Uncle Tom Teachers" [*Ebony*, 1957], "Integration Feud Rocks Alcorn," *Chicago Defender*, 16 March 1957 (second quote), "Ousted Miss. Students on Speech Tour," *Pittsburgh Courier*, n.d. (third quote), and "Alcorn's Situation," Dillard University *Courtbouillon*, n.d., Student Strikes and Protest Movements File, ASUA; Medgar Evers, "Monthly Report: The Alcorn Situation," 25 March 1957 in Myrlie Evers-Williams and Manning Marable, eds., *The Autobiography of Medgar Evers: A Hero's Life and Legacy Revealed Through His Writings, Letters, and Speeches* (New York: Basic Books, 2005), 69 (fourth quote).

15. Trezzvant Anderson, "More Charges Against Boyd Hurled at Alcorn," *Pittsburgh Courier*, 10 September 1960, Student Strikes and Protest Movements File, ASUA; J. D. Boyd to J. A. Morris, et al., 1 May 1959 (quote), enclosure in Corrine Craddock Carpenter to E. R. Jobe, 26 June 1960, AAUPP, Box 4, Folder Corrine Carpenter.

16. The Special Grievance Committee to Administration of Alcorn College, 29 October 1959, and Student Body of Alcorn A&M College to President's Advisory Committee, J. D. Boyd, and Alumni Association, [March or April] 1960, enclosure in Carpenter to Jobe; "More Charges Against Boyd Hurled at Alcorn."

17. "Report of the Special Committee Elected by Faculty," 20 November 1959, 2 (quotes), enclosure in Carpenter to Jobe.

18. Student Body of Alcorn to President's Advisory Committee; Faculty of Alcorn A&M College to J. D. Boyd, 24 March 1960, enclosure in Carpenter to Jobe;

"Hundreds Sent Home," *The Free Press*, 9 May 1964 (first quote), and "Alcorn Education Tragedy Gets Press Cover-Up," *The Free Press*, 9 May 1964 (second quote), AAUPP, Box 4, Folder Frank Purnell; Frank and Rosentene Purnell to Bertram Davis, 11 May 1964, AAUPP, Box 4, Folder A. D. Sumberg.

19. James Meredith, *Three Years in Mississippi* (Bloomington: University of Indiana Press, 1966), 95 (quotes). See also Anne Moody, *Coming of Age in Mississippi* (New York: Dell, 1968); Joyce Ladner interview; Dorie Ladner interview.

20. Meredith, *Three Years*, 93–98; Wallace Dabbs, "Jackson State College Students Stage Protest," *Clarion-Ledger*, 28 March 1961; John A. Peoples, *To Survive and Thrive: The Quest for a True University* (Jackson: Town Square Books, 1995); "Report Classes Boycotted at Jackson State," *Jackson Daily News*, 7 October 1961, SCR 10-105-0-4-1-1-1.

21. Tom Scarbrough, "Marshall County-Mrs. Clarice Campbell, White Female Teacher at Rust College-Also Rust College-All Negro School," 29 May 1961, SCR 2-20-1-50-5-1-1 (quote).

22. Tom Scarbrough, "Marshall County," 14 December 1962, SCR 2-20-1-63-1-1-1 (first quote), 2-20-1-63-2-1-1 (second quote).

23. "Tougaloo: An Introspective Look," *The Student Voice*, 13 March 1964 (first quote), and "Eight Tougaloo Students Locked in Eastman Library During National Library Week," *The Student Voice*, 24 April 1964 (second quote), Demonstrations and Protests Vertical File, TCA; Gershon Konditi to George A. Owens, 8 December 1964 (third quote), GAOP, Box 4, Folder 25.

24. "Student Protest," *Blue and White Flash*, April 1961, 1, JSUA.

25. Moody, *Coming of Age*, 248.

26. Salter, *Jackson, Mississippi*, 19 (quote); John Mangram to Ruby Hurley, 25 January 1960, Box John D. Mangram, TCA; Dittmer, *Local People*; Zack J. Van Landingham, "Boycott by Negroes Jackson, Mississippi, April 10–17," 22 April 1960, SCR 2-135-0-22-1-1-1 through 18-1-1.

27. James "Sam" Bradford interview with Robert Walker [n.d.], "Tougaloo Nine: Demonstration Comes to Mississippi," 1 May 1979, 5 (quote), Tougaloo Nine vertical file, TCA; Cal Turner, "Tougaloo Group Ignore Officers," *State Times*, 27 March 1961, Box Tougaloo Nine, Folder Tougaloo Nine, 1960–1967 clippings, TCA. The students eventually paid a $100 fine and received a thirty-day suspended jail sentence.

28. Moody, *Coming of Age*, 265–266 (quote); Salter, *Jackson, Mississippi*.

29. Moody, *Coming of Age*, 266 (first quote); Salter, *Jackson, Mississippi*, 134 (second set of quotes), 135 (third quote). Salter does not mention salt being thrown in his wounds, but he does discuss pepper being thrown in his eyes.

30. W. C. Shoemaker, "Jackson Negro Boycott Vowed," *Jackson Daily News*, 8 April 1960, SCR 2-135-0-8-1-1-1; "Negroes Free on Bond in Bus Incident Here," *Jackson Daily News*, 20 April 1961, SCR 2-72-1-90-1-1-1; Reverend Johnny Barbour Jr. and Clara M. Barbour interview with Donald Matthews, 25 January 1999, Jackson, Mississippi, http://www.usm.edu/crdp/html/transcripts/barbour_johnny-jr-and-clara-m.shtml (quote).

31. "9 Negroes Face Trial Here Today," *State Times*, 29 March 1961.

32. *Ibid*; Morris, *Origins*; David Garrow, *Bearing the Cross: Martin Luther*

King, Jr., and the Southern Christian Leadership Conference (New York: William Morrow, 1986).

33. "State Reacts to Slaying with Shock," *Jackson Daily News*, 12 June 1963.

34. Moody, *Coming of Age*, 277–278.

35. Meredith, *Three Years*, 51 (quote).

36. Mississippi Improvement Association of Students, "General Boycott Order #1," 23 March 1961, SCR 2-138-0-6-1-1-1 (first quote); Meredith, *Three Years*, 94 (second quote); W. D. Rayfield to Albert Jones, 9 March 1961, SCR 2-138-0-1-1-1 through 2-1-1-1.

37. Mississippi Improvement Association of Students, "Action Order #1," [October or November] 1961, James Meredith Collection, Box 1, Folder 19, UMA.

38. *Ibid.*

39. Edwin King Jr., unpublished manuscript, Clarice Campbell and Oscar Rogers Collection, Box 2, Folder 2–34, TCA; Board of Trustees, "To the Friends of Millsaps College," [21] February 1964, H. E. Finger Papers, Box 24, Folder Segregation, MCA (first quote); Rebel Underground, March 1964, Millsaps College Subject File, MDAH (second quote); "Statement of the Board of Trustees of Millsaps College," 17 February 1965, Millsaps College Subject File, MDAH.

40. Austin Moore to Gary Graffman, 2 February 1964 (first quote), EKP, Box 9, Folder 450; "Mayor Urges White Boycott," *Jackson Daily News*, 21 January 1964 (second quote); Mrs. W. M. Newman, "Hollywood Starts Not Needed Here," *Jackson Daily News*, 13 February 1964, clipped article file, TCA (third quote); King, unpublished manuscript. At least one white citizen wrote a letter to the paper applauding the stars' decision (H. B. Pearsons, "TV Stars' Refusal Portends the Future," *Jackson Daily News*, 28 January 1964, clipped article file, TCA.

41. Henry Raymont, "Cancel Concert, Miss Nilsson Told," *New York Times*, [April 1964] (first quote), EKP, Box 8, Folder 365; King, unpublished manuscript, 57 (second quote).

42. "Negro Girls Turned Away from Church," *Clarion-Ledger*, 14 October 1963; "12 Arrested at Churches Here Sunday," *Clarion-Ledger*, 21 October 1963; Campbell and Rogers, *Mississippi;* Joyce Ladner interview; King, unpublished manuscript.

43. Frank Smith, "A Second Beginning of the End," 11 May 1963, [n.p.], Voter Education Project Papers, James Lawson Files, cited in Payne, *I've Got the Light*, 197(second quote).

44. King, unpublished manuscript, 39–40.

45. "Mr. Phillip Lane Patterson: February 20 through March 9," 1 (first quote), 2–3 (second quote), and no title, *Rebel Underground*, March 1964, 1 (third quote), enclosures in Tom J. Truss Jr. to J. D. Williams, 31 March 1964, General Mississippi Study of Academic Freedom, January–April 1964 File, AAUPA.

46. Clarice Campbell, letter dated 12 April 1961, in *Civil Rights Chronicle: Letters from the South* (Jackson: University Press of Mississippi, 1997), 79–80.

47. Bette Ann Poole, a student at Tougaloo, was named in "Writ of Temporary Injunction," Chancery Court of the First Judicial District of Hinds County, Mississippi, 6 June 1963, EKP, Box 8, Folder 374. Joan Trumpauer was arrested in Louisiana on a Freedom Ride and also had litigation pending against her ("Motion

to Quash," *State of Louisiana vs. Joan Trumpower* [*sic*], [March] 1962, EKP, Box 6, Folder 366).
48. "College Group to Meet Invasion of Northerners," *Jackson Daily News*, 1 May 1964, EKP, Box 16, Folder 834.
49. Moody, *Coming of Age*, 261 (quote); Anderson Crouther interview; James "Sam" Bradford interview with Robert Walker.
50. Morris, *The Origins*; Payne, *I've Got the Light*.

Chapter 4

1. Woodward discusses the loss of academic freedom at colleges and universities, including historically black colleges and universities, in "The Unreported Crisis."
2. Jeff Woods, *Black Struggle, Red Scare: Segregation and Anti-Communism in the South, 1948–1968* (Baton Rouge: University of Louisiana Press, 2004), 5 (quote). There is a handful of literature that discusses race and academic freedom, though not Southern state-based McCarthyism at black colleges. See Stanley H. Smith, "Academic Freedom in Higher Education in the Deep South," *Journal of Educational Sociology* 32, no. 6 (February 1958): 297–308; Marybeth Gasman, "Scylla and Charybdis: Navigating the Waters of Academic Freedom at Fisk University during Charles S. Johnson's Administration, 1946–1956," *American Educational Research Journal* 36, no. 4 (Winter 1999), 739–758; Patrick Gilpin and Marybeth Gasman, *Charles S. Johnson: Leadership Beyond the Veil in the Age of Jim Crow* (Albany: State University of New York Press, 2003). Literature on northern white colleges and academic freedom includes: Richard Hofstadter and Walter P. Metzger, *The Development of Academic Freedom in the United States* (New York: Columbia University Press, 1955); Walter Metzger, ed., *The American Concept of Academic Freedom in Formation: A Collection of Essays and Reports* (New York: Arno Press, 1977); Walter Metzger, *Professors on Guard: The First AAUP Investigations* (New York: Arno Press, 1977); Schrecker, *No Ivory Tower*; Lionel S. Stanley, *Cold War on Campus: A Study of the Politics of Organizational Control* (New Brunswick: Transaction Books, 1988). Literature on Southern McCarthyism includes: M. J. Heale, *McCarthy's Americans* (Athens: University of Georgia Press, 1988); Kenneth O'Reilly, *"Racial Matters": The FBI's Secret File on Black America, 1960–1972* (New York: Free Press, 1989); John Earl Haynes, *Red Scare or Red Menace?* (Chicago: Ivan R. Dee, 1996); William Billingsley, *Communists on Campus: Race, Politics, and the Public University in Sixties North Carolina* (Athens: University of Georgia Press, 1999); George Lewis, *The White South and the Red Menace: Segregationists, Anticommunism, and Massive Resistance, 1945–1965* (Gainesville: University Press of Florida, 2004); Woods, *Black Struggle*.
3. Tom Scarbrough, "Marshall County," 14 December 1962, SCR 2-20-1-63-2-1-1; Meredith interview; Meredith, *Three Years*; Holmes and Jobe interview, 58.
4. A. L. Hopkins, "Continued Investigation of John R. Salter," 11 May 1962, SCR 1-73-0-18-2-1-1; John Held to [Wesley] Hotchkiss, 2 June 1964, American Missionary Association Archives, Addendum (1869–1991, n.d.), Series A, Subseries Tougaloo Correspondence, Box 110, Folder 19, ARC; Tom Scarbrough, "Marshall County (Rust College)," 30 June 1964, 2, SCR 2-20-1-78-1-1-1 through 5-1-1; John

Temple Graves, "See Prof. Clennon King Negroes Man of Destiny," *Jackson Advocate*, [n.d.] April 1957, Clipped Article File, ASUA.

5. Ed King referred to Tougaloo as an oasis of freedom in his interview with the author.

6. Board of Trustees, minutes, 22 April 1954 and 18 March 1959, Board of Trustees Collection, TCA; Campbell, *Civil Rights Chronicle*, 187. Student activism and campus quality are discussed in Orbell, "Social Protest and Social Structure," and Matthews and Prothro, *Negroes and the New Southern Politics*. The fact that Tougaloo was more progressive than certain white colleges is substantiated by Philo Hutcheson, "Reform and Representation: The Uncertain Development of Collective Bargaining in the AAUP, 1946 to 1976," Ph.D. diss., University of Chicago, 1991.

7. United States Senate, 79th Congress, 2d Session, *Hearings Before the Special Committee to Investigate Senatorial Campaign Expenditures, 1946* (Washington, D.C.: Government Printing Office, 1947), 19, 88–90, cited in Dittmer, *Local People*, 3 (first quote); Campbell and Rogers, *Mississippi*, 186; John Mangram to Ruby Hurley, 25 January 1960, John D. Mangram Papers, TCA; Mass Protest Rally Program, 20 April 1961, SCR 2-55-2-16-1-1-1; "Affidavit of Rev. Ralph Edwin King," 6 June 1963, EKP, Box 8, Folder 366; *Council of Federated Organizations, et al., vs. L. A. Rainey, et al.*, [June] 1964, civil action 3599, EKP, Box 16, Folder 834; *State of Mississippi vs. Edwin King, et al.*, Chancery Court, complaint no. 66,011, 19 November 1964, 5, SCR 2-165-2-17-1-1-1 through 5-1-1; King interview (second quote). See Dittmer, *Local People*, and Payne, *I've Got the Light*, for information on the 1963 Freedom Vote campaign.

8. Salter, *Jackson, Mississippi*, 84 (quote); John Salter interview with John Jones, 6 January 1981, 28, OH81–06, MDAH; *City of Jackson vs. John R. Salter Jr., et al.*, Complaint no. 63,429, Chancery Court of the First Judicial District of Hinds County, Mississippi, 6 June 1963, EKP, Box 8, Folder 374. The state of Mississippi identified Salter as a white male, but Salter identifies himself as a Wabanaki (Abenaki) Indian (Salter, *Jackson, Mississippi*, 5).

9. Salter interview, 27; Gabrielle Simon Edgecomb, "Ernst Borinski: Positive Marginality: 'I Decided to Engage in Stigma Management,'" in *From Swastika to Jim Crow: Refugee Scholars at Black Colleges* (Malabar, Florida: Krieger Publishing, 1993), 120.

10. Ernst Borinski, "The Social Science Laboratory at Tougaloo College," *Journal of Educational Sociology* 22, no. 4 (December 1948): 277; Edgecomb, "Ernst Borinski."

11. Dean A. A. Branch, a black man, was considered friendly toward the movement and campus involvement in it (Salter interview; King interview).

12. Frazier, *Black Bourgeoisie*.

13. Edwards, "History of Rust"; Campbell, *Civil Rights Chronicle*; Smith interview; Barbour interview.

14. Ernst Borinski interview with John Jones, 13 January 1980, Ernst Borinski Papers, Box 1, Folder 1, TCA; King interview. Clarice Campbell also sought employment at Tougaloo and Rust as a way to become involved in the movement (Campbell, *Civil Rights Chronicle*).

15. Paul F. Lazarsfeld and Wagner Thielens Jr., *The Academic Mind: Social Scientists in a Time of Crisis* (Glencoe, IL: The Free Press, 1958).

16. Woods, *Black Struggle*.

17. House Committee on Un-American Activities, *Communist Methods of Infiltration (Education)* (Washington, D.C.: Government Printing Office, 1953); House Committee on Un-American Activities, *Hearings Regarding Communist Infiltration of Minority Groups, Part 1* (Washington, D.C.: Government Printing Office, 1949); George Bell Timmerman, "Message to the Legislature," 15 January 1958, cited in "Academic Freedom and Tenure: Allen University and Benedict College," *AAUP Bulletin*, 46 (1960): 87–104, 95 (quote).

18. Hofstadter and Metzger, *The Development*; Schrecker, *No Ivory Tower*. Court cases include *Adler v. Board of Education*, 342 US 485 (1951); *Barsky v. Board of Regents*, 347 US 442 (1954); *Barenblatt v. United States*, 360 US 109 (1959). The AAUP's allowance for the firing of faculty involved in the Communist Party is included in Report of a Special Committee of the AAUP, "Academic Freedom and Tenure in the Quest for National Security," *AAUP Bulletin*, 42 (1956), 49–107.

19. Walter P. Metzger, "Academic Freedom in Delocalized Academic Institutions," in *Dimensions of Academic Freedom* (Urbana: University of Illinois Press, 1969), 3 (quote); AAUP, "Statement"; Resolution endorsed at the Annual Meeting of the AAUP, 1956, *AAUP Bulletin* 42 (Summer 1956): 352–353.

20. Justice Felix Frankfurter concurring opinion in *Wieman v. Updegraff*, 344 U.S. 183 (1952) (first quote); *Sweezy v. New Hampshire*, 354 U.S. 234 (1957) (second quote). See also *Shelton v. Tucker*, 364 U.S. 479 (1960).

21. The 1961 survey is David Fellman, "Academic Freedom in American Law," *Wisconsin Law Review* 3, reprinted in William Murphy, "Academic Freedom—An Emerging Constitutional Right," in *The Constitutional Status of Academic Freedom*, edited by Walter P. Metzger (New York: Arno Press, 1977). The distinction between academic freedom and freedom of speech is taken from William Van Alstyne, "The Specific Theory of Academic Freedom and the General Issue of Civil Liberty," in *The Concept of Academic Freedom*, edited by Edmund L. Pincoffs (Austin, Texas), reprinted in Metzger, *The Constitutional Status*. Court decisions against faculty include *Adler v. Board of Education* and *Barenblatt v. United States*.

22. *Trustees of Dartmouth College v. Woodward*, 17 US 518 (1819); *Meyer v. Nebraska*, 262 US 390 (1923); *Pierce v. Society of Sisters*, 268 US 510 (1925); *Farmington v. Tokushige*, 273 US 284 (1927).

23. "Academic Freedom in Mississippi," *AAUP Bulletin* (Autumn 1965): 341–356, 356 (quote).

24. Borinski interview, 10; "Second Integration Speech at Millsaps," *Jackson Daily News*, 5 March 1958.

25. Borinski interview; "Citizens' Council Demands Trustees Announce Stand," *Jackson Daily News*, 14 March 1958 (first quote); Silver, *Mississippi* (second quote). In 1964, the AAUP issued a statement in support of a student organization's right to invite controversial speakers to campus (American Association of University Professors, draft of "Statement on Faculty Responsibility for the Academic Freedom of Students," March 1964, 3, EKP, Box 3, Folder 112).

26. "White Citizens Council Challenges Millsaps Head," *Concern*, 28 March 1958, 1 and 8 (quote), H. E. Finger Papers, Box 24, Folder Ernst Borinski, MCA; Fred McEachin, editorial, *State Times*, 13 March 1958, EKP, Box 2, Folder 107.

27. L. G. Patterson, editorial, *State Times*, 9 (first quote), March 1958, EKP, Box 2, Folder 107; Hodding Carter, "Ellis Wright and Bill of Rights," *Delta Democrat-Times*, n.p. (second quote), 11 March 1958, H. E. Finger Papers, Box 24, Folder Ernst Borinski, MCA; Craig Castle, editorial, *State Times*, 9 March 1958; Charles Majure, editorial, *State Times*, 9 March 1958, EKP, Box 2, Folder 107; Anonymous, Letter to the Editor, *The Purple and White*, 6 March 1958, 2, MCA.

28. H. E. Finger, "From the President of Millsaps College," 12 March 1958, *Mississippi Methodist Advocate*, 2 (quotes), H. E. Finger Papers, Box 24, Folder segregation, MCA.

29. "Dr. Otto Nathan Rips Communist Hunters," *Jackson Daily News*, 2 March 1962 (first quote), SCR 3-74-1-8-1-1-1; "Is This the Same Dr. Otto Nathan," *Jackson Daily News*, 2 March 1962 (second quote), SCR 3-74-1-8-1-1-1; "Tougaloo Defends Visit of Nathan," *Jackson Daily News*, 3 March 1962, 6 (third quote).

30. Schrecker, *No Ivory Tower*, 10; "Tougaloo College, January 13, 1964," Kammerer to Adams (quote).

31. Schrecker, *No Ivory Tower*, 289 (first quote). Conversely, Lazarsfeld and Thielens found that institutions at the margins were the most prone to external pressures during the same era under consideration (*The Academic Mind*). Shelby Rogers to Earle Johnston, memo, 2 (second quote), 4 (third quote), SCR 3-74-2-13-1-1-1 through 9-1-1.

32. Katagiri, *The Mississippi State*.

33. "Statement of the Board of Trustees Concerning Allegations Relative to the University of Mississippi," 27 August 1959, 2, Board of Trustees, minutes, MDAH.

34. Corrine Craddock Carpenter to E. R. Jobe, 17 June 1960, 2 (first, second, and third quotes), 3 (fourth quote), 6 (fifth quote), AAUPP, Box 4, Folder Corrine Carpenter.

35. E. Phillip Trapp to Robert Van Waes, 29 May 1961, 3, AAUPP, Box 4, Folder Corrine Carpenter.

36. *Ibid.*, 3 (first quote); "Academic Freedom and Tenure: Alcorn Agricultural and Mechanical College," *AAUP Bulletin* (Fall 1962), 248–252, 252 (second quote); "Report of Committee A on Academic Freedom and Tenure," *AAUP Bulletin* (Fall 1973), 364.

37. WLBT TV and WJDX Radio, editorial, n.d., cited in Sansing, *Making Haste*, 173 (first and second quote); text of Barnett speech reprinted in *Clarion-Ledger*, 14 September 1962, cited in *Ibid.*, 168 (third quote); no title, *Franklin County Advocate*, 1 November 1962, cited in Neil R. McMillen, *The Citizens' Council: Organized Resistance to the Second Reconstruction, 1954–1964* (Urbana: University of Illinois Press, 1971), 248 (fourth quote).

38. Henry King Stanford, "Statement on the Mississippi Situation," 28 September 1962, AAUPP, General Copies of the Report of the Special Commission to Survey Conditions of Academic Freedom in Mississippi File, AAUPA; "AAUP Statement on Mississippi Situation," *AAUP Newsletter*, 23 October 1962, University of Mississippi,

1962 Crisis File, AAUPA; Postcard, Eugene Cox Materials, Mitchell Memorial Library, cited in McMillen, *The Citizens' Council*, 246 (first quote); Louis Joughin, "The University of Mississippi Situation: A Review of the Association's Interest and Action," *AAUP Bulletin*, 48 (Winter 1962), 317–320, cited in McMillen, *The Citizens' Council*, 247 (second quote); "Simple Matter of Morality," *The Citizen*, 7 (November 1962): 2, cited in McMillen, *The Citizens' Council*, 246 (third quote).

39. Board of Trustees, minutes, 18 October 1962 (first quote), MDAH; Ross R. Barnett to Henry King Stanford, 25 October 1962, General Copies of the Report of the Special Commission to Survey Conditions of Academic Freedom in Mississippi File, AAUPA; Board of Trustees, minutes, 15 November 1962, MDAH.

40. Silver, *Mississippi*, 154.

41. "Asks Silver Resign," *Clarion-Ledger*, 25 March 1964, General Mississippi Study of Academic Freedom, May–June 1964 File, AAUPA; Kenneth Toler, "Williams Blasts Professor's Talk on Racial Issue," *Commercial Appeal*, 12 November 1963, General Mississippi Study of Academic Freedom, May–June 1964 File, AAUPA; *Rebel Underground*, 5 March 1963, General Mississippi Study of Academic Freedom, January–April 1964 File, AAUPA. Trustees also punished Russell Barrett, another tenured liberal Ole Miss faculty member, in response to his book *Integration at Ole Miss* (Chicago: Quandrangle Books, 1965).

42. Rosentene Purnell to William P. Fidler, 3 May 1964, 3 (first quote), and Frank D. Purnell to J. D. Boyd, 1 May 1964, 2 (second quote), AAUPP, Box 4, Folder A. D. Sumberg.

43. E. R. Jobe to Bertram Davis, 20 April 1964 (first quote), J.D. Boyd to Bertrand [*sic*] Davis, 15 December 1964, Robert Van Waes to J. D. Boyd, 29 March 1965 (second quote), Bertram H. Davis to E. R. Jobe, 15 May 1964, and Robert Van Waes to Franklin D. Purnell, 29 March 1965 (third quote), AAUPP, Box 4, Folder A. D. Sumberg. Purnell's firing also violated the AAUP's 1964 "Statement on the Standards for Notice of Nonreappointment," which would have granted him twelve months' notice.

44. No author, "Background for Office Conference with Paul L. Taylor and Bessie Taylor," 20 July 1965, J. H. White to William Fidler, 8 February 1965 (first quote), Paul L. Taylor to Bertram H. Davis, 8 May 1964, 2 (second quote), and Bertram H. Davis to E. R. Jobe, 18 May 1964, AAUPP, Box 84, Folder Taylor, Evans, Tyler, Gregory, Marshall, Closed 3/15/65 (third quote).

45. E. R. Jobe to Bertram H. Davis, 28 July 1964 (first quote), PD to File, 30 July 1965, 1 (second quote), and Bertram H. Davis to Files, 21 May 1964, 1, AAUPP, Box 84, Folder Taylor, Evans, Tyler, Gregory, Marshall, Closed 3/15/65.

46. "Academic Freedom and Tenure: Allen University and Benedict College" (first quote); CM to File, 19 June 1964, AAUPP, General Mississippi Story of Academic Freedom, May–June 1964 File, AAUPA; HIO to File, 26 October 1966; "Report of the Special Committee to Survey Conditions of Academic Freedom in Mississippi," 17 (second quote), AAUPP, General Copies of the Report of the Special Committee to Survey Conditions of Academic Freedom in Mississippi File, AAUPA. For cases on the unconstitutionality of requiring affidavits of membership, see *NAACP v. Alabama*, 357 US 449 (1958); *Bates v. Little Rock*, 361 US 516 (1960); *Shelton v. Tucker*.

47. "Report of the Special Committee"; enclosure in Kammerer to Adams; "Academic Freedom in Mississippi." Belhaven College (private), Blue Mountain College (private), and Delta State Colleges (public) were the white institutions that had no AAUP chapters ("List of AAUP chapters," [1964], AAUPP, Folder General Mississippi Study of Academic Freedom January–April 1964, AAUP).

48. "Jackson State College, January 13, 1964," 1 (first quote), and "Interview with Dr. Jobe, January 15, 1964," 1 (second quote), enclosures in Kammerer to Adams; "Report of the Special Committee," 18 (third quote); "Academic Freedom in Mississippi."

49. Board of Trustees, minutes, 20 August 1964, 5, MDAH. The board's first speaker ban was enacted 17 February 1955.

50. AAUP, draft of "Statement on Faculty Responsibility for the Academic Freedom of Students," March 1964, 1 (quotes), EKP, Box 3, Folder 112.

51. *Ibid.*, 5.

52. William P. Fidler, "Academic Freedom in the South Today," *AAUP Bulletin* (Winter 1965), 413–421; AAUP, "Declaration of Principles," 1915 (first quote); Woodward, "The Unreported Crisis," 89 (second quote).

Chapter 5

1. Jimmy Ward, "Crossroads," *Jackson Daily News*, 3 June 1963.

2. "Tougaloo Bill Appears Dead," *Clarion-Ledger*, 14 April 1964, Subject Files Tougaloo College, 1960–1969, MDAH. The statement was made about Tougaloo specifically, but it fits securely with the government's attitude toward the other private black colleges in the state.

3. Erle Johnston to John Salter, 17 August 1981, Tougaloo Office File Register, Brown University–Tougaloo College Cooperative Program, BUA.

4. McLemore interview.

5. Hal DeCell to Governor J. P. Coleman, 16 December 1957, 1, SCR 2-5-2-16-1-1-1 (first quote); Sherman L. Greene Jr., "The Urgency for Unification of the A.M.E. Church System of Education," *A.M.E. Church Review* 78, no. 210 (October–December 1961): 28 (second quote).

6. Southern Conference Educational Fund pamphlet, "A Faith for the South: The Role of the Southern Conference Educational Fund in the Struggle for Integration," n.d., SCR 13-59-0-3-1-1-1; "Report of the Florida Legislative Investigation Committee to the 1961 Session of the Legislature," 1961, SCR 13-0-3-31-9-1-1; W. C. Shoemaker, "NAACP-Leftists Link is Charged," *Jackson Daily News*, 19 November 1959, SCR 6-7-0-11-1-1-1 through 2-1-1; "Mississippians Are Listed in Red 'Infiltrated' Groups," *Commercial Appeal*, 14 November 1958, SCR 6-7-0-7-1-1-1 (quote).

7. "Negro Leader Predicts More Suits over Ballot," *Clarion-Ledger*, 31 March 1958, SCR 2-5-1-39-1-1-1; Zack J. Van Landingham, "Progressive Voters' League," 9 October 1958, SCR 2-4-0-1-1-1; Zack J. Van Landingham, "G. R. Haughton," 23 July 1959, SCR 1-55-0-1-1-1-1; Edward J. Odum to Reverend (form letter), 20 March 1959, SCR 2-5-2-41-1-1-1; "Negro Ministers Release List of Main Objectives," *Clarion-Ledger*, 5 October 1957, SCR 2-3-0-9-1-1-1; "State Negro Leaders

Group to Meet in Mound Bayou," *Jackson Daily News*, 11 April 1959, SCR 2-2-0-36-1-1-1.

8. Percy Greene, "State Negro ROTC Training," *Jackson Advocate*, 13 January 1962, SCR 9-1-2-60-1-1-1 (first and second quotes); Percy Greene, "A Real Challenge for Martin Luther King," *Jackson Advocate*, 23 July 1962, SCR 9-1-2-63-1-1-1 (third quote); Katagiri, *The Mississippi State*; Zack J. Van Landingham to File, "George Newman," 4 May 1960, SCR 9-1-2-37-1-1-1.

9. Zack J. Van Landingham, "Memo to File 1–23," 2 June 1960, SCR 1-23-0-70-1-1-1; Zack J. Van Landingham, "Boycott by Negroes Jackson, Mississippi, April 10–17, 1960," 22 April 1960, SCR 2-135-0-22-7-1-1; clipped article from United Press International, 8 April 1960, SCR 2-135-0-3-1-1-1.

10. [No first name] Hopkins and [no first name] Downing, "Investigation of Student 'Walk-out' from Burglund Negro High School, McComb, Mississippi; Parade and Demonstrations; Their Arrest, and Hearing in City and Youth Court," 19 October 1961, SCR 1-98-0-25-1-1-1; Payne, *I've Got the Light*; Dittmer, *Local People*; Jacqueline Byrd Martin interview.

11 No title, United Press International clipping, 8 April 1960, SCR 2-135-0-3-1-1-1; Salter, *Jackson, Mississippi*; John Her[unreadable], "City Declares Segregation Not Enforced in Terminals," *Clarion-Ledger*, 10 April 1962, SCR 2-72-2-36-1-1-1; Tom Scarbrough to File, 8 May 1961, SCR 2-65-0-42-2-1-1 (quote).

12. Zack J. Van Landingham to Meady Pierce, 13 April 1960, SCR 2-72-1-56-1-1-1 (quote); State Sovereignty Commission requisition paid to Percy Greene and T. S. J. Pendleton, 22 January 1962, SCR 97-98-1-317-1-1-1.

13. R. A. *Scott, et al. v. J. P. Campbell College, et al.*, February 1962, Chancery Court of the First Judicial District of Hinds County, Mississippi, SCR 3-78-0-1-1-1-1 through 19-1-1; A. L. Hopkins to Members of the Sovereignty Commission, 1 May 1962, SCR 7-4-0-77-1-1-1.

14. *Scott v. Campbell College*, 3 (quotes).

15. *Ibid.*, 3–4.

16. *Ibid.*, 4.

17. R. A. *Scott, et al. v. J. P. Campbell College, et al.*, Agreed Decree, 29 March 1962, SCR 3-78-0-2-1-1-1 through 3-1-1; "Suit Settled at Campbell," *Jackson Daily News*, 28 March 1962; "Stevens Restored as President of Campbell," *Jackson Daily News*, 2 July 1962, SCR 10-35-1-136-1-1-1.

18. For discussions of the state's quest to close Campbell, see Barbour interview; Lawrence Guyot interview; Hollis Watkins interview with Charles Payne, 15 June 1981, Jackson, Mississippi, cited in Payne, *I've Got the Light*, 461n37; Erle Johnston to File, 13 July 1964, SCR 3-78-0-4-1-1-1 (quote). Campbell appeared in a different iteration, Bonner-Campbell College in Edwards, Mississippi, in 1982.

19. Daniel Thompson, *Private Black Colleges at the Crossroads* (Westport, Connecticut: Greenwood Press, 1973).

20. Comments made by Mr. Ricketts, Board of Trustees, minutes, 12 March 1955, 2–3, Board of Trustees Collection, TCA; Board of Trustees, minutes, 16 April 1957, 1–2, Board of Trustees Collection (quote).

21. Faculty Meeting, minutes, 8 March 1961, 4, Faculty Meetings Collection, TCA (quote). Beittel's experience at Talladega is taken from Henry N. Drewry and

Humphrey Doermann, *Stand and Prosper: Private Black Colleges and Their Students* (Princeton: Princeton University Press, 2001), 148–152.

22. W. C. Shoemaker, "'Federal Judges Undecided on Jackson Mixing Case," *Jackson Daily News*, 12 March 1962, 1, 7 (first and second quote); W. C. Shoemaker, "President Quells Student Disorder," *Jackson Daily News*, 28 March 1961; A. D. Beittel interview with WLBT, September 1961, cited in Campbell and Rogers, *Mississippi*, 198–199 (third quote).

23. Board of Trustees, minutes, 18 May 1961, 7 (first quote), and 9 November 1961, 3–4 (second quote), Board of Trustees Collection, TCA.

24. Board of Trustees, minutes, 10 November 1961, 4, Board of Trustees Collection, TCA.

25. W. Webb Burke to David Fleming, "Mississippi Council on Human Relations," 2 August 1972, SCR 2-1-0-45-1-1-1 (quote); Campbell and Rogers, *Mississippi*.

26. Wesley Hotchkiss, "The Social Revolution," *Journal*, [spring] 1963, 3, Vertical File Demonstrations and Protests, TCA.

27. *Writ of Temporary Injunction*, Chancery Court of the First Judicial District of Hinds County, Mississippi, 6 June 1963, EKP, Box 8, Folder 374.

28. Erle Johnston to File, 13 April 1964, SCR 3-74-2-17-1-1-1 (first quote); Mr. Zero to Sovereignty Commission, 5 May 1964, SCR 3-74-2-19-1-1-1 (second and third quotes).

29. "Church Group Cancels Support of Tougaloo," *Jackson Daily News*, 20 September 1963, A. D. Beittel (Unprocessed), Folder Board of Trustees Fall 1963, TCA. In 1954, Tougaloo merged with Southern Christian Institute, and the Tougaloo campus absorbed the Institute's student body.

30. Barnaby Keeney to Lawrence Durgin, 9 March 1964, 1, Barnaby Keeney Office File Register, Tougaloo College, 1964–65, Miscellaneous Correspondence, BUA (quote); Wesley Hotchkiss to Robert Wilder, 10 April 1964, Barnaby Keeney Office File Register, Tougaloo College, 1964–65, Miscellaneous Correspondence, BUA; King interview.

31. Robert O. Wilder to A. D. Beittel, April 20, 1960, American Missionary Association Archives, Addendum (1869–1991, n.d.), Series A, Subseries Touglaoo Correspondence, Box 110, Folder 17, ARC; A. D. Beittel to Barnaby Keeney, 5 April 1964, American Missionary Association Archives, Addendum (1869–1991, n.d.), Series A, Subseries Touglaoo Correspondence, Box 110, Folder 18, ARC (quote); Wesley Hotchkiss to Mr. and Mrs. George Owens, 20 April 1964, American Missionary Association Archives, Addendum (1869–1991, n.d.), Series A, Subseries Tougaloo Correspondence, Box 110, Folder 18, ARC.

32. "Tougaloo Bill Appears Dead," *Clarion-Ledger*, 14 April 1964; Senate Bill No. 1672, Regular Sess., 1964, Tougaloo College History, Folder Accreditation Revocation (State), TCA (first quote); "Action on Tougaloo Is Due for Delay," *Clarion-Ledger*, 6 March 1964 (second quote); Senate Bill No. 1794, Regular Sess., 1964, Tougaloo College History, Folder Accreditation Revocation (State), TCA.

33. A. D. Beittel to William Fidler, 6 June 1964, A. D. Beittel to Hollis Price, 27 May 1964, and A. D. Beittel to Gordon Sweet, 6 June 1964, Tougaloo College History, Folder Accreditation Revocation (State), TCA; William Fidler to Gover-

nor Paul B. Johnson Jr., 28 February 1964 and Tom J. Truss Jr. to Scott Osborn, 9 March 1964, General Mississippi Study of Academic Freedom, January–April 1964 File, AAUPA.

34. Johnston to File, 24 April 1964, SCR 3-74-2-16-1-1-1. Ed King's name and title are blacked out in the record, but it is certain that he is the individual to whom the report refers.

35. Wesley Hotchkiss to Robert Wilder, 10 April 1964, Barnaby Keeney Office File Register, Tougaloo College, 1964–65, Miscellaneous Correspondence, BUA.

36. Reverend Bernard Law, Reverend Duncan M. Gray Jr., and Rabbi Perry E. Nussbaum to Board of Trustees, American Missionary Association Archives, Addendum (1869–1991, n.d.), Series A, Subseries Tougaloo Correspondence, 4 May 1964, Box 110, Folder 18, ARC.

37. Wesley Hotchkiss to Reverend James Lightborne Jr., 10 June 1964, Box 1, Brown-Tougaloo Collection, TCA; Truman Douglass to Ray Gibbons, 5 June 1964, 2, Box 1, Brown-Tougaloo Collection, TCA (quote).

38. Erle Johnston to Paul Johnson and Carroll Gartin, 5 May 1964, SCR 3-74-2-23-1-1-1.

39. Tom Scarbrough, "Marshall County," 19 April 1963, SCR 2-20-1-67-2-1-2 (quote); McLemore interview; "No Room for Communists," *South Reporter*, 30 July 1964; "Book Boom," *Bearcat*, 15 July 1964, Folder *Bearcat* 1964, RCA; Naomi K. Nero to G. Menshik, 24 May 1989, cited in Edwards, "History of Rust," 145–146.

40. Tom Scarbrough, "Marshall County, 14 December 1962," SCR 2-20-1-63-2-1-1 and 3–1–1 (all quotes). President Smith grew up in Alabama. He received his undergraduate degree from Rust, a master's from Oberlin, and had additional schooling at the University of Hartford. Before returning to Rust as president, he served as Rust's chaplain and pastor of a church in San Antonio, Texas (Edwards, "History of Rust").

41. Earnest Smith interview; McLemore interview; Sam Coopwood to Bishop Marvin Franklin, 29 June 1964, SCR 2-20-1-80-1-1-1 (first quote); Tom Scarbrough, "Marshall County," 19 April 1963, SCR 2-20-1-67-1-1-1 (second quote).

42. Scarbrough, "Marshall County-Mrs. Clarice Campbell," SCR 2-20-1-50-7-1-1 (quote).

43. M. L. Malone to Zack J. Van Landingham, "A Report of Activities of NAACP in Columbus, Mississippi," 9 February 1959, SCR 2-94-0-2-1-1-1; Zack J. Van Landingham to Director of the State Sovereignty Commission, 6 March 1959, SCR 2-4-10-6-1-1-1; Tom Scarbrough, "Lowndes County," 6 September 1961, SCR 2-94-0-56-1-1-1 through 2-1-1; Malone to Van Landingham, "A Report of Activities of NAACP in Columbus, Mississippi" (first quote); Scarbrough, "Marshall County-Mrs. Clarice Campbell," 2-20-1-50-4-1-1 (second quote); Rust College General Catalogue, 1963–1964, RCA. Commission documents list Hunt as both the Superintendent of Negro Schools in 1959 and a principal of a black school in Columbus, Mississippi in 1961. Regardless, the commission speaks favorably in both instances.

44. Erle Johnston Jr. to Herman Glazier, 9 June 1964, SCR 2-20-1-77-1-1-1 (first quote); Smith interview; Tom Scarbrough, "Marshall County (Rust College),"

SCR 2-20-1-78-2-1-1(second quote) and 2-20-1-78-3-1-1 (third and fourth quotes); "No Room for Communists" (fifth quote).

45. "A Statement to the [CME Church] by the College of Bishops," *Christian Index*, 4 August 1960, 5–7, cited in Sommerville, *An Ex-Colored Church*, 114 (quote).

46. *Ibid.*; Edwards, "History of Rust"; Anderson Crouther interview; Clark White interview; Bernard White interview. Mississippi Industrial College, like Campbell College, no longer exists and its records have been lost. Therefore, intimate information on President Rankin, the faculty, and students is severely limited.

47. Tom Scarbrough, "Marshall County," 9 April 1963, SCR 2-20-1-67-1-1-1.

48. Tom Scarbrough, "Marshall County (Rust College)," 30 June 1964, 5, SCR 2-20-1-78-1-1-1 through 5-1-1.

49. Matthews and Prothro, *Negroes and the New Southern Politics*; Oppenheimer, "The Genesis"; Orum, *Black Students*.

50. Anderson Crouther interview.

51. The discussion of the Dartmouth case is taken from Frederick Rudolph, *The American College and University: A History* (Athens: University of Georgia Press, 1990), 207–210.

52. See, for instance, Anderson, *The Education of Blacks*.

53. Morris, *The Origins*, 196–197.

Chapter 6

1. Dittmer, *Local People*, 38; Payne, *I've Got the Light*, 42; B. R. Brazeal, "The Present Status of Desegregation in Higher Education in the South: Some Problems in the Desegregation of Higher Education in the 'Hard Core' States," *Journal of Negro Education* 27, no. 3 (summer 1958): 352–372; Percy Greene, "More Uncle Toms Greatest Need of Southern Negro," *Jackson Advocate,* 19 January 1957 (quote).

2. *Dixon v. Alabama State Board of Education*, 294 F2D 150 (1961); a federal court found similarly in *Knight v State Board of Education*, 200 F. Supp. 174 (1961); Robert M. Hendrickson and Annette Gibbs, *The College, the Constitution, and the Consumer Student: Implications for Policy and Practice* (Washington, D.C.: Association for the Study of Higher Education, 1986).

3. American Opinion Speakers Bureau information sheet on Reverend Uriah J. Fields [n.d.], SCR 10-105-0-15-1-1-1 (first quote); Erle Johnston Jr., "Rev. Uriah J. Fields, Negro Clergyman, Evangelist, Author, and Lecturer of Montgomery, Alabama," 23 September 1963, SCR 10-105-0-13-1-1-1 (second quote). According to White, the fact that black activists shunned Fields boded well for his invitation to campus. He reported to the Commission, who solicited his advice on Fields, that Fields was "very unpopular with the Negroes in Alabama due to his unveiling the facts about [Martin Luther] King and others. . . . Therefore, I feel he is all right" (J. H. White to Virgie S. Downing, 26 September 1963, SCR 9-20-0-25-1-1-1). Still, White and Boyd warned the commission that inviting out-of-state speakers to the

campus was a slippery slope. According to Boyd, he "would be obligated to the student body to invite other speakers, such as possibly Martin Luther King, Jr. or other agitators that planned on creating strife and disruption with college students" (Virgil Downing, "Reverend Uriah Fields' Proposed Speaking Engagement," 27 September 1963, SCR 2-109-0-42-1-1-1 [quote]; Virgil Downing, "Reverend Uriah Fields' Proposed Speaking Engagement," 25 September 1963, SCR 2-45-2-5-1-1-1 through 2-1-1).

4. Jacob Reddix, *A Voice Crying in the Wilderness* (Jackson: University Press of Mississippi, 1974).

5. Posey, *Against Great Odds*, 30–34.

6. White, *Up from a Cotton Patch;* Board of Trustees, minutes, 18 January 1951, cited in Tinsley, "A History," 83. Katagiri mentions White's relationship with the Sovereignty Commission in *The Mississippi State*, 38, 48.

7. Mississippi State University's President Benjamin F. Hilbun (1953–1960) did not have an earned doctorate, but his successor, President Dean W. Colvard (1960–1966), did.

8. John A. Peoples, *To Survive and Thrive: The Quest for a True University* (Jackson: Town Square Books, 1995), 45–46; Zack Van Landingham, "Possible Negro Informants," 24 August 1959, 1, SCR 9-20-0-3-1-1-1 (quote). Boyd's predecessor, Jessie R. Otis, had an earned doctorate from Cornell University. E. R. Jobe, a member of the Negro Education Committee of the Board of Trustees, remembered that the board selected Otis to head Alcorn in 1948 rather than James H. White (who had applied for the job) because Otis had an advanced degree (Sammy Jay Tinsely interview with E. R. Jobe, 8 December 1971, cited in Tinsley, "A History of Mississippi Valley State College," 41). The board's choice was more for the appearance of propriety than a demonstration of support for the upgrade of Alcorn.

9. White, *Up from a Cotton Patch;* Reddix, *A Voice;* "Readers Respond to Plan for Positive State Action," *State Times*, 5 November 1961, Clipped Article File, ASUA.

10. Mathews and Prothro found that colleges in isolated locations and those in areas with a large proportion of black residents were less likely to have active student bodies (*Negroes and the New Southern Politics*, 415–416, 427).

11. Byrd Martin interview.

12. Mathews and Prothro, *Negroes and the New Southern Politics*, 425–429; and Orbell, "Protest Participation," 446–456.

13. Sansing, *Making Haste*, 148–154; A. Maurice Mackel to Walter White, 11 August 1954, National Association for the Advancement of Colored People Papers, Manuscripts Division, Library of Congress, cited in Dittmer, *Local People*, 44 (first quote); Zack Van Landingham, "Clyde Kennard," 28 August 1959, SCR 1-27-0-27-1-1-1 (second and third quotes); Zack Van Landingham, "Clyde Kennard," 3 September 1959, 2, SCR 9-20-0-1-2-1-1 (fourth quote). For White's role in off-campus activities see Zack Van Landingham, "Integration, White Churches," 3 May 1960, SCR 1-16-1-40-1-1-1 through 2-1-1; Zack Van Landingham, "NAACP, Clay County, Mississippi," 24 May 1960, SCR 3-71-0-1-1-1-1; Zack Van Landingham, "Informants," 3 May 1960, SCR 9-20-0-13-1-1-1 through 2-1-1.

14. Tom Scarbrough, "Dewey Green Jr.," 6 November 1962, SCR 2-45-1-57-2-1-1 (quote); Tom Scarbrough, "LeFlore County," 6 March 1963, SCR 2-45-1-65-1-1-1 through 5-1-1-1.

15. J. H. White, "You Can't Have Something for Nothing," Convocation Address, 3 October 1956, SCR 9-20-0-4-8-1-1; J. H. White, "The Amazing Progress of Our Southern Negroes," *The Enterprise Journal*, 13 October 1958, SCR 9-20-0-5-1-1-1; White, *Up from a Cotton Patch*, 151.

16. Committee on Un-American Activities, *Hearings Regarding Communist Infiltration of Minority Groups, Parts 1 and 2*, Washington, D.C.: Government Printing Office, 1949.

17. See entire special issue of *Journal of Negro Education* 27, no. 3 (summer 1958).

18. John Temple Graves, "See Prof. Clennon King Negroes Man of Destiny," *Jackson Advocate*, [n.d.] April 1957, Clipped Article File, ASUA.

19. "Sixth Annual Meeting of the Regional Council of Negro Leadership," 26 April 1957, 15, SCR 2-2-0-4-15-1-1 (first quote); Wright, "What Happened," 349 (second quote).

20. "Interview with Dr. Jobe," January 15, 1964, enclosure in Kammerer to Adams; Holmes and Jobe interview, 59.

21. List of grievances, [n.d.] 1966, Reel 107, *Evers v. Birdsong* File, SCRLR (all Reel materials are from the SCRLR); Crosby, *A Little Taste*.

22. J. D. Boyd to C. E. Tellis, 24 March 1966, Reel 107 (first quote); SMAC, "To the Alcorn College Student Body," n.d., Reel 107 (second quote); "Notice," 20 April 1966, Reel 107.

23. *Evers v. Birdsong*, 287 F. Supp. 900 (1968); Crosby, *A Little Taste*.

24. "Readers Respond."

25. Posey, *Against Great Odds;* Crosby, *A Little Taste*.

26. Crosby, *A Little Taste*.

27. Zack J. Van Landingham, "Boycott by Negroes, Jackson, Mississippi, April 10–17, 1960," SCR 2-135-0-1-1-1-1 through 13-1-1; "Boycott Scheduled as Jackson Protest," *Times Picayune*, 9 April 1960, SCR 2-135-0-10-1-1-1 (quote).

28. Jackson State College Student Handbook, September 1961, 40, JSUA. Reddix suspended Coetee Moore (Jacob Reddix to Albert Jones, 1 April 1961, SCR 10-105-0-2-1-1-1). Moody discusses Reddix's harsh response in *Coming of Age*.

29. Alex Poinsett, "Abolish Student Government at Miss. College: President's Action Chokes Off Anti-Segregation Activities," *Jet*, [n.d.] October 1961, 24 (first quote), 25 (second quote).

30. Dorie Ladner interview; Joyce Ladner interview; Williams interview; MIAS, Policy Letter #3, 20 April 1961, James Meredith Collection, Box 1, Folder 19, UMA.

31. William Peart, "Ross Risks Jail to Halt Mixing," *Jackson Daily News*, 14 September 1962, James Meredith Collection, Folder Newspaper Clippings 1962, JSUA (first quote); Sansing, *Making Haste;* James Meredith, "Behind the Scenes at Jackson State University," *Outlook* 9, no. 2 (September 1983): 1, James Meredith Collection, Folder Weekly Communicator, JSUA (second quote).

32. Reddix, *A Voice*, 222.

33. Peoples interview; Frazier, *Black Bourgeoisie*, 75; Ralph Ellison, *Invisible Man* (New York: Vintage, 1995), 143. Walter Williams also recalled that Reddix maintained a life membership in the NAACP. With regard to President Boyd, according to a personal communication with Emilye Crosby, some former Alcorn employees construed Boyd's caution against allowing Uriah Fields (the former member of the Montgomery Improvement Association turned racial conservative) to speak on campus as an example of how Boyd challenged the board of trustees and protected the college from external interference.

34. Benjamin Mays interview with Aldon Morris, 20 September 1978, Atlanta, Georgia, cited in Morris, *Origins*, 196 (quote).

35. *McAuliffe v. Mayor of New Bedford*, 29 N.E. 517, 517–18 (Mass. 1892). The Supreme Court reversed this decision and extended First Amendment protections to public employees in *Pickering v. Board of Education*, 391 U.S. 563 (1968).

Chapter 7

1. Stokely Carmichael and Charles V. Hamilton, *Black Power: The Politics of Liberation in America* (New York: Vintage Books, 1967), viii (first quote), 44 (second quote); Peniel Joseph, *Waiting 'Til the Midnight Hour: A Narrative History of Black Power in America* (New York: Henry Holt, 2006).

2. Roy Wilkins, "Whither 'Black Power'?," *Crisis*, August–September (1966): 353–354, 354 (quotes).

3. Sellers, *The River of No Return*, 234.

4. Long, "Black Protest."

5. Joyce Ladner, "The New Negro Ideology: What 'Black Power' Means to Negroes in Mississippi," *Trans-Action*, November 1966, 7–15, 8 (quote).

6. Bob Howie, cartoon, *Jackson Daily News*, 24 June 1966, EKP, Box 4, Folder 176 (first quote); James Ward, "It Doesn't Make Sense," *Jackson Daily News*, 8 June 1966, 10 (second quote).

7. Andrews, *Freedom Is a Constant Struggle*; "Stop, Think, Consider: Awake White Mississippi," *Commercial Appeal*, 17 August 1967, personal papers of William Forrest Winter.

8. Liberal white students in Mississippi also participated. They sometimes organized under the banner of the Students for a Democratic Society, but they also created the Southern Students Organizing Committee and the Young Democrats Club and media like the newspaper, *Kudzu*, which were fully supportive of the black freedom struggle.

9. Tougaloo students published *Harambee* and *Nitty Gritty*, and Jackson State students published *Gadfly*.

10. Gurin and Epps, *Black Consciousness*; Long, "Black Protest"; Morris, *The Origins*.

11. Joyce Ladner interview; Dorie Ladner interview; Moody, *Coming of Age*, 273 (quote).

12. "Jackson State," 445; Peoples, *To Survive*; Peoples interview.

13. Peoples, *To Survive*, 163 (quote); Rhodes, *Jackson State*, 137–139; O'Neil, Morris, and Mack, *No Heroes*, chapter 2.

14. Constance Slaughter Harvey interview; Minion K. C. Morrison, *Black Political Mobilization: Leadership, Power and Mass Behavior* (Albany: State University of New York Press, 1987).

15. *Ibid.;* Letter to the President, 16 May 1967, GAOP, Box 4, Folder 17 (quote). George A. Owens, Tougaloo's Business Manager under President Beittel, became Tougaloo's first black president in 1965 after serving as interim president during the 1964–65 academic year.

16. "Stokely Blamed in Jackson Riots," *Nashville Banner,* 13 May 1967, Tougaloo Nine Collection, Folder 1960–1967, TCA; "Jackson Boycott Demands," *Mississippi Newsletter,* 26 May 1967, EKP, Folder 269.

17. Jefferson, "Report of the Commissioners."

18. Gurin and Epps, *Black Consciousness;* Long, "Black Protest;" Morris, *The Origins.*

19. "Major Demands as Presented to the Administrative Council," 1960, cited in Tinsley, "A History of Mississippi Valley," 225–226; Tinsley, "A History of Mississippi Valley," 222–223, 227.

20. "Construction of Events Leading to the Closing of Mississippi Valley State College on February 11, 1970," 11–12, Vertical File 1970 Boycott, MVSUA (first quote); "Mrs. Fannie Lou Hamer's Speech," February 1970, included in "Construction of Events," (second, third, and fourth quotes); *Tyrone Gettis, et al. v. J. H. White, et al.,* Complaint filed 12 February 1970, cited in Tinsley, "A History of Mississippi Valley," 231; James M. Moreland, "Weekly Report," 2, SCR 9-20-0-79-1-1-1 through 2-1-1.

21. Exhibit A in Board of Trustees, minutes, 19 February 1970, MDAH (first quote); J. H. White to Mississippi Legislature, letter reprinted in *Commercial Appeal,* 26 March 1971, 3, cited in Tinsley, "A History of Mississippi Valley," 243 (second quote).

22. Nadine Cohadas, *The Band Played Dixie: Race and the Liberal Conscience at Ole Miss* (New York: Free Press, 1997); "Campus Units Join Forces to Seek Ole Miss Accord," *Commercial Appeal,* 6 March 1970, SCR 3-9-3-10-1-1-1.

23. Cohadas, *The Band,* 154 (first, second, and third quotes), 150 (fourth quote); Joseph interview; "College Board Sits at Ole Miss," *Commercial Appeal,* 24 April 1970.

24. Bob Ingram, "Roberts Addresses AAUP," *The Student Printz,* 11 December 1969, 1, Verner Holmes Collection, Box 3, Folder 6, UMA.

25. *Jones v. State Board of Education of Tennessee,* 397 U.S. 31 (1970); *Healy v. James* (quote).

26. *Jones v. Board* (quote). Other cases involving Mississippi college students include *Wilson v. White,* Civil Action 6852–S, 9 December 1968; *Joseph v. White,* Civil Action No. GC 969–S, 13 February 1969; and *Gettis v. White,* "Order handed down by U. S. District Judge William R. Keady, 4 September 1970," in Tinsley, "A History." Also, University of Mississippi School of Law professors working with the North Mississippi Rural Legal Services Program, a federally subsidized program to help black Mississippians gain their legal rights and whose members defended the black Ole Miss students, had only recently won the right to engage in outside employment (*Trister v. University of Mississippi,* USCA Miss, 420 F. 2d 499 [1969]).

27. J. D. Boyd to Nettie Ruth Brandon, 9 March 1966, and Dorothy Mae Brandon, affidavit, 14 March 1966 in *Brandon v. Alcorn*, Reel 108.

28. Charles Merten to Files, 12 December 1966, in *Brandon v. Alcorn*, Reel 108.

29. Crosby, *A Little Taste.*

30. Board of Trustees, minutes, 20 May 1965, 7 (quotes).

31. Board of Trustees, "Resolution," 17 November 1966, MDAH, cited in Donald Reagan Stacy, "Mississippi's Campus Speaker Ban: Constitutional Considerations and the Academic Freedom of Students," *Mississippi Law Journal*, 38 (1966–1967), 488–507.

32. Donald Cunnigen, "Standing at the Gates: The Civil Rights Movement and Liberal White Mississippi Students," *Journal of Mississippi History*, 67, no. 1 (Spring 2000), 1–19; Board of Trustees, minutes, 16 January 1969; Sam Lowe, "Mississippi College Students Challenge the Courthouse Gang," *New South*, 24 (Spring 1969), 17–21; *Stacy v. Williams*, (1969) N.D. Miss. 306, F 2d Supp. 963.

33. *Molpus v. Fortune*, 311 F. Supp. 240 (1970).

34. Alexander W. Astin, "New Evidence on Campus Unrest, 1969–1970," *Educational Record* 52, no. 1 (Winter 1971), 41–46.

35. Carter G. Woodson, *The Mis-Education of the Negro* (Nashville: Winston-Derek, 1933/1990); W. E. B. DuBois, "On the Dawn of Freedom," in *The Souls of Black Folk*, edited by Henry Louis Gates Jr. and Terri Hume Oliver (New York: Norton, 1999); Frazier, *Black Bourgeoisie;* Harold Cruse, *The Crisis of the Negro Intellectual* (New York: Morrow, 1967); Frantz Fanon, *Black Skin, White Masks* (New York: Grove, 1967).

36. Vincent Harding, "Black Students and the Impossible Revolution," *Journal of Black Studies* 1, no. 1 (September 1970): 75–100, 76 (quote).

37. "Student Doubts Reddix," *Mississippi Independent*, 28 April 1967, JSUA.

38. Harding, "Black Students," 87.

39. Sylvester Oliver Jr., "Civil Rights History in Marshall County, Mississippi from 1957 to 1989," RCA; Campbell and Rogers, *Mississippi;* "Alcorn Explodes Again," *MFDP Newsletter*, 26 February 1968, EKP, Folder 699; "Notice Students," n.d. Reel 107 (quote).

40. Albert N. Whiting, "Position Paper on the Role of Negro Colleges and Universities," November 1971, 2 (first quote), 3 (second quote), in Faculty Meeting, minutes, 10 November 1971, TCA.

41. "An Overview: The First Year of the Tougaloo College–Brown University Cooperative Program," February 1965, GAOP, Box 1, Folder 27 (quote); Dittmer, *Local People.*

42. Faculty Meeting, minutes, 26 March 1969, 2 (first and third quotes), 1, second quote, Faculty Meeting Collection, TCA.

43. Nathan Hare, "The Case for Separatism: 'Black Perspective,'" in *Black Power and Student Rebellion*, eds. James McEvoy and Abraham Miller (Belmont, CA: Wadsworth), 234 (quote).

44. Roy Wilkins, "The Case Against Separatism: 'Black Jim Crow,'" in McEvoy and Miller, *Black Power*, 235–237, 235 and 236 (quote); Noliwe M. Rooks, *White Money/Black Power: The Surprising History of African American Studies and the*

Crisis of Race in Higher Education (Boston: Beacon, 2006); William E. Sims, *Black Studies: Pitfalls and Potential* (Washington, D.C.: University Press of America, 1978).

45. University of Mississippi admitted its first black student in 1962, Mississippi State University in 1965, Mississippi University for Women and Delta State University in 1966, and University of Southern Mississippi in 1967. The University of Mississippi, Mississippi University for Women, and the University of Southern Mississippi hired their first black faculty members in 1970, and Delta State hired theirs in 1973. The state's black college faculties desegregated before the white college faculties: Alcorn hired its first white faculty member in 1966, Jackson State in 1967, and Mississippi Valley in 1968 (Sansing, *Making Haste*).

46. Proposal, 10 October 1963, GAOP, Box 4, Folder 7; Dittmer interview; John A. Dittmer to Members of the Faculty, 12 May 1969, Faculty Meeting, minutes, 2 (quotes).

47. Rooks, *White Money/Black Power*, 106.

48. *Kenyatta v. Moore*, 744 F.2d 1179 (5th Cir.1984); *Kenyatta v. Moore*, 623 F.Supp. 220 (D.C.Miss.1985) (first and second quotes); Campbell and Rogers, *Mississippi*, 230 (third quote).

49. W. Webb Burke to James O. Eastland, 28 March 1969, SCR 1-109-0-10-1-1-1 (first quote); Jim Cline to Charles Griffin, 3 March 1969, SCR 1-109-0-8-1-1-1 (second quote); Joseph interview.

50. "The Alcorn Student Demands," *MFDP Newsletter*, 5 April 1968, Reel 83; Posey, *Against Great Odds;* Campbell and Rogers, *Mississippi*.

51. "Jackson State," 444 (first quote); "Obscenities Blamed," *Delta Democrat Times*, 27 May 1970 (second quote); "Our Own Affairs," *Daily Corinthian*, 1 June 1970 (third quote); "Jackson State, 454 (fourth quote); and "JSC Fracas, Racial Mix Top AP Stories," n.p., 27 December 1970, clipped article file, Gibbs-Green Collection, JSUA.

52. Cohadas, *The Band*, 153 (quotes); Chester M. Morgan, *Dearly Bought, Deeply Treasured: The University of Southern Mississippi, 1912–1987* (Jackson: University Press of Mississippi, 1987).

53. John Donald, testimony at student hearings, February 1969, SCR 3-9-3-15-33-1-1.

54. Urban Research Corporation, *Student Protests.*

55. Gurin and Epps also critique this claim in *Black Consciousness.*

56. Clayborne Carson, "Civil Rights Reform and the Black Freedom Struggle," in *The Civil Rights Movement in America: Essays*, edited by Charles W. Eagles (Jackson: University Press of Mississippi, 1986), 27–28.

57. Payne, *I've Got the Light*, 424.

58. Sanford Jay Rosen, "Report of the President's Commission on Campus Unrest," *Columbia Law Review* 71: no. 6 (June 1971): 1120–1133, 1120 (quote).

Chapter 8

1. William Van Deburg, *New Day in Babylon: The Black Power Movement and American Culture, 1965–1975* (Chicago: University of Chicago Press, 1992), 294.

2. Long, "Black Protest."
3. *United States v. Fordice*, 505 U.S. 717 (1992).
4. Van Deburg, *New Day*, 306 (first quote); www.stg.brown.edu/projects/
FreedomNow; www.olemiss.edu/winterinstitute (second quote).
5. Anderson, *The Education of Blacks*.
6. Long, "Black Protest"; Matthews and Prothro, *Negroes and the New Southern Politics;* Douglas Rossinow, *The Politics of Authenticity: Liberalism, Christianity,
and the New Left* (New York: Columbia University Press, 1998); Orum, *Black Students*, 69 (quote).
7. Todd Gitlin, *The Sixties: Years of Hope, Days of Rage* (New York: Bantam
Books, 1987); "Why Mississippians Ignored San Francisco's Free Advice," *Clarion-
Ledger*, 2 June 1962, 2.
8. Bob Moses, quoted in Charles Payne, *I've Got the Light*, 284.
9. Augustus B. Cochran III, *Democracy Heading South: National Politics in
the Shadow of Dixie* (Lawrence: University Press of Kansas, 2001); John Mickleth-
wait and Adrian Wooldridge, *The Right Nation: Conservative Power in America*
(New York: Penguin, 2004); Kevin Michael Kruse, *White Flight: Atlanta and the
Making of Modern Conservatism* (Princeton: Princeton University Press, 2005).
10. Ray Delgado, "Ford Foundation Grant Moratorium Lifted, Provost Says,"
Stanford Report, 26 January 2005; Section 215, *Uniting and Strengthening America
by Providing Appropriate Tools Required to Intercept and Obstruct Terrorism (USA
PATRIOT Act)*, Public Law 107–56, 107th Cong. (26 October 2001) (first quote); David
Horowitz, *The Professors: The 101 Most Dangerous Academics in America* (Washington, D.C.: Regnery Press, 1996), 50 (second quote); /www.studentsforacademicfreedom
.org; http://www.uclaprofs.com/ (third quote);
11. "Academic Freedom and National Security in a Time of Crisis," *Academe*
(November/December) 2003, 7 (first quote); *Sweezy v. New Hampshire* (second
quote).
12. Du Bois, "On the Dawn of Freedom," 29.

Index

About the Author

Joy Ann Williamson is associate professor of the history of American education at the University of Washington's College of Education, where she teaches courses on the history of higher education, education for liberation, and theoretical debates in the history of education. Her body of work examines the reciprocal relationship between social movements of the middle twentieth century and institutions of higher education. She has published a book entitled *Black Power on Campus: The University of Illinois, 1965–1975*, (2003), articles in *History of Education Quarterly*, *History of Higher Education Annual* (now titled *Perspectives on the History of Higher Education*), *Journal of Negro Education*, and *Review of Research in Education*, as well as book chapters in several edited volumes. She is the recipient of the Spencer Foundation/National Academy of Education's Post-Doctoral Fellowship, campus-wide teaching awards, and the Association for the Study of Higher Education Council on Ethnic Participation's Early Career Award.